RD
HOME
HANDBOOKS

COOK'S
INGREDIENTS

RD
HOME
HANDBOOKS

COOK'S INGREDIENTS

Contributing editor
Adrian Bailey

The Reader's Digest Association, Inc.
Pleasantville, New York

This is an RD Home Handbook
specially created for
The Reader's Digest Association, Inc.,
by Dorling Kindersley Limited.

First American edition, 1990
Copyright © 1990 by Dorling Kindersley Limited, London

Published in the United States
by The Reader's Digest Association, Inc.,
Pleasantville, N.Y.
Published in Great Britain
by Dorling Kindersley Limited, London
Printed in Singapore

Designed and edited by Swallow Books,
260 Pentonville Road, London N1 9JY

Library of Congress Cataloging in Publication Data

Cook's ingredients.
    (RD home handbooks)
    1. Food—Encyclopedias.   I. Bailey, Adrian, 1928–
II. Reader's Digest Association.   III. Series.
    TX349.C66 1990   641'.03   90-8303
    ISBN 0-89577-356-2

CONTENTS

Introduction 6

INTRODUCTION

In days past, when a main meal consisted of meat and vegetables, the most difficult culinary question was: how to do the spuds? Things have changed.

Today's cook has an enormous range of options, both in menu and in variety of ingredients. On the one hand, consumers have begun to scrutinize labels to see what they're *really* giving the family to eat – good wholesome food, or a plateful of preservatives. On the otherhand, the various ethnic cooking traditions have made a huge impact, with a greater variety of foods being eaten in ordinary households. These two factors have led to a demand for top quality natural ingredients ... resulting in a remarkable growth in the range of foodstuffs available.

The choices, however, can be bewildering. Can you tell tagliatelle from tagliarini? Do you know what "vegetable spaghetti" is? How many different types of lettuce are there? Rice is no longer "just rice", it's basmati, arborio or brown, and now a vast range of other grains offers further alternatives: do you know what polenta, soy flour or matzo meal are, or how to use them? The cheeses and salamis of a delicatessen are a feast for the eye and nose, but which ones are best suited to your needs and tastes?

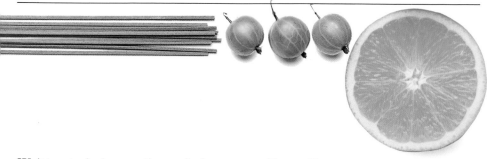

Written to help you through the maze of ingredients that can be found throughout the world, this book is the ultimate international shopping guide, giving new breadth to your repertoire, whether you are a beginner or an experienced cook. It tells you where these primary foods originated, how they are produced, what nutritional values they have and how they are prepared for the table. Mouth-watering photographs accompany most entries.

The ingredients are grouped together with their near relatives: vegetables and beans, herbs and spices, pastas and noodles, fruits and nuts, fish and seafood, grains, dairy products and meats. There are hundreds of hints and tips on using each ingredient – is it best dried, flaked, sliced or peeled; how should it be cooked, or is it served raw; and what other foods does it complement?

Good cooking and good eating depend on a knowledge of ingredients and the best way to prepare them. With the needs of the modern cook and consumer at its heart, this book makes fascinating reading and is an essential work of reference that will make shopping and cooking more enjoyable – and eating a whole new pleasure.

VEGETABLES

VEGETABLES, LIKE FRUITS, ARE the edible products of certain plants. They share several characteristics: they are savory rather than sweet; we add salt to them; and in most countries, they are associated with poultry, meat or fish as part of a meal, or as an ingredient. Some vegetables are botanically classified as fruits: tomatoes are berries, and avocados are drupes, but both are commonly used as vegetables because they are not sweet. Some people would also add the distinction that vegetables are usually cooked, while fruits are eaten raw, but this is a very loose definition since we frequently eat vegetables raw in salads, and many dishes call for cooked fruit.

The history of vegetable cultivation
All our cultivated vegetables have derived from primitive varieties whose origins are, in some cases, unknown, but we do know that many of our present-day vegetables have been cultivated since prehistoric times. We have evidence that peas were grown in Turkey by 6500 BC, from the wild pea (*Pisum elatus*) and that gourds, lima beans and perhaps maize were grown in Mexico before 5000 BC. It is also possible that the potato was then being harvested, and probably the tomato, too.

There was probably a spontaneous genesis of primitive vegetable farming in widely separate parts of the world – in China, the Middle East and South America. By 3000 BC the farmers in Mesopotamia were growing crops of turnips, onions, fava beans, peas and lentils, leeks, garlic and radishes.

From this early cultivation of food crops in western Asia, varieties began to spread towards Europe. The Greeks and Romans encouraged vegetable production on a fairly large scale and, in the wake of the Roman armies, local farmers began to grow the crops that the Romans had introduced – carrots, leeks, artichokes, cauliflower, garlic, onions and lettuces. The Islamic invaders of Spain, thrusting northward toward France, paused long enough to plant rice, spinach, eggplants, carrots and citrus fruits.

By the Middle Ages, extensive vegetable farming was carried out in Europe, especially in the Low Countries, where market gardeners were able to export a proportion of their harvest. Following the Spanish conquest of South America in the late fifteenth century, there was an important exchange of crops between the Old World and the New. Throughout the sixteenth and seventeenth centuries crops were gradually established in both continents. From the Americas came maize, potatoes, sweet potatoes, tomatoes, sweet peppers, kidney beans, pumpkins, Jerusalem artichokes and, despite their name, French beans. Settlers from Europe introduced to America fava beans, chick-peas, black-eyed peas, radishes, carrots, cabbages, okra and yams – black-eyed peas, okra and yams being brought on the slave ships from Africa.

The production of vegetables for the table became a well-developed industry, especially in France, when the chemist Nicolas Appert pioneered canned foods at the end of the eighteenth century. Appert's technique was soon to revolutionize the marketing of vegetables, and was not to be equaled in importance in this field until the American physicist, Clarence Birdseye, introduced a new process of freezing foods in 1929, which is still widely used today.

Composition of vegetables
Flavor accounts for a very small percentage of a vegetable's composition. Most contain at least 80 per cent water, the remainder being carbohydrate, protein and fat. Squashes, in particular, contain a high percentage of water, while potatoes contain a great deal of starch, used by the vegetable as a reserve food supply. Invert sugars are also a food source, and sucrose is present in corn, carrots, parsnips, onions, and so on. When vegetables age, the woody lignin increases, water evaporates, and sugars become concentrated: old, raw carrots appear to be sweeter than young ones. But sugars change as soon as the vegetable is separated from the plant. (A good

example is corn, which is often rushed straight from the stalk to the pot in order to preserve its taste.)

Protein accounts for about 1 per cent of a vegetable's composition but can be as high as 4 per cent in corn and 8 per cent in legumes. Vegetables are also a useful source of vitamins, which can vary according to the time of day, the temperature, and when the vegetables were harvested. Sunshine increases the vitamin C in turnips, which also have more vitamin B if harvested in the morning; cabbages grown at 50–60°F have a greater concentration of B vitamins, and a higher nutritive value when freshly harvested. These nutrients tend to concentrate in the outer leaves and stem.

Each vegetable owes its unique character to the arrangement of cells and the various substances it contains. The cell walls are made of cellulose and lignin – a cell-building substance that produces such textures as fibrousness (globe artichokes), stringiness (celery) and crispness (carrots); crispness also depends on the water content. Cells are cemented together by pectin, a form of carbohydrate. Common factors in vegetables are water and starch.

The familiar qualities of some vegetables are due to small amounts of chemical compounds, such as sulphur in brassicas – hence the far-reaching smell of boiled cabbage – while onions contain an enzyme that brings tears to the eyes. In addition, there are lipids or fats, organic acids, and pigments such as green chlorophyll (cabbages), yellow and orange carotenoids (carrots and pumpkins), and purple or blue anthocyanins (broccoli and red cabbage).

Vegetables in the kitchen

When choosing vegetables you should obviously avoid those that are limp and wilting, discolored or damaged by harvesting. Leaf vegetables need careful inspection to avoid serving garden pests on the plate. Vegetables should be prepared for cooking as simply as possible just before cooking. When peeled and cut, vegetables lose vitamins and nutrients if they are left in the air, or even more rapidly if they are left to soak in water. They should only be peeled thinly: vitamins are usually found just under the skin.

We cook vegetables in order to break down the starch and cellulose, and render them more digestible; heat achieves this, however we apply it. Ideally, most vegetables should be cooked as briefly as possible, to preserve their character, taste and freshness. Although boiled vegetables lose a quantity of their nutrients, the actual volume of cooking water makes no difference once the vegetable has been immersed. The cooking water of vegetables often contains valuable minerals and vitamins and is useful for soups. A good alternative to boiling or stir-frying is to cook vegetables in a steamer, while both pressure-cooking and microwave cooking preserve the maximum amount of nutritive elements present in vegetables.

On contact with air certain vegetables tend to discolor, regardless of whether they are cooked or raw. This is because certain enzymes cause oxidization. This activity can be halted by the addition of an acid, which is why cooks plunge celeriac and apples into acidulated water (water with a little lemon juice added) after peeling them. Blanching helps to preserve color, especially in green vegetables, but some vegetable dyes are lost in the cooking process. Purple broccoli contains both chlorophyll (green) and anthocyanin (purple), the latter being water-soluble, so cooked broccoli always looks green. Red cabbage reacts like litmus paper – it turns blue in the presence of an alkali (the lime in tap water), so you need to add a dash of acid, such as vinegar, to preserve the color .

Vegetables can be classified according to their botanical family, such as the brassica (cabbages) group, or by identifying the edible part: root, leaf, shoot and stem or bulb.

Leaf Vegetables

LETTUCE (*Lactuca sativa*)

Probably native to the Mediterranean region, but now cultivated worldwide, there are three main varieties of lettuce: crisphead or roundhead, which has a tight solid head (the variety shown is "iceberg"); romaine or cos, which has elongated coarse leaves; and butterhead or cabbage, which varies from the very soft-leaved to the robust. The little gem lettuce is a compact variety of dwarf cos. Although they may be braised or used in soups, lettuces are normally used raw in salads; lettuce hearts are an ingredient in *petits pois à la française*. Other varieties with red-tinged leaves have been developed over the past few years. Lettuces are available all year round.

WATERCRESS
(*Nasturtium officinale*)

High in vitamins, the clean, fresh, peppery taste of watercress greatly recommends it for salads. It is also used in soups, in Oriental stir-fry dishes and as a garnish. Native to Europe, watercress was normally gathered from the wild. It is cultivated throughout the world and is available most of the year.

SPINACH (*Spinacea oleracea*)

Thought to be of Persian origin, spinach has a pleasant acidic taste due to oxalic acid. It is an annual plant, but obtainable all year round. It is at its best eaten raw in salads or lightly cooked (usually boiled in a little water). The word "Florentine" denotes its use in recipes. New Zealand spinach (*Tetragonia expansa*), although not botanically related to spinach, looks and tastes similar and is prepared in the same way. It is a summer vegetable.

Romaine or cos lettuce

Watercress

Butterhead lettuce

Crisphead lettuce

Spinach

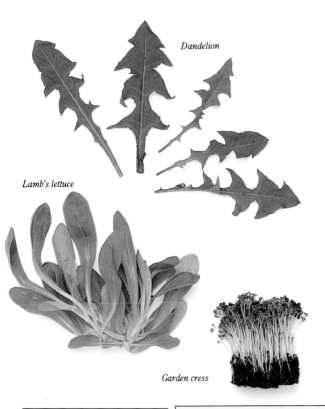

Dandelion

Lamb's lettuce

Garden cress

DANDELION
(*Taraxacum officinale*)

A wild meadow plant with a bright yellow flower and long tap root, dandelion leaves should be eaten young, before the plant flowers, as they become bitter. The blanched leaves are used for salads, especially in France and the American South. The roots make a coffee substitute, and are used in Japan as a vegetable.

LAMB'S LETTUCE
(*Valerianella olitoria*)

A wild plant indigenous to Europe, but now grown worldwide, this is also known as corn salad and in France as *mâche*. The leaves have a delicate, slightly bitter taste and are useful in winter salads.

GARDEN CRESS
(*Lepidium sativum*)

Garden cress is eaten at the seedling stage. It has a peppery taste and is used raw in salads and sandwiches. Available all year round, and is easy to grow yourself.

ARUGULA (*Eruca sativa*)

Native to the Mediterranean, this plant, known as rocket in Europe, is grown for its leaves, which are slightly pungent and peppery in taste. They are used raw in salads or cooked like spinach.

Arugula

OTHER LEAF VEGETABLES

CALALOU
(*Colocasia esculenta*)
The West Indian and Creole name for the tops of the taro plant or Caribbean spinach is "callalloo greens". The leaves are used like cabbage.

CELTUCE (*Lactuca sativa*)
Originally from China, celtuce is a sort of hybrid lettuce with a celery texture and taste. The crunchy stalks can be used raw in salads, and the leaves can also be cooked like Swiss chard.

LAND CRESS
(*Barbarea verna*)
Also known as American cress and winter cress, this is indigenous to America and Europe. It has a slightly

peppery taste, is available in winter, and can be used in the same way as watercress, which it resembles.

SAMPHIRE
There are two unrelated samphires, both wild plants indigenous to Europe: rock samphire (*Crithmum maritimum*) and marsh samphire or glasswort (*Salicornia europaea*). Marsh samphire, a small, succulent plant, is used in summer salads or cooked as a vegetable; rock samphire, with fleshy, aromatic leaves, is cooked as a vegetable and can be pickled.

GRAPE LEAF (*Vitis vinifera*)

The grape vine, originally from the Mediterranean region, is now found worldwide. It is much used in Turkish, Greek and Middle Eastern cooking, and is best known in the form of *dolmades* (leaves stuffed with rice and ground meat). Sold fresh or packed in brine, they are also wrapped around game and used decoratively in fresh fruit dishes.

Grape leaf

Sorrel

Radicchio

Curly endive

SORREL (*Rumex acetosa*)

There are several varieties, but the main ones are common sorrel (shown here) and French sorrel (*Rumex scutatus*). A perennial plant native to Europe and Asia, and now also found in America and Australia, it has a refreshing, slightly sour taste (the name "*acetosa*" implies its acid character, mainly from oxalic acid). It is related to rhubarb. Sorrel can be used as a vegetable (raw, in salads, or cooked as a type of purée, like spinach) and as a herb (in soups and sauces and, with other herbs, as a stuffing for fish). It is available in the summer.

RADICCHIO (*Cichorium endivia*)

This red-leafed member of the chicory family is from the Treviso area in northern Italy. The leaves are firm and crisp, with a slightly bitter, peppery taste. Its rich red colour makes it a dramatic addition to mixed salads and an excellent garnish. It is available all year round.

ENDIVE (*Cichorium endivia*)

This curly-leaved and slightly bitter-tasting plant is native to southern Asia and northern China. There are several varieties, including the curly endive or French frisée shown, and the more wavy Batavian endive or escarole. Used mainly in salads, they can also be braised, and are generally available all year.

Swiss chard

Nettle

SWISS CHARD
(*Beta vulgaris,* var. *cicla*)

Swiss chard is closely related to
beets; but the root is not used. The
green-leaved, cream-stemmed
variety has a similar taste to
spinach. The red varieties are
known as rhubarb chard. The
plants are valued for their leaves,
and stalks. It is available from
winter to spring.

NETTLE (*Urtica dioica*)

Available worldwide, nettle is a
perennial plant that can be cooked
in the same way as sorrel and
spinach. The stinging hairs are
destroyed by cooking. It is the
basic ingredient of nettle soup, and
is also used to make beer and tea.

Cabbage family

SPRING GREENS
(*Brassica oleracea*, spp.)

All brassicas are native to Europe
and western Asia. These greens –
which are cabbages without hearts
and are harvested when young
cabbages are being thinned – are
sold primarily in England.
They are a good source of green
vegetables from the home garden
when mature cabbages are scarce.

CAULIFLOWER
(*Brassica oleracea*, spp.)

Often referred to as the aristocrat
of the cabbage family, cauliflowers
were first cultivated in the Middle
East, and known in Europe by the
thirteenth century. Its flowers or
"curds" are eaten raw or lightly
cooked, and it is often served
au gratin with a white or
cheese sauce.

Spring greens

Cauliflower

Green kohlrabi

KOHLRABI (*Brassica oleracea*)

Kohlrabi, German for "cabbage-
turnip", is a cabbage mutant that
can be either purple or green.
Available in winter, the stem has a
delicate taste and may be cooked
or grated raw into salads. The
leaves can be used like spinach.

Purple kohlrabi

BROCCOLI
(Brassica oleracea, spp.)

Related to the cauliflower, there are several varieties: white sprouting, purple sprouting, green or calabrese, purple hearting or purple cauliflower, and a perennial variety. They are eaten raw but are best steamed, and are excellent served with melted butter, Hollandaise or Béarnaise sauce. Broccoli is also used for hors d'œuvres and in soups. It is available all year round.

KALE (Brassica oleracea, spp.)

There are many varieties of kale, both crinkly and smooth-leaved. It and its close relative collard greens probably originated in the eastern Mediterranean, where they have been cultivated for 2000 years. They are closely related members of the cabbage family. A winter vegetable, kale is rather coarse in texture but offers a good source of vitamin A in the winter months. Kale is best steamed or boiled and served with butter.

Green broccoli; calabrese

Purple broccoli; purple cauliflower

Kale

BRUSSELS SPROUTS
(Brassica oleracea, spp.)

A type of miniature cabbage, Brussels sprouts are thought to have originated in Belgium. They grow from tall, woody stems, and should ideally be harvested as small buds, and cooked just long enough to retain some firmness and bite. They are available from August to April. Recipes include cooking sprouts with chestnuts or onions. They can be cooked and creamed, sautéed, or made into soup. The leaves from the top of the main stalk can also be used as a vegetable.

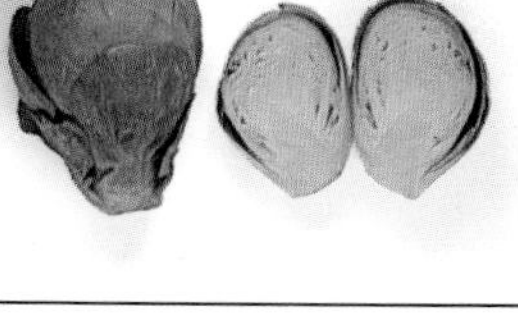

Brussels sprouts

Cabbage varieties

Cabbages are classed according to season
(spring, summer, autumn and winter varieties)
and to type (semi-hearted, green-hearted,
hard white and red). Spring cabbages are
smooth-leaved, loose and small-hearted.
Green-hearted may have round or conical
hearts, and include the Savoy. Hard whites are
sometimes called drumheads. Chinese leaf
has a more subtle taste than ordinary cabbage.

Savoy cabbage

SAVOY CABBAGE
(*Brassica oleracea*, spp.)

The Savoy is a type of green
cabbage, probably of Italian origin.
It is eaten both cooked and raw – it
is very good sliced in salads – and
its wrinkly leaves, which make a
decorative alternative to the plain
ones of the green cabbage, are
those used in recipes for stuffed
cabbage leaves.

GREEN CABBAGE
(*Brassica oleracea*, spp.)

Also known as the common
cabbage, this is eaten raw or
lightly cooked. Like the conical-
shaped cabbage, it is available all
year; most plentiful in winter.

Green cabbage

Chinese cabbage

Bok choy

Red cabbage (whole)

Red cabbage (cut)

White cabbage

CHINESE CABBAGE
(*Brassica pekinensis*)

With its long shape, this variety of cabbage is similar to the cos lettuce. It is used a great deal stir-fried in Chinese cooking, but can also be eaten raw, and is interchangeable with ordinary cabbage. The midribs of the outer leaves can be cooked like asparagus. It is known in Japan as *hakusai*.

BOK CHOY (*Brassica chinensis*)

Also known as Pak-choi, the plant does not form a heart and the leaf is reminiscent of spinach or Swiss chard. It is usually stir-fried with rice but can be eaten raw in salads. It is used extensively in Chinese cooking.

RED CABBAGE
(*Brassica oleracea*, spp.)

Usually cooked with vinegar to preserve its colour, this is often served with game. In Britain, red cabbage is pickled, while the Dutch, Danes and Swiss stew it with apples and spices. It can also be eaten raw.

WHITE CABBAGE
(*Brassica oleracea*, spp.)

Also known as drumhead or Dutch cabbage, this variety keeps well and is good for storing. Its crisp, tight head is particularly good for coleslaws and sauerkraut.

Shoot Vegetables

GLOBE ARTICHOKE
(*Cynara scolymus*)

Really a type of thistle, the globe artichoke is the flower head of a perennial plant native to north Africa, but now cultivated in Europe as a winter vegetable and in North America all year round. It can be pickled whole when small, and its tender base or "heart" is also sold canned and, in some countries, frozen. It can be baked, fried, boiled, stuffed and served with various sauces and dressings, such as vinaigrette, mayonnaise and Hollandaise sauce. Young, fresh artichokes may also be eaten raw.

BAMBOO (*Bambusa vulgaris*)

The white inner part of the young bamboo plant, bamboo shoots are conical and sold fresh in Far Eastern markets, but cooked and canned everywhere else. Their crispness and slight acidity provide a good complement to pork in particular.

PALM HEARTS
(Family: *Palmaceae*)

A tropical delicacy, these are the tender terminal shoots of some varieties of palm trees. They may be eaten raw, but are usually sold pre-cooked and canned.

ASPARAGUS
(*Asparagus officinalis*)

The young shoot of a plant native to Europe, there are about 20 varieties, the most common being green (a weedier version is known in England as "sprue") and white, preferred by the French, Belgians, Italians and Germans. Asparagus is served hot with butter, or cooked and cold with vinaigrette. It is also used in soups, quiches, soufflés and other dishes, and is available fresh in spring and early summer.

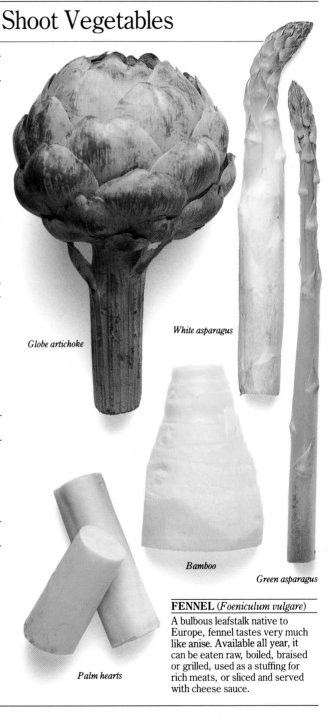

Globe artichoke

White asparagus

Bamboo

Green asparagus

Palm hearts

FENNEL (*Foeniculum vulgare*)

A bulbous leafstalk native to Europe, fennel tastes very much like anise. Available all year, it can be eaten raw, boiled, braised or grilled, used as a stuffing for rich meats, or sliced and served with cheese sauce.

CELERY (*Apium graveolens*)

Developed by Italian gardeners in the sixteenth century, there are several varieties of celery, some self-blanching, and some which need earth piled around the stems to blanch them. Available all year round, celery is eaten raw or cooked.

Belgian endive

Celery

BELGIAN ENDIVE
(*Cichorium intybus*)

Native to Europe and western Asia, but also grown in America, Belgian endive is available from autumn to early summer. Slightly bitter, it is used raw in salads, braised or fried.

Fiddlehead fern

Fennel

FIDDLEHEAD FERN
(*Pteridium aquilinium*)

Many varieties of this tender fern, also called bracken, grow wild in America and Europe. Frozen varieties can be served cooked, with Hollandaise sauce, or raw in salads.

OTHER SHOOT VEGETABLES

CARDOON
(*Cynara cardunculus*)
A thistle related to the globe artichoke, cardoon is indigenous to the Mediterranean region. Its blanched stalks are similar to celery, and are eaten raw, steamed or braised.

SEAKALE
(*Crambe maritima*)
A wild seashore plant indigenous to western Europe, seakale may also be grown as a cultivated crop. It is gathered for its white stems which are steamed and eaten in the same way as asparagus.

Fruit Vegetables

EGGPLANT
(*Solanum melongena*)

Also known as aubergines, eggplants are probably native to India. They can be various shapes and colors ranging from deep purple to white, although purple is the most common. Available all the year round, the mealy yellow-green flesh is eaten cooked, and may be sliced, hollowed and stuffed. Typical recipes include *ratatouille*, *moussaka* and *eggplant parmigiana*.

TOMATO
(*Lycopersicum esculentum*)

Originally from South America, and once known as the "love-apple", the tomato is in fact a berry and a relative of the potato. There are numerous varieties, shapes and sizes of this attractive fruit, including green, plum, ridged and cherry tomatoes. Available throughout the year, tomatoes can be bought fresh or canned and are eaten raw or cooked. Red tomatoes are available as juice, purée or sauce, while green tomatoes are often used in pickles, pies and chutneys.

Italian eggplant

Early long purple eggplant

Oriental eggplant

Cherry tomato

Beefsteak tomato

Eggplant

SWEET PEPPERS
(Capsicum annuum)

Native to tropical America and the West Indies, peppers are either sweet (capsicums) or hot (chiles) and come in many colors and sizes (the green capsicum is the unripe red or yellow capsicum). Both varieties are available fresh or canned all year round.
Sweet peppers are mild in taste and can be eaten raw or cooked. Hot peppers are used almost exclusively as a seasoning in southwestern, Indian, Mexican and Latin American dishes.

AVOCADO (Persea americana)

This nutritious buttery fruit is grown in many tropical countries, but originated in Central America. Also known as the alligator pear, there are two main varieties, one with dark-green smooth skin and one with warty black skin. A wild variety, *aguacate*, can be found in the American south-west.
Available fresh all year, avocados are used in salads, sauces, dips and mousses or as an hors d'œ uvre, and form the main ingredient in the Mexican dish *guacamole*.

Avocado

Sweet peppers

Early tomato

Hot peppers

OTHER FRUIT VEGETABLES

AKEE (*Blighia sapida*)
History maintains that akee fruits were introduced to the West Indies by Captain Bligh of the *Bounty,* hence the botanical dedication. The outer pink covering of the medium-sized fruit is poisonous, but benign portions are used as a vegetable with salt cod in Jamaica. It is mostly available canned.

BREADFRUIT
(*Artocarpus communis*)
Like the akee, this is also associated with Captain Bligh, who introduced it to the West Indies. The large fruits contain a pulp used as a vegetable, generally roasted.

Squash and Pumpkin

Squash and pumpkin, together with melons cucumbers and gourds, share the distinction of being native to both the Old World and the New. There are many different varieties – some soft-skinned, some hard – and all belong to the climbing family known as Cucurbitaceae.

SPAGHETTI SQUASH
(*Cucurbita pepo*)

Also known as vegetable spaghetti, this melon-shaped squash is available in winter. Usually boiled in its skin, the white flesh, which resembles spaghetti, is taken out, seasoned and eaten hot with butter, tomato sauce or other seasonings, or chilled and served with meats or salads.

Acorn squash

Spaghetti squash

ACORN SQUASH
(*Cucurbita pepo*)

Harvested in autumn, this thick-skinned American variety, also known as winter squash, keeps well for several months in a cool, airy place before it is used. It is usually cooked whole, because of its tough skin, but peeled it can also be cut into rings and steamed. It is particularly suitable for stuffing and baking.

SCALLOPED SQUASH
(*Cucurbita pepo*)

Also known as patty-pan squash and custard squash, this is a summer squash with a somewhat buttery taste which is at its best when very ripe. The skin, flesh and seeds can all be eaten, and it can be steamed, boiled or stuffed and baked.

GOLDEN NUGGET
(*Cucurbita pepo*)

Orange with greenish flesh, this small native pumpkin is usually eaten when immature and tender and can be steamed, boiled or stuffed and baked like a squash. It can also be left on the vine to ripen and develop a thicker skin that must be peeled before cooking, but that allows it to be stored for several months. When mature, it can be boiled and mashed with butter and seasonings, or baked.

Custard squash

Golden nugget

OTHER SQUASH

CHAYOTE (*Sechium edule*)
This squash is also called christophene or chaci. The name, from the Aztec *chayotl*, reveals the Central American origin of this squash. Varying widely in size, shape, shade and texture, it has a high water content: the bigger it grows, the more insipid it becomes. Chayote can be prepared in the same way as smaller squashes, used in chutneys, baked or stuffed. In Central and South American cooking it is also eaten as a dessert.

CROOKNECK SQUASH
(*Cucurbita moschata*)
This bright-yellow squash has a distinctive hooked shape, hence its name. It is a summer variety, with a thin skin. Younger squashes can be eaten seeds and all.

WEST INDIAN PUMPKIN
(Cucurbita pepo, spp.)

A close relative of the common pumpkin, the West Indian pumpkin (or calabaga or winter squash) lacks the dense texture and sweet taste necessary for pumpkin pie, but can be used as a substitute for other winter squash.

Pumpkins are similar in shape, but usually have a bright orange skin and are used mostly in pies. They may also be used as a vegetable either lightly boiled, sliced and fried, or puréed and used for soups; in France pumpkin jams are made and in Italy mashed pumpkin is used as a filling for sweet ravioli. Pumpkin seeds are rich in fats and proteins and an edible oil is produced from them.

West Indian pumpkin

SNAKE SQUASH
(*Trichosanthes cucumeriana*)

This curled, eye-catching squash also known as gooseneck squash is native to southeast Asia and Australia, but it can be grown in America and Europe. Eaten in the summer when immature and thin-skinned, it is usually sliced in rounds and steamed, or boiled and served with butter, salt, pepper and herbs such as tarragon, dill or marjoram.

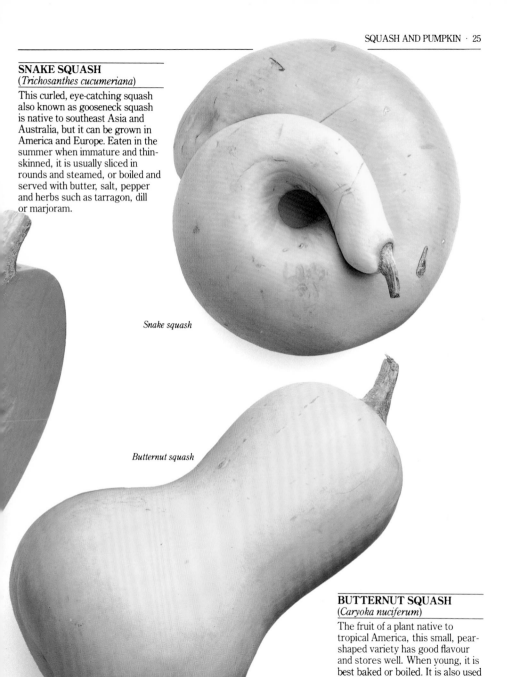

Snake squash

Butternut squash

BUTTERNUT SQUASH
(*Caryoka nuciferum*)

The fruit of a plant native to tropical America, this small, pear-shaped variety has good flavour and stores well. When young, it is best baked or boiled. It is also used to make pies and pickles.

SUMMER SQUASH
(*Cucurbita pepo*)

An edible gourd indigenous to the Americas, this versatile vegetable should be firm and heavy, and about 12 inches long. It can be steamed, boiled, stuffed and baked, cubed and served *au gratin* or made into tasty breads.

Striped summer squash

ZUCCHINI (*Cucurbita pepo*)

Also known as courgette and Italian squash, young zucchini can be harvested before it has a chance to grow into the huge vegetable so loved by gardeners. Available in green-skinned and golden-skinned varieties, it does not need peeling, but can be simply trimmed, sliced and eaten raw, steamed, baked, sliced and fried in batter, made into soups and stews, or used in *ratatouille*; zucchini flowers can be served Italian style, dipped in batter and deep-fried.

Zucchini

CUCUMBER (*Cucumis sativus*)

Although not generally thought of as a squash, the cucumber does belong to the same family. An ancient cultivated fruit thought to be indigenous to India, there are three basic types: the long, thin, smooth variety known as the Oriental, hot-house or greenhouse or frame cucumber; the shorter, thicker, slicing cucumber; and the small round varieties known as pickles. Available all year round, cucumbers can be bought fresh or pickled, and may be eaten raw or cooked. In India cucumber is added to yogurt to make the refreshing *raita*, used to temper curry dishes. Northern Europeans combine it with sour cream and the French garnish cucumber salad with salted whipped cream. Cucumbers may be pickled, used in soups, in a sauce (especially with poached salmon) and in salads.

Young zucchini

Cucumber

Oriental cucumber

Bulb Vegetables

LEEK (*Allium porrum*)

Not as pungent as onions or shallots, the leek is native to Europe. Available from autumn to spring, leeks can be braised, served with sauces, *au gratin*, or in soups and stews. Welsh onions, native to Siberia, not Wales, are small leeklike bulbs with a delicate flavor which can be used to flavor stews.

PICKLING ONION (*Allium cepa*)

Picked when the plant has just formed bulbs, the small size of these onions makes them ideal for pickling. They are also good boiled and served in sauce.

YELLOW ONION (*Allium cepa*)

Dubbed "The King of Vegetables" because of its dominant taste, long reign and widespread influence, the onion is extremely versatile. There are two general types, mild or pungent, and two shapes, globe and elongated. Available all year round, they are eaten raw, boiled, steamed, braised, fried and in many prepared dishes, stuffings and sauces. Like all varieties, the yellow onion originated in central Asia and is today found worldwide. Unlike most white varieties, it is mild and keeps well. Onions are available all year round, both fresh and dehydrated.

Pickling onions

Yellow onion

Leek

ITALIAN RED ONION (*Allium cepa*)

Oblong, mild and sometimes sweet, this variety is grown in many places. It is attractive when sliced thinly in rings and used raw as a garnish, as cooking blanches red onions. Like all onions, leeks and shallots, this variety becomes bitter when its cut flesh is exposed to the air too long before use.

Italian red onion

GARLIC (*Allium sativum*)

Garlic is probably of central Asian origin, as both Chinese and Egyptians were using it early in their history. It is sold all year round in heads, but usually used in small amounts of one or two cloves at a time. It can be used simply as a vegetable, but compounds the taste of an infinite variety of savory dishes (one of the most notorious is *lièvre à la royale,* a French dish that calls for some 30 cloves). Garlic cloves can be planted .

Shallot

SHALLOT (*Allium ascalonicum*)

Unknown in ancient times and of uncertain origin, this is a close relative of, but less pungent than, the onion. It is widely used in France, where there are gray, pink and golden-brown varieties, and is mostly available in summer and autumn. Mainly used in sauces, the elongated varieties tend to be stronger-tasting.

SCALLION (*Allium cepa*)

Picked when young and tender before the bulb forms, scallions, or green onions are available all year and are used fresh and in salads and stir-frys.

Scallion

Garlic

RED ONIONS (*Allium cepa*)

This variety, sometimes called Spanish onion, is mild and often sweet. It can be eaten raw in salads, boiled or baked, or used to flavor soups, sauces and stews.

Red onion

Root Vegetables

WHITE RADISH
(*Raphanus sativus*)

Grown since prehistory in the
Middle East, radishes were a
favourite in ancient Egypt. The
wild radish probably originated in
southern Asia. White cultivated
varieties are found in many
countries, and are usually at their
best in the spring. Available
throughout the year, the white
radish is primarily used as a
salad vegetable.

DAIKON RADISH
(*Raphanus sativus*)

This traditional Japanese radish is
often sold in Far Eastern markets.
Milder than other types, it can be
grated and used as a garnish, or
pickled. In Japan it is finely sliced
and cooked with other vegetables
or used in soups.

Daikon radish

Navette

White radish

NAVETTE (*Brassica rapa*)

A type of French turnip available in
Europe in winter and early spring
this can be boiled or used in
casseroles, soups and stews. The
flesh is usually white.

Scorzonera

SCORZONERA
(Scorzonera hispanica)

Scorzonera and its close relative salsify (also called oyster plant because of its delicate flavor) have long tapering roots and are members of the daisy family. Native to Europe and the Mediterranean and also grown in some parts of America, scorzonera has a black skin and salsify a white skin. Both plants can be used for soups, salads, as a cooked vegetable, puréed, in hors d'œuvres or casseroles. Also known as black salsify, scorzonera is at its best in late autumn.

PARSNIP *(Pastinaca sativa)*

A sweet root vegetable native to Europe, it is sold fresh all year round but is at its best in winter. It can be braised, boiled, roasted, puréed, candied or even – in some parts of Europe – made into wine.

Turnips

Parsnip

TURNIP *(Brassica rapa)*

The swollen root of a plant thought to be native to Europe, this can vary considerably in size, shape and color. Available all year round, turnips are cooked whole when young and small, and puréed or used in stews and soups when older. The green-leaved tops can be cooked like spinach.

RUTABAGA
(*Brassica napobrassica*)

This heavy, coarse-skinned root vegetable originated in Europe but is also common in America. It is at its best in winter and resembles the turnip, but has yellow-orange flesh. It can be baked, roasted with meat, sliced and fried, boiled and mashed (delicious mixed with potatoes and carrots) or cubed, blanched and added to stews. In Finland it is cooked with cream and spices.

RADISH (*Raphanus sativus*)

Native to southern Asia, cultivated varieties of red radish are sold all year round but taste less peppery in spring. Usually eaten raw in salads or with bread and butter as an hors d'œuvre, its leaves add pungency to salads. They can be lightly stir-fried.

BEET (*Beta vulgaris*)

Beet and its close relatives all developed from *Beta maritima*, a Mediterranean seashore plant whose root was cultivated in Germany in the Middle Ages. Widely grown around the world, it is sold throughout the year. Available fresh or canned, it can be boiled or baked and served hot, or cooled and pickled. The beet is an ingredient in the classic Russian soup *bortsch*, and is much used as a salad vegetable. In America, small beets are served in orange juice as Yale beets, and in a sweet-sour sauce as Harvard beets.

Radish

Rutabaga

Beet

CELERIAC
(*Apium graveolens*, var. *rapaceum*)

This special variety of celery, with a similar taste, is cultivated for its thick, tuberous root. A winter vegetable, it should be firm and must be peeled before cooking – this is easier if it is cut into slices first. It can be eaten raw, grated, or boiled until tender and served with sauce, blanched and dressed with vinaigrette sauce, or puréed and used in soups and stews. Celeriac tends to discolour when cut, so a few drops of lemon juice should be added to the cooking water or salad to prevent this.

Celeriac

OTHER ROOT VEGETABLES

Carrot

CARROT (*Daucus carota*)

Thought to be native to Europe, wild carrots were cultivated by the Dutch in the Middle Ages. Carrots are available all year round but are most tender in early summer when they are also smaller and sweeter. Sold fresh, canned and frozen, carrots are good steamed or boiled, or sautéed in butter and herbs, roasted with meat or used in stews and soups. They are also used to make carrot cake. Their fresh juice is nutritious and delicious.

APIO and ARRACACHA
(*Apios tuberosa*)
Members of the legume family, these are native to North America and are cooked like potatoes or used in desserts. They are very similar in flavor and are interchangeable.

A similar plant from South America, and also called Arracacha, is the Peruvian carrot (*Arracacia xanthorrhiza*). Cultivated in the Andes – and native to Colombia, not Peru, despite the name – the roots may be baked, fried or used in soups and stews, like potatoes. A flour from the roots is used to make breads and pancakes.

ARROWHEAD
(*Sagittaria sagittifolia*)
Tule potato or wappato are other names for this water plant with arrow-shaped leaves. Both leaves and root are used in Chinese cooking.

BITTERROOT
(*Lewisia rediviva*)
This plant of the purslane family is native to North America's north-west. The roots are fleshy, succulent and nutritious and, despite the name, are not bitter when peeled.

BLACK RADISH
(*Raphanus sativus*)
Unlike the more common radishes, the black winter variety is the size of a small turnip. It is used mostly as a winter salad vegetable.

BURDOCK (*Arctium lappa*)
This is a wild, thistlelike plant common to the northern hemisphere. Young leaf stems are used in salads; in Japan, where it is called *gobo,* the entire plant is used.

CHINESE ARTICHOKE
(*Stachys affinis*)
Native to China and developed in Europe by the French, this tuber can be grated raw into winter vegetable salads, used as an accompanying vegetable to meat dishes, and in Chinese mixed vegetable dishes. It is available in late autumn and early winter.

HAMBURG PARSLEY
(*Petroselinum hortense*)
Also called turnip-rooted parsley, this plant is cultivated for its root, which is white, slender and closely resembles a parsnip. Its popularity in eastern and northern Europe may help to account for its name. Used in soups and stews, it can also be an accompanying vegetable like celeriac. It has a slightly nutty flavor.

HORSERADISH
(*Armoracia rusticana*)
Native to southeast Europe and western Asia, this root is usually crushed and made into a sauce. It has a pungent flavor and is a popular ingredient in cocktail sauces.

LOTUS
(*Nelumbium nuciferum*)
This sacred plant of India and China is used extensively in the cooking of the Far East, where it is indigenous. The cut root is perforated with holes, a decorative quality exploited in Chinese and Japanese dishes. It is available fresh, dried or canned, and can be served as a starch, pickled or steamed. The raw leaves are used in salads.

Tubers

WEST INDIAN YAM
(*Dioscorea batatas*)

Native to Africa and Asia, yams are also grown in tropical America. There are many varieties of this mild, tuberous root, which is high in starch. In Africa, yams are mashed, peppered and spiced to make *foufou* and *kalajoum*. They may be cooked in the same way as potatoes and are a popular feature of West Indian cooking.

JERUSALEM ARTICHOKE
(*Helianthus tuberosus*)

Indigenous to North America and introduced to Europe in the seventeenth century, there are several varieties, ranging from beige to brownish red. It has a nut-like taste, and can be eaten raw in salads, or cooked in sauces and casseroles. It is mainly a winter vegetable.

Jerusalem artichoke

SWEET POTATO/YAM
(*Ipomoea batatas*)

Sweet potatoes are not related to ordinary potatoes, although both hail from Central America. They arrrived in Europe before the common potato, and were highly regarded. There are two main types: the reddish sweet potatoes, commonly called yams, have sweet orange flesh and are good with roasts, or mashed and used in cakes, souffles, pies and stuffings; the white varieties, with drier yellow flesh, can be fried, boiled or used in casseroles. Both types of potato are traditional at Thanksgiving.

West Indian yam

White sweet potato

Red sweet potato

OTHER TUBERS

CASSAVA
(*Manihot utilissima*)
Also known as manioc, this starchy tuber from Central America is used to make tapioca (page 106). Fermented, it is used in an alcoholic drink and the leaves can be eaten as a vegetable. Cassava flour is used in cakes and pies.

TARO (*Colocasia antiquorum*)
This tuber contains fine-grained and digestible starch and is used as a vegetable in West Indian cookery, cooked like the potato. In the West Indies the leaves are eaten, like cabbage.

POTATO
(Solanum tuberosum)

The potato plant is a member of the nightshade family whose edible tuber is one of the world's most important food crops. (A tuber is a growth that forms underground on the plant's stems; potato plants may have from 3 to 20 tubers each, depending on variety, weather, and soil conditions.) Indigenous to South America, the potato is now cultivated worldwide in hundreds of varieties.

Potatoes were first cultivated by South American Indians of the high Andes. Spaniards brought potatoes to Europe in the early 16th century; Sir Francis Drake is believed to have introduced them into England in 1586. From there, potato cultivation spread to Ireland, where they quickly became the principle crop. Potatoes did not become an important food crop in the American colonies until the early 18th century, when Irish immigrants brought the tubers with them when they settled in New England.

In the United States potatoes are generally divided into four basic categories: Round Whites, also sold as Maine, Eastern, or All-purpose potatoes, are good for boiling, mashing, and frying; mealier varieties can also be baked. Round Reds and California Long Whites are good for boiling. Russet Burbank, or Idaho, potatoes are the choice for baking; they are also good french-fried.

A potato that is harvested young, usually in the spring or early summer, and is sent directly to market instead of being stored, is known as a new potato. Tender and thin-skinned, new potatoes are best scraped and simply boiled in their skin. Serve them with butter, salt, and pepper or in salads.

Illustrated on this page are two popular American varieties. The Kennebec is a thin-skinned, creamy white potato that is excellent for baking and frying. The Red Pontiac is a non-mealy,

white-flesh potato with red or pinkish-white skin; it boils well without disintegrating. Also shown are two new potatoes and several common British and European varieties.

Look for new potatoes in the spring and early summer. Mature potatoes are available throughout the year. All potatoes should be firm, clean but not washed, fairly smooth, and well shaped, with no sprouts, wilting, or decay. Avoid any with "light burn" (green discolorations which must be cut away). Also avoid potatoes with numerous "eyes," cuts, or bruises. Store potatoes in a cool, dark, well-aired bin rather than in the refrigerator.

New potato

Red pontiac potato

Desiree potato

Cyprus new potato

Maris Piper potato

Pentland Squire potato

Pentland Hawk potato

King Edward potato

Pentland Crown potato

Pods and Seeds

PEA (*Pisum sativum*)

Possibly the earliest of all cultivars, the pea was first grown in the Middle East. Garden peas are sold fresh, frozen, canned and dried (page 39), and may be puréed, used in soups, stews and as a cooked vegetable. The pods are usually discarded, but may be used to make pea soup.

SNOW PEA (*Pisum sativum*)

Also called the mangetout, sugar pea or snap pea, this is an early variety of pea (usually available in winter and spring) which has very tender pods. They are eaten pod and all.

PETITS POIS (*Pisum sativum*)

These are garden peas picked very young while they are sweet and tender. Particularly popular in France, they are often considered to be the finest of all varieties.

Petits pois

Snow pea

Garden pea

OKRA (*Hibiscus esculenta*)

Also known as lady's finger or gumbo, this pod is the fruit of an annual plant of the cotton family, native to tropical Africa. Widely used in the South, in okra soup and dishes with rice, it appears in Indian cooking as *bindi*, and as *bamia* in the Middle East, cooked in a lamb stew. Available fresh, canned, or frozen, it may be used to thicken soups and stews, or fried and eaten as a vegetable.

SWEET CORN (*Zea mays*)

Also named maize, this variety is indigenous to America, but now grown throughout the world. It may be fresh, frozen or canned, and is used as a vegetable, boiled or roasted and eaten with butter. Also used in soups, it may be puréed, made into fritters, cornmeal, corn bread, corn pone and hominy.

Okra

Sweet corn

BEAN SPROUTS
(*Phaseolus aureus*)

Virtually any grain or large seed can be sprouted, but the one most frequently sprouted commercially is the mung bean (page 41). Used as a vegetable in Oriental cooked dishes, bean sprouts may also be eaten raw in salads.

Sprouting mung beans

Alfalfa sprouts

Bean sprouts

Fava bean

Mature runner bean

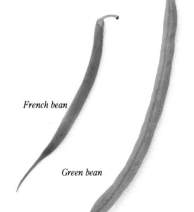

French bean

Green bean

FAVA BEAN (*Vicia faba*)

The only bean native to the Old World, this seed has been grown and eaten throughout Europe and the Middle East since prehistoric times (pages 38 and 42). A brown Egyptian variety provides the staple *ful.* They may be creamed, served with a sauce or puréed, and are the traditional complement to ham or bacon. Fava beans are available frozen or canned, and fresh in winter and spring. Normally shelled, very young pods may also be cooked and eaten.

GREEN BEAN
(*Phaseolus vulgaris*)

Native to Central America and grown for their pods, there are many varieties, including runner, Lima and French beans. Green beans need only be trimmed before cooking; runner beans must have their tough strings stripped off even when they are very young. There is also a yellow variety, known as wax bean or butter bean, which is sweetest if picked when young.

DRIED PEAS, BEANS AND LENTILS

PEAS, BEANS AND LENTILS are the edible seeds of certain plants of the legume family. Some, like green beans, fava beans, lima beans and green peas are eaten fresh; others are eaten dried and in this form have been a staple food in many parts of the world for thousands of years.

Archaeological research into plant origins has shown that beans were among the first plants cultivated when agriculture began. The "common bean" (which includes kidney and its many varieties such as pinto and black) was first cultivated in Mexico; lima beans in Peru; fava beans and chick-peas in the Middle East; soy- and aduki beans in China, and black-eyed peas and pigeon peas in Africa. All have become widely naturalized outside their native regions, however, so that today most of them are available worldwide.

Beans remain as popular as ever in the cooking of the Middle East, Asia, the Caribbean, Mexico and Central and South America, while in North America and Europe there is an ever-growing interest in them due in part to the high cost of meats and to the increasing popularity of vegetarian cooking.

Methods of processing
Beans are dried as quickly as possible after picking to preserve their flavor, plumpness and texture. They are then graded and any stones removed before packing. Most are now artificially dried and graded by machine. Mung beans and soybeans may also be sprouted for their shoots, which are eaten as a fresh vegetable.

Dried beans, peas and lentils are in some cases also available cooked and canned and a few types are fermented or processed into some other form, such as flour, oil, fresh pressed bean curd or dried bean curd sheets. The fermentation processes that are used vary considerably. In China black beans are fermented in salt, and in Africa in wood ash. The process may continue for months, as for the soybeans used to make soy sauce.

In the kitchen
Most peas, beans and lentils are widely available and the lesser-known varieties can usually be found in shops specializing in Oriental and health foods. They keep well and are easily reconstituted but should be stored in a cool, dry place and used within 6 to 9 months.

Peas, beans and lentils may be used whole in casseroles, salads and vegetable dishes, puréed in soups or ground and used for croquettes and dips. All types of beans and lentils are high in protein and 30 per cent more is released if they are eaten with grains; this is why there are many dishes around the world in which beans are served with rice or bread.

In many recipes, one type can be successfully substituted for another, but variation in flavor and texture should be taken into account since this makes some much more suitable than others for certain dishes. Those peas, beans or lentils that become very tender with cooking will absorb other flavors well and are particularly good in spicy or herbed casseroles, while those with a firmer texture are the best to serve whole as a vegetable or in salads.

Remember that most beans need soaking and cooking, the exact times depending on the particular type and quality of the bean. Pick over the beans before washing and soaking them to remove any stones or pieces of grit, and add salt toward the end of cooking time, as this will make the beans soften more quickly.

Peas

DRIED PEA (*Pisum sativum*)

Dried peas were an important vegetable before frozen peas appeared, but they have now lost much of their popularity. In Germany, whole dried peas are still baked with sauerkraut and soured cream. The blue boiling pea is one of the most tasty of several varieties of dried peas. Its texture is coarse, but it retains its shape when cooked.

Whole peas

SPLIT YELLOW PEA (*Pisum sativum*)

Like the split green pea, these make excellent purées for soup and for vegetable dishes served with ham.

Split yellow peas

CHICK-PEA (*Cicer arietinum*)

Also known as garbanzo, ceci (Italy) and chana dal (India), there are several varieties of this large pea, native to western Asia. Available whole and split, they can be served in casseroles, soups and stews and are the main ingredient of *humus*, a savory dip, or *felafel*, deep-fried patties. A staple food of the Middle East, chick-peas also appear in many European and Oriental dishes.

Middle Eastern chick-peas

SPLIT GREEN PEA (*Pisum sativum*)

It cooks to a purée to make the traditional English pease pudding served with salt pork, a complementary combination that is also successful in split pea soups made with a ham bone, and may be used in vegetable dishes.

Mediterranean chick-peas

Split green peas

Split skinless chick-peas

Beans and Lentils

GREEN LENTIL
(*Lens esculenta*)

Lentils are particularly rich in protein. This variety, also known as the continental lentil, is popular in European cooking. It retains its shape after cooking and may be served as a vegetable. There are large and small varieties.

Large green lentils

Small green lentils

Puy lentils

YELLOW LENTIL
(*Lens esculenta*)

Because of their Asian origin, many lentils are often referred to by their Indian names as types of dal. Also known as yellow dal, this lentil is often served as a main or side dish with curry.

Yellow lentils

Orange lentils

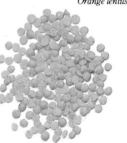

Indian brown lentils

ORANGE LENTIL
(*Lens esculenta*)

There are many different varieties of lentil, usually identified by and named after their color. They all have the same flattish round shape, but vary in size and may be sold split or whole. Lentils play an important part in Indian cookery, where they are usually served as a main or side dish with curry, and the split orange variety is a staple food throughout the Middle East, where it is often served with rice. Lentils do not need soaking before cooking. This familiar orange lentil quickly cooks to a purée.

FLAGEOLET
(*Phaseolus vulgaris*)

A small green variety of common bean (haricot) native to the Americas, this can be eaten fresh or dried and is also available pre-cooked and canned. Its fresh texture and delicate taste make it especially good as a vegetable or in salads. In France it is traditionally eaten with roast lamb.

Flageolets

OTHER BEANS

PINTO BEAN
(*Phaseolus vulgaris*)
These beans are kidney-shaped and beige dappled with brown flecks. They lose their color but not their flavor when cooked.

PUY LENTIL
(*Lens esculenta*)

These dark French lentils, which vary in size, are highly regarded and considered the best of their type. They retain their shape when they are cooked.

INDIAN BROWN LENTIL
(*Lens esculenta*)

Also known as masoor dal, these are red lentils with their seedcoats. They become a purée when they are cooked.

MUNG BEAN (*Phaseolus aureus*)

Also known as moong dal or green gram, these are widely cultivated in India and China. They have a good flavor and very high vitamin content, and are available whole, split or skinless. Probably best-known in the form of bean sprouts (page 37), mung beans are widely used in China, where the sweet tender shoots are used to make *fen tiao* noodles, and in India where they are curried. They are used in stews.

Whole mung beans

Skinless mung beans

Split mung beans

GREAT NORTHERN BEAN (*Phaseolus vulgaris*)

A large, creamy-white, flat variety of the common (haricot) bean, this is used in stews and casseroles, and is generally interchangeable with other types of white beans.

Great Northern beans

NAVY BEAN (*Phaseolus vulgaris*)

This small white variety of common bean is also known as pearl haricot, Boston bean and pea bean. It is used to make the French dish *cassoulet* and the traditional Boston baked beans, the forerunners of modern, canned baked beans.

Navy bean

URD BEAN (*Phaseolus mungo*)

Also known as urd dal or black gram, this bean is sold in several forms. It is thought to be native to India and is widely grown both in India and the Far East.

Whole urd beans

Skinless urd beans

Split urd beans

FAVA BEAN (Vicia faba)

Native to north Africa, this was cultivated by the ancient Egyptians and Greeks. It is available fresh (page 37), dried or canned. The dried beans have a fine texture and can be eaten on their own or in stews and salads.

Fava beans

BLACK BEAN
(Phaseolus vulgaris)

This shiny black variety of common bean, tender and sweet-tasting, is a staple food in the Caribbean, Mexico and Central and South America. Fried black beans and rice *(gallo pinto)* is the national breakfast dish of Costa Rica, while *feijoada completa,* a dish of mixed meats and black beans served with cassava meal *(farofa),* diced oranges, hot fresh pepper sauce and collard greens is the national dish of Brazil.

Black beans

BORLOTTI BEAN
(Phaseolus vulgaris)

Also known as saligia beans, borlotti beans come from Italy. They cook to a creamy consistency and are baked in spicy casseroles or may be used in dips and salads.

Borlotto beans

RED KIDNEY BEAN
(Phaseolus vulgaris)

This sweet-tasting bean with a firm texture comes in many varieties ranging from dark pink to maroon. It is most readily identified with Mexican cooking, particularly for its use in the hot, spicy dish *chilli con carne.*

Red kidney beans

CANNELLINO BEAN
(Phaseolus vulgaris)

A creamy-white kidney bean, this is slightly larger than the navy bean and with a fluffier texture. Used mostly in Italian cooking, cannellini beans (or fagiola beans) are often used with tuna fish to make *tonno e fagioli.*

Cannellino beans

BLACK FERMENTED CHINESE BEAN (Glycine max)

These are smallish black beans – usually soy – which, in China, are fermented in salt and added to meat and vegetable dishes.

Black fermented Chinese beans

LIMA BEAN (Phaseolus lunatus)

There are two sizes and several varieties of these kidney-shaped beans which are eaten both fresh and dried. Available fresh, dried and frozen, they are usually pale green or cream, which accounts for the fact that they are sometimes referred to as butter beans. They are also known as Madagascar beans because they are grown there so extensively, although they were originally found in South America. Dried limas retain their shape well and are often served by themselves as a hot vegetable, or in succotash.

Lima beans

FUL MEDAMES
(Lathyrus sativus)

A small variety of broad bean widely eaten in the Middle East, where it originated, its white counterpart is called ful nabed. Dried bean patties or *taamiya* are eaten throughout the Middle East and ful medames have given their name to one of Egypt's national dishes, in which they are baked with eggs, cumin and garlic. They are also good when cooked and served as a vegetable.

Ful medames

ADUKI BEAN
(Phaseolus angularis)

Also called adzuki beans, these small dark red or black beans are very tender when cooked and have an unusually sweet, quite strong flavor. The seeds of a bushy annual native to China, they are valued in the Far East for their medicinal properties and have been eaten in rice dishes and soups for thousands of years. Their sweetness has also made them a common ingredient in Oriental confectionery.

Aduki beans

BLACK-EYED PEAS
(Vigna senensis)

Native to China, this pea has come to be identified with the cooking of the southern states of America, where it has given its name to a classic dish of salt pork and beans. Also known as cowpeas and black-eyed beans, in China they are stir-fried and mixed with meat or fish to make *chiang ton chia*.

Black-eyed peas

RICE BEAN
(Phaseolus calcaratus)

Rice beans are grown in limited amounts in China, India and the Philippines. They are named because of their rice-like taste.

Rice beans

LABLAB BEAN
(Dolichos lablab)

Hard-skinned beans from the hyacinth plant, also known as hyacinth beans, these originated in India but are now eaten throughout Asia and the Middle East, particularly in Egypt. They must be shelled before cooking.

Lablab beans

PIGEON PEA *(Cajanus cajan)*

Also known as gandules and toor dal, these beige beans take their name "pea" from their shape and size and have a sweetish flavor. Native to Africa, they are a staple food in the Caribbean, used in dishes such as *jugjug* from Barbados and pigeon pea soup from Trinidad.

Pigeon peas

SOYBEANS *(Glycine max)*

Soybeans range in color from yellow, green and red to black. They are very high in nutrients, especially protein, and have been an important part of Oriental diets for many years. They are used for making bean curd (also known as *tofu*), delicate noodles called *harusame* and a sweet confectionery paste. The beans are also fermented and used to make flavoring pastes and condiments, notably soy sauce (called *shoyu* in Japan), *tempeh* from Indonesia and *miso* from Japan. More recently, soybeans are used for making a variety of basic western foodstuffs, as well as for industrial purposes such as the manufacture of plastics. They provide an important oil (page 75), can be ground to make a flour (page 107) and are the basis of most meat substitutes. Soybeans are also often used for their milk.

One of the "five sacred grains" of ancient China, soybeans require lengthy preparation for cooking, but a pre-cooked variety known as soy splits is available. The beans may be sprouted for their long, crisp shoots, which are best cooked.

Black soybeans

Yellow soybeans

MUSHROOMS AND TRUFFLES

CONFUSION EXISTS OVER THE terms "mushrooms" and "fungi". Here we use the term "mushroom" to describe all forms of edible fungi. Mushrooms can be wild, cultivated, fresh, canned, pickled and dried. They are made into sauces and are used in a great variety of dishes in most countries throughout the world. Mushrooms contain about 80 per cent water, 8 per cent carbohydrate and 1 per cent fat. They are also a good source of protein, and other vitamins and minerals, such as riboflavin and thiamine, iron and copper, potassium and phosphates.

Mushrooming is a favorite pastime in many countries, though the mushrooms sought are different. In America alone there are about fifty edible wild species. However, not all mushrooms are edible. Certain mushrooms of the Amanita family are deadly, indeed *Amanita phalloides* is known as death cap, or, more picturesquely, the angel of death. Mushrooms of the *Psilocybe* species found mostly in Mexico are hallucinogenic and were once regarded as sacred. Amateur mushroom hunters are urged to gather only those easy to identify, among them the morel, held to be the finest of all mushrooms, the shaggymane and the puffballs. It is important to have all wild mushrooms identified by a reputable source before eating them; in America, membership of one of the mycology societies takes care of the problem with expert identification.

Cultivating mushrooms
Ignorance about the growth and life-cycle of mushrooms was widespread until in 1678 the French botanist Marchant demonstrated that mushrooms grew from spawn, appearing on a lace-like structure, the mycelium, just beneath the surface of the soil. Market gardeners in Paris swiftly put theory into practice and transplanted the mushroom "roots" to a bed of horse manure, and thus bred the ancestors of a remarkably successful commercial product.

In the 1890s, French scientists finally consolidated their long monopoly by developing a pasteurized spawn, and therefore more dependable crops. American growers, who had first raised mushrooms in New York City, adopted the French technique in the late nineteenth century. Today the mushroom industry is a thriving one, with Pennsylvania the center of the industry in America.

Elsewhere the cultivation of mushrooms remains a local industry on a limited scale, mainly in China and Japan, although wild mushrooms have a ready market in Europe. Russia's *Lactarius deliciosus* is gathered in conifer forests and sold in dried form, likewise the boletus, and chanterelles in France, Italy, Poland and Germany, where over 300 species of edible mushrooms are sold. Five types of mushroom are now cultivated: the common mushroom, the French and Italian truffle, China's straw mushroom and cloud ear fungus, and Japan's shiitake. The matsutake, from Japan, while not cultivated, is extensively gathered and canned for export.

Mushrooms in the kitchen
Some mushrooms may need parboiling first, especially chanterelles. Large varieties can be sliced, dipped in egg and breadcrumbs, and fried in bacon fat, while young mushrooms are excellent sliced raw in salads. Dried cepes or porcini mushrooms are a useful standby ingredient, and they keep for over a year. They are dried on wire trays in a current of air maintained at 130°F. Unless their skin is tough and discolored, fresh mushrooms need not be peeled. Wipe the caps with a damp cloth or paper towel. If they are very dirty or sandy and must be washed, do it quickly without letting them soak. Wild specimens should be carefully sorted and checked for insects and grit. Cook as soon as possible after gathering. Dried mushrooms will need soaking in warm water until soft – about 15 minutes. To store fresh mushrooms, put them in an open plastic bag in the refrigerator, where they will keep for four or five days. As little as three ounces of dried mushrooms when reconstituted can yield the equivalent of one pound of fresh mushrooms.

TRUFFLES
(Tuber magnatum, melanosporum)

These are tubers that grow near the roots of oak or beech trees – they are "cultivated" to the extent that oak groves are planted to encourage them. The two main varieties, and the most highly prized in cuisine, are the black Périgord truffle (*Tuber melanosporum*) and the white Piedmontese truffle (*T. magnatum*) of Alba, Italy, both expensive luxuries. There is also the red-grained black truffle (*T. æstivum*), which grows in England but is largely ignored, and the violet truffle of Europe (*T. brumale*). Fresh truffles are gathered in the autumn, and are only marketed locally, so most of us are obliged to buy them cooked and canned, when they have lost some of their characteristic taste and aroma.

White truffles have a powerful taste and aroma. They are usually grated, raw, on pasta, risotto or egg dishes, although one classic recipe suggests cooking them with Parmesan cheese. Black truffles can be used as a decorative garnish, in *pâté de foie gras,* aspic dishes, or cooked with scrambled eggs, as in *brouillade de truffe.*

Périgord black truffle

Piedmontese white truffle

WOOD EAR
(Auricularia polytricha)

This Chinese mushroom is cultivated on wood, or gathered wild from tree trunks on which it grows. It is also known as cloud ear and Chinese black fungus. Dried, it forms a gelatinous, tough product that needs reconstituting in several changes of warm water for about 30 minutes.

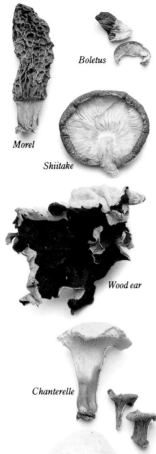

Boletus

Morel

Shiitake

Wood ear

Chanterelle

Rubber brush

RUBBER BRUSH
(Hydnum repandum)

Commonly found in all types of woodland in autumn and early winter, the rubber brush or wood hedgehog is unique in having spines instead of gills. It is a good cooking mushroom.

BOLETUS (Boletus granulatus)

Also known as the yellow mushroom, this is a fruity-smelling, superior-tasting mushroom found in conifer woods in the late summer and autumn. The dried version is shown here.

MOREL (Morchella esculenta)

Not a true mushroom, the morel is easily recognizable by its brown, sponge-like cap, pitted with hollows in which the spores are produced, and which gives rise to its other common name of sponge mushroom. It can be found in woodland clearings during spring and early summer and can also be bought, dried or canned, in speciality food stores.

SHIITAKE (Lentinus edodes)

Also known as Chinese mushrooms, these are the most widely used mushrooms in Oriental cooking and are grown in China and Japan on the wood of dead deciduous trees. *Lentinus edodes* takes its name from the *shii*-tree (*Pasania*), but also grows on the oak and hornbeam. The spawn is planted into holes or wedges cut in the logs, and crops last for 3–6 years. Shiitake are dried by sun or artificial heat. Dried ones should be soaked in warm water for 20 minutes before using.

CHANTERELLE
(Cantharellus cibarius)

Commonly found in European woods, especially beech, from summer to midwinter, the chanterelle (also called girolle or egg mushroom) smells faintly of apricots and, when cooked, tastes slightly peppery with a delicate perfume. Its firm flesh requires longer cooking than other fungi. Chanterelles cannot be artificially cultivated but are available dried or canned in specialty food stores.

Mushrooms

CULTIVATED MUSHROOM
(*Agaricus bisporus*)

The cultivated mushroom comes in three sizes, the smallest or button, the medium-sized, and the largest or open (flat) mushroom, and is available all year round.

FIELD MUSHROOM
(*Agaricus campestris*)

A "wild" version of the cultivated mushroom, this is found from late summer to the end of autumn.

FLAT MUSHROOM
(*Agaricus bisporus*)

Also called the open mushroom, this is the largest and most strongly flavored form of the cultivated mushroom.

BUTTON MUSHROOM
(*Agaricus bisporus*)

The smallest, most immature form of the cultivated mushroom.

BLEWIT (*Lepista,* spp.)

Named for their bluish-violet cast, blewits are found under deciduous trees or conifers. They appear from October to December and are best fried or baked.

FIELD MUSHROOM
(*Agaricus vaporarius*)

One of the many varieties of wild mushroom to be found in meadows and pastures in summer and autumn.

Field mushroom
(Agaricus campestris)

Cultivated mushrooms

Blewit

Button mushroom

Flat mushroom

Field mushroom
(Agaricus vaporarius)

BEEFSTEAK FUNGUS
(*Fistulina hepatica*)
Named after the beef-like appearance of its flesh, this is found occasionally on living trees, especially oaks.

PARASOL MUSHROOM
(*Macrolepiota procera*)
A summer and autumn fungus found standing tall on grassy hillsides, often near trees, its size makes it easy to find. Also known as the umbrella mushroom because of the way in which its cap opens out from its stem on maturing. It should be picked young. Although this is an excellent tasting mushroom, the stalk should not be eaten as it is tough and fibrous.

CEP (*Boletus edulis*)
Also known as the cèpe or boletus (but not to be confused with *Boletus granulatus*), this is a superior-tasting wild mushroom widely eaten in Europe. The Greeks and Romans used the term *bolites* to describe the best edible mushrooms, but this term has since been applied only to the boletus. Found in woodland clearings in late summer and autumn, usually under beech or coniferous trees, they are distinguished by their stout stalks with delicately raised white veins running toward the top, and by the vertical tubes underneath the cap in which the brown spores are produced. Commercially, they are sold in imported dried form.

OTHER MUSHROOMS

GIANT PUFFBALL
(*Lycoperdon giganteum*)
All true puffballs are edible, but can only be eaten when they are young, firm and white. The giant puffball can be found in woods and meadows in late summer and autumn.

HORSE MUSHROOM
(*Agaricus arvensis*)
Similar to the field mushroom in habitat and taste, the horse mushroom has a yellow-tinted cap and grayish gills.

MATSUTAKE
(*Tricholoma matsutake*)
This type of wild mushroom grows on the *matsu* (pine) tree. A cousin of the European blewit, matsutake is a delicate, fine-tasting mushroom which is collected wild, and sold canned or fresh (in Japan). It is used in several Japanese dishes, including *tori mushiyaki*.

OYSTER MUSHROOM
(*Pleurotus ostreatus*)
A wild mushroom, now being cultivated, with a bluish gray cap, this is eaten fried or grilled.

STRAW MUSHROOMS
(*Volvariella volvacea*)
These small, conical mushrooms are grown on wet rice straw beds, and sold fresh, canned or dried. The local industry, in Canton, is probably quite old. They feature in such recipes as the vegetarian dish *sushi-chin,* and steamed or fried chicken dishes.

SHITAKE MUSHROOM
(*Lentinus edordes*)
The meaty, earthy flavor and resilient texture make this Oriental mushroom a substantial treat. Their flat shape makes them ideal for stuffing, but they are usually delicious grilled or in stir-frys, or in stews or soups. They are now cultivated in America.

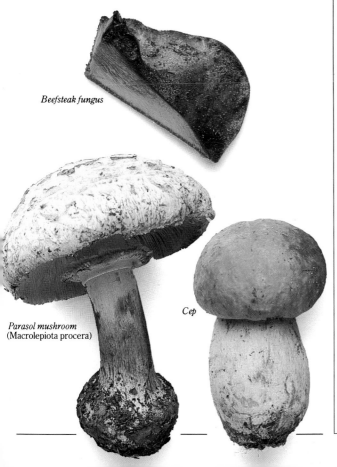

Beefsteak fungus

Parasol mushroom
(Macrolepiota procera)

Cep

Herbs, Spices and Seeds

ERBS ARE NON-WOODY PLANTS – usually annual and mostly grown from seed – of which the flowers, leaves, seeds, stems and roots are used as flavorings in cooking, or for medicinal purposes. The name "herb" comes from the Latin word *herba,* meaning grass or herbage. They are plants of great antiquity going back to earliest civilizations, with records from ancient Persia, Egypt, Arabia, Greece, India and China giving details of their cultivation and use. The names of many are a reminder of the medieval period after the fall of Rome when the monasteries of Europe were centers of agriculture, each having its own herb or "physic" garden.

Herbs gathered for the medicine chest have an alchemistic ring to them, with names like skullcap, St John's wort, wormwood, woodruff, balm and self-heal. All herbs do, in fact, have medicinal qualities and some – rue, for example – still provide a source for a substantial number of vital drugs used in pharmacy. Many have a dual purpose as they are used both in cooking and in medicine and, although the original purpose is unknown, the general consensus is that their primary use was culinary. Centuries before the birth of Christ it was suggested that medicine was a by-product of cooking. One use must have followed the other rapidly since the Sumerians were using thyme and laurel medicinally by 5000 BC and in 2700 BC the Chinese had an herbal listing 365 plants.

Herbs are also credited with magical and religious significance. The Romans, for example, believed that a wreath of bay leaves would protect the wearer from lightning during a storm. Nicholas Culpeper's herbal of 1653 was extremely popular and influential, mixing herbs with magic, medicine and astrology.

Herbs in the kitchen

The use of herbs in the kitchen is ruled by culinary traditions which vary from country to country. Every cuisine has its favorite herbs: oregano, mint and dill are used a great deal in lamb dishes in the Middle East and Greece; in Thailand, coriander leaves garnish almost every dish on the table, and lemon grass flavors fish and chicken dishes. In Britain,

sage is a favorite with pork and gives its green color to Sage Derby cheese, while roast lamb is usually served with mint sauce.

Dill is an important flavoring: for fish in Scandinavia, soups in Russia and Denmark, and for pickling cucumbers in America. Italians acknowledge the happy union of basil with tomatoes and rosemary with lamb, the Germans of savory with beans, and the French of tarragon with chicken and fennel with fish. The herbs of Provence are justly famous for their pungency and aroma: thyme, marjoram, tarragon, juniper, lavender, bay, rosemary and fennel owe much to the soil of the region and to the long hours of sunshine. The amount used in cooking depends partly on individual taste, and partly on the type of herb. Strongly flavored herbs should be used only sparingly.

Fresh herbs are always preferred to dried ones, and many, such as parsley, basil, fennel, marjoram or thyme, can be grown in pots on a window sill. Dried herbs are much more concentrated than fresh because the water content has been removed. For every teaspoon of dried herbs, use 1 tablespoon of fresh.

Bouquet garni, much used in French cooking, is a bouquet of herbs tied with a piece of string or in a small square of cheesecloth and put into sauces, stews or *court bouillon.* Strictly, the herbs are parsley sprigs, thyme sprigs and bay leaf but other seasonings may be added such as celery, garlic, rosemary, marjoram, savory and so on. The bouquet is always removed at the end of the cooking time. Bay leaves put directly into a dish are also removed at the end of cooking, and so are dried sprigs of herbs like thyme or marjoram, as they would be unattractive in a finished dish.

Storing and drying herbs

To store fresh herbs, wrap them separately in paper towels, then put them into plastic bags and keep in the vegetable compartment of the refrigerator. To dry herbs, pick them just as they begin to flower when their flavor will be at its strongest. Gather them on a dry day, tie them in bunches and hang in a warm room away from strong light, or dry them in a very slow oven. Rub the dried leaves and flowers on to paper towels, then sift them into airtight containers and store away from the light in a cool place. Dried herbs will gradually lose their flavor.

SPICES AND SEEDS

Spices – most of which come from the tropics – are dried parts of aromatic plants and include flowers, seeds, leaves, bark and roots. Their use is of great antiquity and they have played a large and important role in human history. Their great value ensured that governments in countries with a big spice trade became rich on the taxes they levied.

Although there are no exact dates, it is believed that the trade in spices that came along the hazardous caravan routes from China, Indonesia, India and Ceylon to the eastern Mediterranean lasted about 5000 years. A favorite route went through Peshawar, over the Khyber Pass, through Afghanistan and Persia, eventually to reach Europe. The Phoenicians were great spice traders, so were the Arabs and the Romans, and later the Venetians and Genoese. After the fall of the Roman Empire there was a long, stagnant period, until the Portuguese found a sea route to the East via the Cape of Good Hope, which led to competition between the Portuguese, Dutch, French and English.

During the centuries of struggle to control the trade, wars raged and empires rose and fell, but the spices that cooks have needed and used since early times – nutmeg, cloves, cinnamon, pepper, ginger, saffron and, from the New World, allspice, annatto, vanilla and chocolate – continued to arrive. Though once as costly as gold, they are today reasonably priced, neatly packaged items on the spice shelves of every supermarket. No longer do they come from a few precious sources; there is now hardly a country that does not produce at least one spice of its own.

The use of spices grew out of the natural cooking techniques of India, China and Southeast Asia, where herbs and spices are still widely employed. The spices indigenous to these areas, such as ginger and nutmeg, provide a lively and enjoyable accent to the blandness of rice and bring out latent flavors in vegetable, fish, poultry and meat dishes; in Southeast Asia spices complement the fiery sambals and fermented fish sauces and are essential in the variety of curries prepared throughout the sub-continent.

Spices in the kitchen

Today, spices still have a wide range of uses. Some, like pepper, are used exclusively in savory dishes. Others, such as ginger, can also be used for baking or pickling. Ginger should be bought fresh, as ginger root, or dried as ginger powder.

Roasting or dry-frying dried seeds, bark or roots helps to release their aromatic essential oils, and thus increases the flavor. Heat must be gently applied, then the spices can be pulverized – it's rather like first roasting then grinding coffee beans for maximum flavor. Spices can be used in whole pieces – in *birianis* and *pilaus* you can add pieces of cinnamon, or whole cloves or cardamoms to perfume the rice. They can also be used singly, as in China, where star anise is used to flavor pork and beef, ginger to add piquancy to fish and chicken, or in combination, as when using five-spice powder, in such dishes as Szechwan duck. In Japan a favorite condiment is *shichimitogarashi*, seven-flavor spice, a seasoning powder which is made from ground hot red peppers, ground Japanese pepper leaf (*sansho*, the leaf of the prickly ash), sesame, mustard, rape and poppy seeds and dried tangerine peel.

The French *quatre épices* is another popular combination of spices consisting of ground peppercorns, nutmeg, cloves and cinnamon. Ginger is sometimes substituted for the cinnamon. Many modern cooks combine allspice berries and black and white peppercorns in pepper mills for on-the-table use. The art of blending spices is as subtle as that of blending teas, perfumes, or liqueurs; cooks usually vary ingredients according to individual preference.

Herbs

TANSY (*Tanacetum vulgare*)

Native to Europe, tansy is now also common in other parts of the world. The leaves are chopped and used fresh. Once widely used to flavor egg and fish dishes, tansy now features as an ingredient in drisheen sausage.

TARRAGON
(*Artemesia dracunculus*)

Tarragon is a very aromatic, distinctive herb, related to wormwood. There are two main species, French tarragon and Russian tarragon, the latter being inferior in flavor, with a coarser leaf. French tarragon, native to Europe, is used for Béarnaise and Hollandaise sauce, *poulet à l'estragon*, savory butters, soups, fish dishes and salads. It is available fresh, as dried leaves.

POT MARIGOLD
(*Calendula officinalis*)

An annual plant native to southern Europe and Asia, the petals of this golden flower were used in medieval cooking, both as a flavoring and a dye to color cheese, in custards and cakes. Today they are used to color and flavor rice, meat and fish dishes, or in soups and salads. The petals are sold dried.

LEMON BALM
(*Melissa officinalis*)

So-called because of its lemony scent (but also known simply as balm), the leaves of this plant native to Europe are used in vegetable and fruit salads, drinks – especially punch and cordials – soups and sauces or wherever a faint lemon flavor is required. Fresh or dried leaves are available.

Tansy

Tarragon

Dried tarragon

Dried pot marigold

Pot marigold

Woodruff

Dried woodruff

Lemon balm

Dried lemon balm

CORIANDER
(*Coriandrum sativum*)

A member of the carrot family, this ancient herb is indigenous to the Mediterranean and the Caucasus, and is often sold as cilantro or Chinese parsley in Latin American and Chinese markets. It has a fresh taste, similar to orange, and is greatly used in India, Asia, Mexico, South America and the Middle East in its fresh, leafy form. The seeds (page 59) are used as an ingredient in curry and to flavor alcoholic drinks such as gin. In Thailand, the roots are used in curries.

Coriander

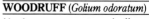

Hop

HOP (*Humulus lupulus*)

Well-known as a flavoring for beer, hops are the flowers of a vinelike plant native to Europe. The young shoots are used as a vegetable, and can also be made into a salad. Pillows stuffed with hops are said to aid insomnia, as is hop tea.

WOODRUFF (*Golium odoratum*)

Also known as sweet woodruff, this perennial herb is native to Europe and Asia. It has a distinctive scented taste, and the leaves can be used fresh or dried. It is used dried in "May Cup" – a traditional English drink – and in champagne, Benedictine and punch.

BORAGE (*Borago officinalis*)

An annual plant native to the Middle East, this is now common Europe and America. The flowers and the leaves are used, fresh or dried, in vinegar, sauces and salads. The taste is reminiscent of cucumber, and may be used in Pimm's wine cups. Finely chopped leaves can be used to flavor cream cheese, dips and yogurt.

BASIL (*Ocimum basilicum*)

A strong and pungent herb, this annual plant is native to India. Also known as sweet basil, the leaves are used, fresh or dried: the fresh leaves have a taste similar to cloves, but when dried they taste more like curry. It has many uses, notably in the Italian pesto sauce.

Borage

Dried borage

Winter savory

Burnet

MINT (*Mentha*, spp.)

There are many varieties, but from the cook's point of view, spearmint (*Mentha spicata; M. viridis*) and apple mint (*M. rotundifolia*) are the two most important. Spearmint is the common or garden mint, used for mint sauce, mint jelly, stuffings, salads and to flavor drinks such as Moroccan mint tea. Apple mint, or round-leaved mint, has a fine flavor. The leaves are covered with a fine down, and such varieties as Bowles mint (*M. villosa alopecuroides*) are recommended for all culinary uses. Orange bergamot mint (*M. citrata*), has a pleasant perfume, and can be used chopped in salads, or to flavor iced summer drinks. Other species of mint include peppermint (*M. piperita*), used for flavoring candies and in crème de menthe, and horsemint (*M. longifolia*), used in curries and chutneys.

BURNET (*Poterium sanguisorba*)

Native to Europe, today burnet (or salad burnet) is used mainly in French and Italian cooking. The leaves are similar to borage in flavor and are used, fresh or dried, in salads, soups, casseroles, and also in wine punch.

WINTER SAVORY (*Satureja montana*)

Both this and summer savory (*S. hortensis*) are very similar and seasonal according to their names, although winter savory is considered by some cooks to possess a coarser flavor than its warm-weather relative. They are fairly strong, aromatic herbs, and can have the same uses as thyme.

SAGE (*Salvia officinalis*)

Native to the northern Mediterranean, sage is a well-known plant with downy leaves and a strongly aromatic flavor. There is much variation in the color of the leaves and the flavor. Garden sage (shown here) is used for stuffings, particularly with pork or duck, and may be used with discretion in meat stews and casseroles, though it tends to overpower subtle flavors.

Dried sage

Sage

Basil

Dried basil

Apple mint
(Mentha rotundifolia)

Spearmint
(Mentha viridis)

Dried spearmint

BAY (*Laurus nobilis*)

Also called sweet bay or laurel, but not to be confused with varieties of laurel that are poisonous, this refers to a leaf of the sweet bay tree native to the Mediterranean, which is usually used dried, although powdered bay is available. Used to flavor meat dishes, milk puddings, soups, stews and sweet white sauces, bay is one of the ingredients in bouquet garni.

THYME (*Thymus* spp.)

There are many varieties of this perennial herb, which is native to southern Europe and the Mediterranean. The leaves (fresh or dried) have many uses and form the basic part of bouquet garni. Thyme has a strong, sharp taste so lemon thyme, which is less strong with a lemon tang, is often used instead. Thyme can be used to flavor soups, stews, roast meat and poultry stuffings.

LOVAGE (*Levisticum officinale*)

This is a large, celerylike plant native to the Mediterranean that yields an essential oil and has a strong aromatic flavor. The entire plant is used: stems and root can be cooked in the manner of celery or candied as for angelica; leaves, roots and seeds are used in salads, soups and sauces; the seeds can be used in baking. Lovage is available dried.

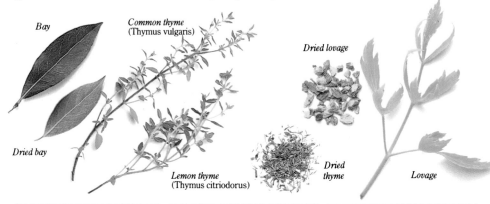

Bay

Common thyme (Thymus vulgaris)

Dried lovage

Dried bay

Lemon thyme (Thymus citriodorus)

Dried thyme

Lovage

LEMON VERBENA
(*Aloysia triphylla*)

Also known as lemon-scented verbena, this herb is a native of South America, and was introduced to Europe by the Spanish. It can be used to impart a lemon flavor to drinks and salads and as an herb. It is available fresh or dried.

PARSLEY
(*Petroselinum crispum*)

Native to the Mediterranean area, there are several varieties of parsley, including flat-leaved parsley, curl-leaved parsley, Hamburg parsley (page 33), grown for its roots, and Neapolitan or Italian parsley, grown for its celery-like stems. Parsley has many uses, not the least of which is as a garnish. It is used in bouquet garni, in *fines herbes*, added to sauces and stuffings or fried as an accompaniment to fish. It is available fresh and dried.

OREGANO (*Origanum vulgare*)

This aromatic herb has been used for centuries in Asia and Europe and is now especially popular in Italy, where it is used in pizzas. Oregano or wild marjoram is also used with tomatoes, cheese, beans and eggplants. There are many Greek varieties, collectively called *rigani*, the flowers of which are used to garnish meat dishes. The leaves are usually used dried.

Lemon verbena

Parsley

Dried parsley

Oregano

Dried oregano

CHIVE (*Allium schoenoprasum*)

A native of Europe, the chive is a member of the onion family. The fine, hollow stems are used fresh and chopped finely in cream soups, scrambled eggs, omelets, salads and hors d'œuvres. Chinese or garlic chives (*Allium odoratum*) have larger leaves and taste of garlic. Flowers smell like roses.

Dried chives

MARJORAM
(*Origanum majorana*)

Although the name "marjoram" covers numerous plants, including wild marjoram (see oregano, opposite) and pot marjoram (*Origanum onites*), the name is normally used to refer to sweet, or cultivated, marjoram. It can be used fresh or dried in omelets, stuffings, sausages, bouquets garnis, meat sauces, potato dishes, soups and stews.

Marjoram

Dried marjoram

MIXED HERBS

A ready-prepared mixture of dried herbs, usually consisting of thyme, marjoram, parsley, rosemary and basil. It can be used in most savory dishes.

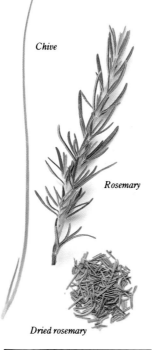

Chive

Rosemary

Dried rosemary

ROSEMARY
(*Rosmarinus officinalis*)

Of Mediterranean origin, rosemary is found growing wild over most of Europe, and in America. Its hard, spiky leaves contain oil of camphor, and are widely used for flavoring meat dishes, most notably lamb, and chicken and fish. Rosemary is seldom used in salads or soups except in powder form, when its qualities become muted. It is available fresh, as dried leaves or in powder form.

Mixed herbs

COSTMARY
(*Chrysanthemum balsamita, Tanacetum balsamita*)

Costmary is similar to tansy, being spicy but less bitter. Native to the Far East, the leaves were traditionally used in Britain and America as flavoring for beer, hence its other name "alecost". Costmary is used with game and veal and in soups, and is sometimes available dried.

EPAZOTE
(*Chenopodium ambrosiodes*)

Also known as Mexican tea, wormseed, goosefoot and Jerusalem oak, epazote grows wild in the Americas and in parts of Europe. It is used as a green herb in Mexican cooking and as a tisane in Europe.

LEMON GRASS
(*Cymbopogon citratus, flexuesus, nardus*)

This includes several species of grass, all possessing the flavor of lemon due to the presence of citric oils. It is native to Southeast Asia, where in some places the lemon tree is absent, and is available as "sereh powder". It is useful in flavoring salads, fish dishes and soups. In Thailand, and other parts of Southeast Asia, the leaves of the Kaffir lime (*Citrus hystrix*) are also used for fish dishes.

ROSELLA
(*Hibiscus sabdariffa*)

A native of tropical Asia, also known as sorrel and flor de Jamaica, rosella is grown for its fleshy red sepals, which are commonly used to make drinks, and preserves.

VERVAIN
(*Verbena officinalis*)

Often confused with lemon verbena, this ancient European herb is mainly used to make herb tea.

BEE BALM (*Monarda didyma*)

There are many varieties of this strongly flavored herb, native to America. Related to the mint family, it is also known as oswego and bergamot. The flowers and leaves are used, fresh or dried, in tisanes and teas in iced tea and cordials. The leaves can also be used in salads.

DILL (*Anethum graveolens*)

A plant of the parsley family native to Europe and western Asia, dill is now grown throughout the world. Dill weed (as it is sometimes called) is best known for its affinity with fish and its use in flavoring dill pickles. Also used in soups, egg dishes and sauces, dill is available as seeds or as dried leaves. The seeds have a more pungent flavor.

NASTURTIUM (*Tropaeolum majus*)

Native to Peru, this annual plant is now available worldwide. The leaves (usually fresh), petals and seeds are all used; the brilliant orange and red flowers and peppery tasting leaves are useful for salads and sandwiches. The seed pods can be pickled and used like capers.

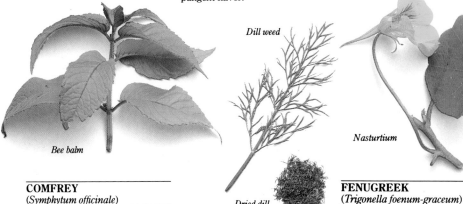

Dill weed

Nasturtium

Bee balm

COMFREY (*Symphytum officinale*)

Native to Europe and Asia, comfrey is related to borage. Its leaves are used either fresh (in salads) or dried and powdered (in tea). The dried root is also used in Europe, as a flavoring for wine.

Dried dill

Dill seeds

FENUGREEK (*Trigonella foenum-graeceum*)

Native to western Asia, fenugreek or methi also grows in the Mediterranean. The young leaves, which have a faintly bitter taste, are used, fresh or dried; also the rock-hard seeds (page 61). It is an important ingredient in curries.

Dried fenugreek leaves

Comfrey root

CURRY LEAF (*Chalcas koenigii*)

Dried curry leaves

Dried comfrey

A relative of the lemon tree, and a native of Southeast Asia, the leaves lend a currylike flavor to foods. They are also used throughout southern India in vegetarian dishes. The curry leaf is available mostly in dried form, although the fresh leaves are usually preferred.

BOUQUET GARNI

A combination of dried herbs such as thyme, parsley and bay used in soups, stews and sauces. Usually wrapped in cheesecloth, they are removed before serving.

Bouquet garni

Comfrey

CAMOMILE
(Chamaemelum nobile)

There are many varieties of this daisylike plant found growing wild in parts of America and throughout Europe. The leaves and flowers are used to make refreshing drinks and tea. It is available fresh or dried.

Camomile

Dried camomile

HYSSOP (Hysoppus officinalis)

The leaves have a pungent and slightly bitter, minty taste and are used for flavoring liqueurs such as Bénédictine and Chartreuse. It may also be used fresh in salads and fresh or dried in soups, stuffings and stews.

Hyssop

Dried hyssop

CHERVIL
(Anthriscus cerefolium)

A native of southern Russia and the Middle East, this parsleylike plant with feathery leaves is considered one of the *fines herbes* in French cuisine. It is used to flavor soups, salads and stuffings and is also employed as a garnish. Available dried, it is best when used fresh.

Dried chervil

YARROW (Achillea millefolium)

A perennial plant native to southern England, yarrow or milfoil is now grown in many countries. The leaves (fresh or dried), seeds and roots are used.

Yarrow

Dried yarrow

Fennel

ANGELICA
(Angelica officinalis, archangelica)

A member of the parsley family, angelica is a native of northern Europe. The entire plant can be used, as even the root provides a drug, but its more familiar form is as a candied stem used in baking (page 125).

Angelica

FENNEL (Foeniculum vulgare)

A tall plant with feathery leaves and yellow seeds, fennel is a native of southern Europe. Like dill, it is frequently used to season fish, and now grows wild throughout the world, although it is produced commercially. The leaves can be used in salads and stuffings, and the stems are cooked as a vegetable (page 18). In Provence, fish are often *flambéed* on a bed of dried fennel stalks. The seeds have a slight licorice taste.

Dried fennel

Fennel seeds

Spices and Seeds

CURRY POWDER

This is a blend of any number of spices, bought ready-prepared. It can vary from mild to hot depending on the spices included, and can be used to season curries, stews and dips.

Curry powder

PICKLING SPICE

A mixture of spices, consisting basically of black peppercorns, red chiles and varying proportions of mustard seed, allspice, cloves, ginger, mace and coriander seed. It is used in pickles, chutneys and vinegars.

Pickling spice

GARAM MASALA

The name means, literally, "hot mixture", and is applied to a combination of roasted spices (such as coriander seed, chili and black pepper) ground into a powder. Although freshly blended and ground in India and the East, in the West it is bought ready-prepared. It is used as a basic seasoning for many Indian dishes.

CHINESE FIVE-SPICE POWDER

This is a Chinese spice mixture consisting of equal parts of finely ground anise-pepper, star anise, cassia or cinnamon, cloves and fennel seed. It has a subtle taste and, apart from its wide use in Oriental cooking, can be used in any pork or beef dish.

Chinese five-spice powder

ANNATTO (*Bixa orellana*)

Also known as achiote, bija, bijoul and roucou, this is the fruit and seeds of a tree native to tropical America. The dye from the fruit is orange and used for coloring foods. Seeds are ground and used as a spice in Latin America, and in Southeast Asian dishes such as rice, or shrimp and potato cakes.

Annatto

Garam masala

GALANGAL

Both greater (*Alpinia galanga*) and lesser (*Alpinia officinarum* – shown here) galangal are root spices related to ginger but with a faint flavor of camphor. Available in root or powder form, they are used in the Far East in curries and in Malay dishes, and also in liqueurs.

Galangal

HORSERADISH
(*Armoracia rusticana*)

The pungent root of the plant may be grated, and is sometimes sold dried. It is often used as the basis for a sauce traditionally eaten with roast beef. It is most pungent when fresh.

Fresh grated horseradish

Dried ground horseradish

CASSIA (*Cinnamomum cassia*)

Similar to cinnamon and often confused with it, cassia spice (or Chinese cinnamon) is the dried bark of an evergreen tree native to Burma. Also used in powder form, it is popular in Oriental cooking.

Cassia bark

Ground cassia

NIGELLA (*Nigella sativa*)

These black seeds have a peppery taste and are sprinkled on bread and cakes. Nigella, or wild onion seed, is often confused with the black variety of cumin.

Nigella

CELERY SEED
(*Apium graveolens*)

The dried seeds of the celery plant, native to Italy, have a rather bitter taste and are used in soups and stews, and to flavor salt.

Celery seed

FENNEL SEED
(*Foeniculum vulgare*)

The aromatic dried seeds of the fennel plant, native to the Mediterranean area, have a slight anise taste and can be used in a wide range of dishes, including apple pie, curries and fish dishes.

Fennel seed

SUNFLOWER SEED
(*Helianthus annuus*)

These are the dried seeds of the sunflower plant native to Peru. Their main use is as a source of oil (page 75), but they can also be eaten roasted in their husks. There are many varieties.

Sunflower seed

TAMARIND (*Tamarindus indica*)

The fruit pods and pulp of an African tree, now grown throughout India. The pods contain a very sour juice used as a flavoring for some Indian curries. Sold as sticky, broken pods minus the seeds, and dried.

Tamarind

SESAME SEED
(*Sesamum indicum*)

The dried fruits of the sesame plant (an annual native to India), the seeds are best known as a source of oil (page 75). In the Middle East they are ground to produce tahini (page 69) and halva. They are often used in the decoration of cakes and breads in America.

Black sesame seeds

White sesame seeds

PUMPKIN SEED
(*Cucurbita maxima*)

The seeds of the native American plant are used as a source of oil, but can also be eaten roasted.

Pumpkin seed

DILL SEED
(*Anethum graveolens*)

The dried fruits of the dill plant, native to southern Europe; the seeds taste like caraway and are used with fish.

Dill seed

CAYENNE PEPPER
(Capsicum frutescens)

Made from a type of red chile pepper said to be native to Cayenne in French Guyana, other seeds, salt and spices are often added to the powder in its commercial form. It is very pungent and thus should be used sparingly. It is used in Southwestern, Mexican and South American recipes.

Cayenne pepper

PEPPER (Piper nigrum)

A type of vine pepper not to be confused with the capsicum varieties, this is native to Asia, but used in most cuisines. Black peppercorns are the sun-dried berries of the pepper vine, picked while still green. White peppercorns are from the same plant, but the berries are picked when ripe and the skin is removed. Both are used as a seasoning, though white pepper is much less aromatic.

Mignonette pepper is a coarse-grained pepper made by grinding and sieving black or white peppercorns. It is used a great deal in French cooking. Szechwan peppercorns, from China, are red and have a fiery effect when roasted.

White peppercorns

Black peppercorns

ANISE-PEPPER
(Zanthoxylum piperitum)

The dried berries of a tree native to China, this is also called Szechuan pepper. It has a hot aromatic flavor and is used in Chinese five-spice powder and Oriental cooking.

Anise-pepper

NUTMEG (Myristica fragrans)

The dried kernel or "nut" of an evergreen of the myrtle family, native to Indonesia, this is encased in a fleshy apricot-like fruit which splits open when ripe. Small quantities are used to season pies, cakes and other foods. It can be purchased whole or ground.

Ground nutmeg

Whole nutmeg

Green peppercorns in brine

CLOVE (Eugenia aromatica)

The dried, aromatic flower buds of an evergreen of the myrtle family native to south-east Asia, cloves are normally used whole, but the central "head" of the bud can also be ground into a powder. They contain an essential oil used for relieving toothache, but are mainly used to flavor baked goods, hot drinks, stews and soups.

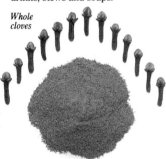

Whole cloves

Ground cloves

GARLIC (Allium sativum)

The bulb of a perennial plant (page 29), garlic can be dried and used as flakes or granules, or ground into a powder. It has a pungent taste and smell, and is used sparingly.

Garlic flakes

Garlic powder

MACE (*Myristica fragans*)

Mace, in blade form, is the outer net-like covering of nutmeg. The blades are pressed flat and dried before use, and can be ground.

Ground mace

Blades of mace

CINNAMON
(*Cinnamomum zeylanicum*)

A member of the laurel family and native to India, cinnamon is used for its aromatic bark. Available in sticks, or as a powder, cinnamon is used for baking and desserts, also to flavor rice dishes and fish, chicken or ham. It keeps well.

Cinnamon stick

Cinnamon quills

Ground cinnamon

PAPRIKA
(*Capsicum tetragonum*)

Made from a type of pepper native to South America, paprika varies in taste from fiery hot to mild and sweet and in appearance from rosy brown to scarlet. The national spice of Hungary – there is also a Spanish version called *pimentón* – it is used in goulashes, sauces, meat, chicken, and fish dishes.

Paprika

POPPY SEEDS
(*Papaver somniferum*)

The seed of the opium poppy flower native to the Middle East, there are two types: white and black. They are used in Indian and Jewish cooking.

White poppy seeds

Blue poppy seeds

CUMIN (*Cuminum cyminum*)

The dried fruit of an annual plant related to parsley and indigenous to the Upper Nile, cumin has a pungent, hot and somewhat bitter taste and is a very popular culinary spice in the East, Mexico and North Africa. It can be used whole or ground.

CORIANDER
(*Coriandrum sativum*)

The leaves are used as an herb (page 50), the seeds as a spice; they are quite different in flavour. Coriander seeds are used in curry pastes and powder. They can be added to lamb and pork, pickles, marinades and *à la grecque* recipes and dishes.

Ground coriander

Coriander seeds

SAFFRON (*Crocus sativus*)

The dried stigmas of a crocus flower native to Greece, saffron is one of the world's most expensive spices. Aromatic, pungent and slightly bitter, it yields a brilliant yellow dye. It is used for coloring and flavoring rice dishes, cakes, breads and soups, particularly in *bouillabaisse* and *paella*. It is available as stigmas or powder.

Saffron

Ground cumin

Whole cumin

CARDAMOM
(Elettaria cardamomum)
The pods are the aromatic dried fruits of a perennial plant of the ginger family native to India. They can vary from green to black; the white pods are sun-bleached and not as aromatic as the green pods. They contain small seeds, which may be ground up and used. Cardomom pods and seeds are used in many Indian recipes, and to flavor rice.

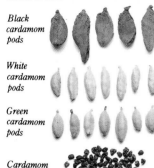

Black cardamom pods

White cardamom pods

Green cardamom pods

Cardamom seeds

ALLSPICE (Pimenta officinalis)
The berries are the dried fruit of the evergreen pimento tree, native to the West Indies. Called allspice for its versatile nature (but also known as pimento and Jamaica pepper), it tastes like nutmeg, cinnamon and cloves. It is used in baking, pickling and savory dishes, and is available whole or powdered.

Ground allspice

Allspice berries

TURMERIC *(Curcuma longa)*
A bright yellow spice obtained from the rhizomes of a plant of the lily family, native to Southeast Asia. It is an inexpensive spice, used in curries, curry powder and pickles. It is available as a powder and a dried root.

Ground turmeric

Turmeric root

CARAWAY *(Carum carvi)*
Well-known in Europe, where the sickle-shaped seeds are used in baking, cheese-making and many savory dishes, caraway is native to Europe and Asia. Related to anise, it has a pungent, characteristic taste and is also used to flavor liqueurs.

Caraway

OTHER SPICES AND SEEDS

GRAINS OF PARADISE
(Amomum melegueta)
Piquant, strongly flavored brown seeds of a plant related to allspice, used as a substitute for pepper. Known as Guinea pepper and malegueta pepper, it is indigenous to west Africa.

MUSTARD *(Brassica,* spp.)
The seeds come from three plants of the cabbage family. The black are hotter than the white; the powder is a mixture of both.

Black mustard seed

White mustard seed

Mustard powder

STAR ANISE *(Illicium verum)*
The small star-shaped seed of a tree native to China, and related to the magnolia, this contains the same essential oils as anise. It is used in Oriental cooking, especially with braised beef, chicken and lamb, and is an ingredient in Chinese five-spice powder.

Star anise pods

Star anise seeds

GINGER (*Zingiber officinale*)

The rhizome or root stem of this plant native to Southeast Asia can be bought whole, sliced or ground. Refreshingly pungent in flavor and slightly hot, it is used in Oriental and Indian dishes, baking, confectionery and also in certain liqueurs.

Chili powder

Chili flakes

Ground ginger

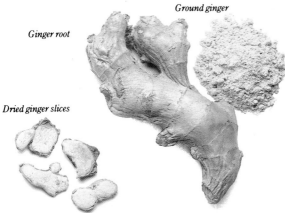

Ginger root

Dried ginger slices

CHILI POWDER
(*Capsicum frutescens*)

Powder made from dried ground chile peppers. Not to be confused with paprika, it can vary from mild to very hot. Chili powder can often contain other spices such as cumin.

FENUGREEK
(*Trigonella foenum-graceum*)

The pods of a flowering plant native to western Asia contains seeds which are dried and then ground into powder. The leaves are used as a herb (page 54).

Ground fenugreek

Fenugreek seeds

ANISE (*Pimpinella anisum*)

Grown for the seed which yields a sweet-scented anise flavor, it is used mainly in confectionery and baking; it is also used to flavor Anisette and other anise-flavored alcoholic drinks. Both the seeds and fresh leaves are used.

JUNIPER (*Juniperus communis*)

Native to the Old World, juniper is used to flavor gin, game and pork. In Germany it is used in sauerkraut and in preserves. The dried berries are often used in a marinade for venison.

Ground anise

AJOWAN (*Carum ajowan*)

The seed of a plant native to India, this has a strong taste of thyme and is used extensively in Indian and Middle Eastern cooking.

Juniper

Anise seeds

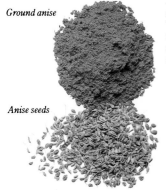

Ajowan

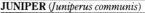

FLAVORINGS

PEOPLE HAVE NEVER BEEN content merely to accept nourishment for its own sake: the pursuit of taste to enliven a staple diet has always been an important part of eating habits, and as new and interesting flavors were discovered so were they adapted and incorporated. In Central America the staple ingredients of maize and potatoes were heightened by the use of chiles. Chiles were eventually to make an enduring impact on the curries of India and the sambals of Southeast Asia. In the same way two plants originally enjoyed only by the Aztecs – chocolate and vanilla – were destined to contribute enormously to international cooking.

Many synthetic flavorings have been developed which are by and large preferred by some sections of the industry because they are concentrated, more stable at high temperatures, and have a reduced moisture content.

There is, however, still a demand for the real thing. Extracts, mainly essential oils, are produced from the plant by processes which soften and break down the oil-bearing cells. Essences are extracted from various parts of the plant according to its nature: from crushed seeds or pits, from flowers and leaves, or the dried bark and roots.

Flavorings in the kitchen

Flavoring extracts will keep indefinitely stored in tightly sealed bottles, and in a cool, dark place. If a recipe demands "a few drops" of some essence, add the essence drop by drop until the desired strength is reached. Ice cream needs stronger flavoring than temperate foods, because mixtures lose their flavor as they get progressively colder – also, cold numbs the taste buds.

Vanilla pods are preferable to vanilla extract. Whole pods can be cooked in sweet sauces to flavor them, after which the pods can be washed, dried, and used again. Vanilla sugar is a useful form of flavoring, and a pod of vanilla can be kept in a jar of fine sugar for adding to cakes and confectionery.

DRIED CHILES
(Capsicum frutescens)

Many varieties of pungent chiles are dried and used to flavor foods, particularly in Latin American cooking. They include ancho, jalapeño, mulato, pasilla, and the familiar traditional red chile pepper.

VANILLA (Vanilla planifolia)

The cured pod of a climbing orchid native to Central America, vanilla is used as a flavoring in sweet sauces, cakes, cookies, puddings and ice creams.

LICORICE (Glycyrrhiza glabra)

One of the most ancient of flavorings, licorice is the root of a small perennial plant grown in southern Europe and the Middle East. Used in confectionery, desserts, cakes and drinks, the root can be sliced or ground.

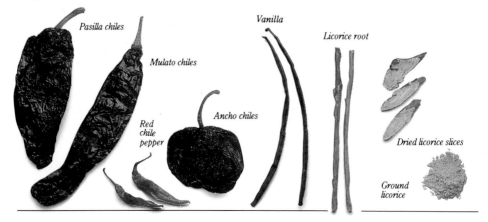

Pasilla chiles

Mulato chiles

Vanilla

Licorice root

Red chile pepper

Ancho chiles

Dried licorice slices

Ground licorice

DRIED MANGO
(Mangifera indica)

The mango fruit (page 92), native to India, is often dried and sliced as shown and used as a flavoring for curries. It is also used to make mango chutney (page 67), or may be pickled.

Dried mango

ANGOSTURA BITTERS

These bitters, named after an old Venezuelan town, are made in Trinidad. They consist of cloves, cinnamon, mace, nutmeg, prunes, quinine, rum and gentian. Their most popular use is in cocktails, but they are also used in ice cream, fruit juices, preserved fruits and puddings.

GRENADINE

A popular term for the extract of pulp from the pomegranate *(Punica granatum)* native to Kurdistan. It is used in soft drinks, cocktails, ice cream and confectionery.

Angostura bitters

Grenadine

8 fl oz
230 ml

OTHER FLAVORINGS

BITTER ALMOND ESSENCE

This commercial almond essence, much stronger than sweet almond extract, is derived from the bitter *Prunus amygdalus* and from the kernels of peaches and apricots. It is used in baking, confectionery and desserts.

CAROB

A flavoring from the pulp of the carob or locust bean *(Ceratonia siliqua)* originating in the Middle East, this chocolate substitute is used in soft drinks, and baked goods and candies.

CHOCOLATE

Chocolate and cocoa come from the fruit of the Mexican *Theobroma cacao,* in beans containing 20–30 white seeds which, when fermented, dried, then roasted are a source of cocoa butter, cocoa powder, drinking chocolate and baking chocolate (page 125). Milk chocolate contains dried milk solids. Apart from the familiar use of chocolate in baking and confectionary, it is also used, unsweetened, to flavor some Mexican meat dishes.

COLA

Extract from the nuts of *Cola nitida,* native to west Africa, and a main ingredient of cola drinks. The nuts are macerated to obtain an extract, then mixed with syrup.

NEROLI BIGARADE

The fruit and flowers of the bitter orange tree *(Citrus aurantium var. bergamia,* the Bergamot orange), yield a powerful, aromatic oil, called neroli oil, which is used in soft drinks, ice cream, confectionery and baked goods.

ORRIS

The peeled rhizomes, "orris root", of *Iris germanica,* native to the Far East, yield orris extract which is used in ice cream, confectionery and baked goods.

PEPPERMINT

Steam distillation of the flowering plant *Mentha piperata* gives peppermint oil, which is used in soft drinks, beverages, confectionery, ice cream and also in icings.

SANDALWOOD

The dried bark of a tree native to southern India is distilled to yield an essential oil, containing aromatic sanatol. It is used in perfumes, soaps, confectionery and baked goods.

SARSAPARILLA

The roots from the Mexican tree *Smilax aristolochiaefolia* yield an extract with a bitterish, licorice taste. It is used in soft drinks, ice cream, confectionery and baked goods, and also in medicine.

SASSAFRAS
(Sassafras albidum)

The roots, bark and leaves of this tree native to North America are used and steam-distilled to produce a lemon-scented oil with a spicy flavor. It is used in soft drinks, confectionery and ice cream.

YLANG-YLANG

The flowers of a large tree *(Cananga odorata)* native to the Philippines are steam-distilled to obtain their oil, which has a strong, flowerlike scent and a bitter aromatic taste. Used in soft drinks, ice cream, confectionery and baked goods.

Seasonings and Extracts

The purpose of seasonings is to enhance and accentuate flavors, especially flavors dormant in food, or to create a dominant taste to bland foods. In the West salt is the principal seasoning, and in the East soy, either as soy sauce or as a paste.

SALT

Salt is the mineral sodium chloride; when obtained from the evaporation of sea water it is sea or bay salt; when mined from deposits left by primeval seas, it is rock salt. Although salt contains no calories, proteins or carbohydrates, traces of other minerals are present in unrefined salt, including calcium, magnesium, sulphur and phosphorus; magnesium in salt gives it a bitter aftertaste.

The mineral elements in unrefined sodium chloride can affect foods cooked with salt. For example, rock salt contains calcium, which will toughen the skin of beans and peas – for this reason we are advised not to boil corn in salted water. Calcium also increases the moisture retention of salt, so that anti-caking agents are needed; the hygroscopic properties of salt cause it to solidify or to become heavy with moisture in damp conditions. Manufacturers have now improved their techniques by treating salt with YPS (sodium ferrocyanide), a chemical that causes small tentacles to form on each grain, preventing them from sticking together.

A measure or a "pinch" of salt is an essential ingredient in a limitless variety of recipes, savory and sweet. Salt enhances the taste of foods, and actually reduces the sourness of acid, and increases the sweetness of sugar. Salt and sugar react together as balancing agents: sugar will reduce saltiness, while over-sweet foods can be moderated by adding a touch of salt.

You will need salt in the majority of bread recipes, for it strengthens the gluten – the building fiber of wheat – and helps to form a crisp crust on bread. Yet too much salt will inhibit the action of yeast, so bakers must measure carefully, according to the recipe. The best salt to use in the kitchen is the fine, free-flowing table salt, or pure sea salt.

FOOD EXTRACTS

Meat and vegetable extracts further fulfil the purpose of seasoning, since they are concentrates and have excellent keeping properties. Although commercial extracts are a fairly recent invention – the German chemist Justus von Liebig developed a concentrated beef paste at Fray Bentos, Uruguay, in 1847 – the usefulness of food concentrates must have been evident to the first cooks who used meat gravy, and to the Chinese who, thousands of years ago, made a paste from fermented soy-beans, an early type of yeast extract. In the late nineteenth century, it was found that autolysis of brewer's yeast with salt made a vegetarian equivalent of beef extract.

Food extracts have a long shelf life, though stock cubes may absorb moisture if stored in a damp place. Soybean pastes have a shelf life of over six months, and once opened tend to slowly dry out; they can be moistened with a small quantity of oil.

STOCK BOUILLON CUBES

These contain monosodium glutamate, herbs and spices, yeast extract, starch, caramel, lactic acid, sugar, salt, fat, onion, celery and pepper. Stock cubes are available in beef, chicken, lamb and vegetarian flavors.

Stock bouillon cubes

STOCK BOUILLON POWDER

This is powdered dehydrated meat extract containing herbs. As its name implies, it is used for stocks, gravies and soups and occasionally in sauces.

Stock bouillon powder

SALT

Bay salt is obtained by the evaporation of sea water in pits by the natural heat from the sun. Kosher (or block, lump or coarse) salt is a refined purified rock salt without additives, most commonly used for pickling or curing meat. Flavored salts, including garlic salt and celery salt, and the spiced seasoned salt, or *sel épice*, are a mixture of salt and other ingredients and are useful seasonings. Freezing salt is a rough, coarse version of salt in crystals, not considered fit for human consumption. Pretzel salt is currently mined on the Gulf of Mexico, where there is a rare deposit of salt that forms large, regular, flat flakes that are perfectly suited to coating pretzels. Rock salt is purified by a similar process to sea salt – boiling down and crystallizing the saline to varying degrees of fineness, to produce cooking or kitchen salt, and table salt. Sea salt is produced from tidal pools of concentrated saline, filtered and heated in shallow pans, left to crystallize and artificially evaporated.

Seasoned salt

Rock salt

Common salt

Garlic salt

Table salt

Sea salt

Celery salt

BENTOO NO TOMO

A Japanese seasoning compound consisting of dried fish, salt, soy sauce, seaweed and monosodium glutamate, this is also used in Oriental cooking.

Bentoo no tomo

MONOSODIUM GLUTAMATE

The salt of glutamic acid, one of the amino acid food proteins, this is flavorless in itself but enhances other foods. Also known as MSG and Ve-tsin, monosodium glutamate may be used as a salt substitute.

Monosodium glutamate

ASAFETIDA

A resin from the plant *Ferula asafoetida*, this is sold as shown or as a powder, and only minute quantities are needed. It is particularly useful in fish recipes and is often used in Indian cooking as a salt substitute.

GRAVY POWDER

This is a dehydrated meat extract with added thickening agents, such as cornflour or wheat flour. It can be used to thicken stews and casseroles.

SETO FUUMI

A Japanese seasoning compound consisting of dried seaweed, tuna, sesame seed and monosodium glutamate, this is widely used in Oriental cooking.

Gravy powder

Seto fuumi

Asafetida

SOY PASTES

There are two types of paste made from soybeans, the fermented and the unfermented. The Japanese *miso* shown here is a fermented type, made by cooking the beans, mixing them with *koji* (steamed rice treated with a growth of the fungus *Aspergillus oryzae*), salt and water, then inoculating the mass with yeast. It is then left to ferment for several months. Extracts from the red, yellow and black varieties of soybean are shown, *Natto* is a similar preparation. *Tempeh* is fermented bean cake from Indonesia. Unfermented bean pastes are prepared as *tofu* or Chinese bean curd, and the sweet red paste used in confectionery.

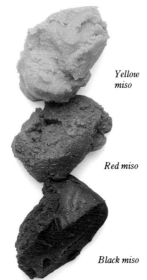

Yellow miso

Red miso

Black miso

GRAVY BROWNING

This is basically a coloring agent which enhances the appearance of brown sauces and gravies. It should be used with caution. The usual composition is simply caramel, salt and water. Sometimes flavors are added, such as hydrolized vegetable protein and MSG.

Gravy browning

MALT EXTRACT

Malt extract is made by soaking powdered malt in water, heating, and then reducing the mixture to a syrup or paste. It is used in brewing and distilling, in the manufacture of breakfast cereals, as a coffee substitute, and in baking. It gives a moist texture to brown bread, helps the dough to rise, and imparts a sweet flavor.

YEAST EXTRACT

The liquid from fresh yeast is separated, evaporated and added to vegetable extract. It has similar characteristics to meat extracts and is used as a seasoning.

Yeast extract

Malt extract

Beef extract

BEEF EXTRACT

A concentrated meat soup reduced by evaporation to a thick dark-brown salty paste.

OTHER EXTRACTS

MALTED MILK
Malted beverages arose from the pioneer work done during the mid-nineteenth century on invalid diets and infant foods. In 1869, an English immigrant to America, William Horlick, developed a maltose-dextrin-milk powder that found favor with the medical profession, and was marketed as Horlicks in 1887. Malted milk, one of the drinks originally sold in America's drugstores and soda fountains, is itself an ingredient, used to make crackers, cookies, cake mixes, frostings, and ice cream.

PICKLES, CHUTNEYS AND PASTES

PICKLES, CHUTNEYS AND PASTES are flavorings, designed to enliven or to provide a contrast to their accompanying foods. Most are products of preserving techniques using oil or vinegar, sugar and salt.

Pickles are vegetables or fruits (either whole or coarsely chopped) which are preserved in brine or vinegar. The word "pickle" also describes a brine or spiced vinegar solution for preserving meat, fish, fruit or vegetables.

Chutneys are mixtures of fruits or vegetables, either fresh or cooked in a thick sauce. They are sweet-tasting, thick and spicy, and generally darker in color than pickles. Fresh chutneys, as made in the East, need no preservative, but the chutneys made in the West are cooked preparations, and so always include vinegar.

Pastes are finely-ground products based on a main ingredient such as nuts, meat or salted fish. Their keeping qualities are due to the presence of oil (as in peanut butter) or salt (as in anchovy paste).

The word "relish" is often used to describe any chutney or sweet pickle preserved in a sweet-sour foundation. Certain foods are traditionally connected with certain types of relishes. Indian curries, for example, are linked with many such accompaniments, including mango, tamarind and coriander chutneys, pickled limes and cauliflower. Indonesian pickles, or *sambals,* also vary in taste.

HORSERADISH RELISH

The grated root of the horseradish is mixed with cream, agar-agar, vinegar and salt in this relish, which is used with hot or cold meats and fresh or smoked fish.

Horseradish relish

TOMATO CHUTNEY

A rich and tangy blend of tomatoes, gherkins, chiles and spices, this can be eaten with cold meats and cheese.

CUCUMBER RELISH

A sweet-tasting mixture of cucumbers, mustard seed, sugar, vinegar, onions, peppers and spices, which goes well with cold meats, cheeses and barbecues.

Cucumber relish

MANGO CHUTNEY

Perhaps the best-known Indian chutney, this can be hot or mild. It is usually eaten with curries.

Mango chutney

Tomato chutney

OTHER CHUTNEYS

APPLE CHUTNEY

Made with cooking apples, this relish can be sweet or savory. Similar chutneys can be made with green tomatoes or pears. They are all best served with cold meats.

APRICOT CHUTNEY

An excellent blend of apricots, raisins, chiles and spices, this is a hot chutney with a very good flavor. It can be eaten with cold meats and curries, or used for canapés and other savory fillings.

CORIANDER CHUTNEY

Fresh coriander leaves pounded with green chiles, yogurt, and spices make this slightly sour chutney that is eaten with fish, meat or vegetables.

MINT CHUTNEY

Made using mint leaves, tomatoes, apples, onions and raisins, this is excellent with cold meats and curries.

Pickles and Pastes

SWEET PICKLE

Despite its name, this is more like a sweet chutney. It contains a wide range of fruits and vegetables and is best eaten with cheese and most cold cuts.

Sweet pickle

CAPER
(*Capparis spinosa*, var. *rupestris*)

Members of the *Capparidaceae* family, capers are the unopened buds of a shrub native to the Mediterranean region. They are used only in their pickled form, as a flavoring and a garnish, in salade Niçoise and butter sauces. French capers are reputed to be the best and include Capucines and Nonpareilles.

Capers

LIME PICKLE

A spicy mixture of limes, chiles spices and vinegar, this can be eaten with bland foods.

Lime pickle

MIXED PICKLES

A mixture of cauliflower, onions and gherkins in a vinegar solution, these can be eaten as an accompaniment to cheese and roast chicken.

Mixed pickles

PICKLED WALNUTS

The nuts are picked while still green, retained in their shells, steamed and packed in a solution of vinegar, caramel, black pepper and other spices. They are eaten with cold cuts and cheese.

Pickled walnuts

PICKLED ONIONS

Onion pickling is one of the most ancient forms of pickling – evidence of it was found in the ruins of Pompeii. They are best eaten with poultry or lamb.

Pickled onions

PICCALILI

Also known as mustard pickle, there are two main types: American and English. The American is made with green tomatoes, onion and sweet pickles in spices and sweet vinegar. The English is made with mixed vegetables. It is used mainly to accompany cheese and cold meat.

Piccalili

INDONESIAN RELISH

Really a pickle containing a variety of vegetables such as cabbage, onions, leeks, carrots and cucumbers, this is mild in taste and is eaten with smoked fish.

Indonesian relish

PICKLED RED CABBAGE

The cabbage is machine-shredded, packed in brine, then drained and repacked in spiced vinegar. Pickled cabbage is used in salads.

Pickled red cabbage

PICKLED GHERKINS

These small cucumbers, grown exclusively for pickling, can be eaten with grilled meats, sausages and in salads.

Pickled gherkins

ANCHOVY PASTE

A preparation based on anchovies, butter, herbs and spices, this was invented in 1828. It is used for canapés, pasta sauces and mixed with tuna for a sandwich filling.

Anchovy paste

OLIVE (*Olea europea*)

A member of the Oleaceae family, this is the fruit of a tree native to Mediterranean coasts. The difference between green and black olives is simply that the black ones are fully ripened. There are several varieties, as shown here, and they are used only in their pickled form in recipes and as finger food. Some olives are pitted, then stuffed and used for canapés and hors d'œuvres.

JAPANESE PICKLED RADISH

The Japanese *daikon* radish (page 30) is pickled in a solution of soy sauce and sugar, and is often eaten with fish. It is also sold shredded.

Japanese pickled radish

PEANUT BUTTER

A paste made from crushed peanut seeds, this is used mainly as a spread. In Indonesian cooking it is used to thicken sauces.

Peanut butter

TAHINI PASTE

A paste made from crushed sesame seeds, this is widely used as a flavoring in Middle Eastern and Latin American cooking.

OTHER PICKLES

DILL PICKLES

There are four main types: fermented (usually in brine); unfermented (packed in brine with vinegar); sour (prepared in fermented salt stock, then packed in a vinegar solution); and sweet (packed in brine, then drained and packed in a sugar syrup with vinegar). Dill pickles are often eaten with cold cuts and hamburgers.

SAUERKRAUT

Finely shredded green or white cabbage, fermented in brine and flavored with juniper berries, sauerkraut or choucroute is sold canned or in plastic packs in supermarkets and speciality food stores. It is frequently used to accompany smoked sausages and frankfurters.

Tahini paste

Spanish Sevillana olives

Olives with almonds

Olives stuffed with red peppers or pimento

Dried olives

Pitted olives

Black olives

MUSTARDS, VINEGARS AND OILS

MUSTARD IS A CONDIMENT PRODUCED from three different plants of the *Cruciferae* family, the color of the seeds giving the name of the mustard type: *Sinapis alba* is white mustard (sometimes called "yellow mustard"), *Brassica nigra* is black mustard and *Brassica juncea* brown mustard (sometimes also called "black mustard"). In fact, when black mustard is used, it is normally the *B. juncea* variety rather than *B. nigra*, which is now considered unsuitable for modern farming. Although mustards are sometimes thought of as hot – as their name would imply – the majority are mild, and only freshly prepared English, Chinese and Japanese mustards are really fiery.

Types of mustard

The pungency of mustard is due to an essential oil that is only formed by the action of water on pulverized seeds. Only *B. nigra* and *B. juncea* contribute the familiar "hot" or pungent flavor of mustard, the black being the stronger of the two. White mustard contributes its own, characteristics flavor, and commercial mustard powders – basically the dry residue after oil has been extracted from the seeds – are a combination of the two types.

Mustards are made in a wonderful variety of flavors, derived from the addition of herbs and liquids such as beer, wine, vinegar, lime or lemon juice. They may be prepared with whole mustard seeds, or with tarragon, allspice, peppercorns, mint, chiles and garlic. There are also green mustards, which are mild and flavored with herbs.

Mustard in the kitchen

Mustard can be used in the form of whole seeds (page 60), but is more often used in its prepared form, or as a powder. Mustard powder should be prepared with cold water to make a smooth paste. Hot water or vinegar will inhibit the action of the enzyme, and result in a mild mustard. The pungency is fully developed after about ten minutes. After a while the pungency deteriorates, although the typical mustard flavor may be retained.

In the preparation of sauces, mustard should be made into a paste (or used straight from the jar) and added only after the sauce has completed cooking. Mustard powder alone makes a sauce lumpy, and excess heat destroys pungency. Prepared mustard may be used in mayonnaise, and the French Dijon mustard is an ingredient for many sauces.

All types of mustard can be used in the kitchen. Although the black mustard is stronger, white mustard also has its advantages; its enzymes are not so easily damaged, and it is strongly preservative, discouraging molds and bacteria, which is why it is often included in pickles (page 67). It also helps prevent mayonnaise from separating.

VINEGAR

Vinegar is a by-product of fermentation and should, strictly speaking, be made from wine (the word "vinegar" comes from the French *vin aigre*, meaning "sour wine").

Vinegar develops through a completely natural process involving two fermentations, the alcoholic and the acetous. The first occurs when natural yeasts present in the air or on fruit turn the sugar content into alcohol. Vinegar yeasts, also natural but usually added by the manufacturer, are then introduced. These acetobacters multiply to form the vinegar plant, a floating raft of yeast cells called the vinegar mother, which converts the alcohol into acetic acid (the main component of vinegar), thus completing the second stage of the process, acetous fermentation. (Anyone can, in fact, make their own vinegar by obtaining a vinegar mother.)

Strengths and types

The strength of acetic acid varies considerably with each type; wine vinegar is stronger than malt or cider vinegars, while distilled or fortified vinegars are the strongest of all. The minimum level of acetic acid required by law in America and Britain is 6 per cent and above for wine vinegars and 4 per cent and above for other types.

Regional and national varieties depend on the raw materials available. In the Far East vinegar is made from rice wine and from fruit.

Vinegar in the kitchen

Vinegar was originally used as a preservative. Over the years, however, it has also become a valued aromatic condiment.

Wine vinegars particularly lend themselves to herb, spice and fruit flavorings; these include rosemary, tarragon, dill, garlic, chiles, peppercorns, lemons, raspberries, rose petals and violets. Cooks should keep a selection of these vinegars, as different types suit different recipes. As a general rule, the choice of vinegar depends upon the country of origin of the recipe: rice vinegar should be used in Chinese and Japanese recipes, wine vinegar in Mediterranean recipes, cider vinegar in traditional American recipes, and malt vinegar in English and Australian recipes.

Other points worth bearing in mind are that cider or wine vinegar can be used for general cooking purposes, wine, rice, sherry or any herb vinegar for salads, and distilled, spirit or malt vinegar for pickling.

OILS

Oil is the vehicle that moves mayonnaise so smoothly over vegetables, salads and eggs. Italians pour it into soup, over pasta, over salads and practically everything else. Its lubricity makes salads palatable, when mixed with vinegar or lemon juice to make a vinaigrette dressing. Bakers use oil to encourage the expansion of bread dough, and to coat their baking tins. Cooks brush oil over meat prior to roasting or broiling, and fry potatoes in one of the many oils on the market. Sources of oil include sesame seeds, poppies and olives.

Modern agriculture has substantially added to the primitive and unrefined oils used by our ancestors. The sunflower, first cultivated by the American Indian, was introduced to Europe during the sixteenth century and first became established as an oil crop in Russia, where it was produced commercially in the 1830s. Also, corn, cottonseed, soybean, colza and peanut oil have all substantially overtaken poppy, olive and almond oil in productivity.

Types of oil

Each oil has its specific character, color and culinary purpose. Some are naturally darker than others, and darken with age, but because consumers prefer light-colored oils, color is bleached out – except for olive oil, which is often green or deep yellow.

The majority of oils possess two main characteristics: they tend to collapse or revert during cooking, and they may solidify in cold weather or in the refrigerator. You may have noticed how, in cold weather, oil has a tendency to go opaque in the bottle. The first manufacturers of commercial mayonnaise found that their products were inclined to "de-emulsify" in low temperatures as the oil gradually hardened. It was for this reason that winterized oils were developed. "Winterizing" means artificially freezing the oil until the solids can be separated off. The remaining oil can then be marketed as "salad oil".

Several types of oil are unstable, and break down during increases in temperature to give strong or unpleasant flavors. Safflower, sunflower and soybean oil can develop a fishy taste, and this is why most oils are now stabilized during processing, by a hardening technique known as hydrogenation.

There are basically three types of fat: saturated, unsaturated and polyunsaturated. Saturated fats are considered to increase levels of cholesterol in the blood, and oils containing polyunsaturated fatty acids, such as safflower, sunflower and corn oil, are thought by some to be beneficial to the diet-conscious. Compounds such as emulsifiers may be added – a chemical, lecithin, is important to cooking oils, since it is a natural emulsifier, and helps to prevent food from sticking to the pan and water droplets from splattering.

When frying food in oil, you need to maintain a constant correct temperature to prevent the oil from entering the food and making it greasy. The temperatures should not be too high – from 325°F to 385°F depending on the type of food. If the oil gets too hot it darkens and burns the outside of the food, while frequently leaving the inside undercooked.

Mustards

MUSTARD WITH GREEN PEPPERCORNS

This mustard, containing crushed green peppercorns, is one of the Dijon varieties from Burgundy. It is fairly hot and therefore goes best with bland foods, such as broiled steaks and chops.

DIJON MUSTARD WITH WHITE WINE

Popular as a cooking ingredient for seafood and veal dishes. Its additional wine flavoring makes it suitable for many sauces and dressings.

MOUTARDE DE MEAUX

Whole seed mustard, known as moutarde de Meaux, is Dijon mustard containing the seeds of brown mustard, so that biting into the seed releases a quantity of the pungent oil. There are many varieties, and some may contain coarse mustard seeds and include white wine, spices, vinegar and salt will add zest to bland foods which need to be enhanced.

GREEN HERB MUSTARD

A very mild mustard, delicately combined with a mixture of herbs, this should be eaten with cold cuts and sausages.

FRENCH MUSTARD WITH TARRAGON

One of the darker Bordeaux mustards, this variety containing tarragon is mild and therefore good with cold meats and spicy food.

Green herb mustard

Mustard with green peppercorns

Dijon mustard with white wine

French mustard with tarragon

Moutarde de Meaux

Coarse-grain mustard

ORIENTAL MUSTARD

CHINESE MUSTARD
Usually prepared from dry mustard and water or flat beer, this is an extremely hot preparation. It is traditionally served with egg rolls.

COARSE-GRAIN MUSTARD

This is a coarse-grained variety of moutarde de Meaux and may contain white wine. It is excellent with different types of bland food.

DUSSELDORF MUSTARD

The most popular type of German mustard, this is similar to the Bordeaux mustards. It is mild, and is eaten with spicy food.

ENGLISH WHOLE-GRAIN MUSTARD

This is a hot, pungent mustard made from whole mustard seeds, white wine, allspice and black pepper. It goes with bland foods.

English whole-grain mustard

AMERICAN MUSTARD

This mustard, made from *Sinapis alba* seeds, is mild and an excellent accompaniment to hot dogs and hamburgers.

Plain Dijon mustard

ENGLISH MUSTARD

English mustard is made of *Brassica nigra* seeds blended with *Sinapis alba* seeds, plus a quantity of wheat flour and, sometimes, a very small amount of turmeric. It is used as an accompaniment to boiled and roast beef, boiled ham, hamburgers, broiled herrings, chops and steaks, sausages and meat pies. As an ingredient, it is used on toasted cheese dishes (Welsh rarebit) and in mustard sauce. Bear in mind that English mustard, if freshly made, is quite hot. It *should* be hot, for that is its true character.

PLAIN DIJON MUSTARD

There are four traditional types of French mustard: Dijon, whole seed, Bordeaux and Florida. Dijon mustard, from Burgundy, is the best known outside France. It is usually paler than its Bordeaux counterpart because it is made from *Brassica nigra* without the seed husk (the husk darkens the mustard). It is also the hotter of the two, and should be used with foods where the flavor needs enhancing, such as steaks, hamburgers and beef, and is also used in sauces such as ravigote, rémoulade, Dijonnaise and Russian dressing.

American mustard

English mustard

Bordeaux mustard

German mustard

Dusseldorf mustard

Florida mustard

BORDEAUX MUSTARD

This is a plain mild French mustard. Bordeaux mustards contain the seed husk and are, therefore, dark, though they can vary slightly in color. They may contain a veriety of herbs – particularly tarragon-vinegar and sugar. They are mild, with a sweet-sour taste, and as such are best used in sandwiches or with spicy sausages. Bordeaux mustard can also be used in salad dressings, and makes a delicious sauce when mixed with honey or brown sugar and lemon juice.

GERMAN MUSTARD

This sweet-sour mustard contains herbs, spices and caramel. It is lighter than the popular Dusseldorf mustard (left), is mild-tasting and is best eaten with cold meats and, of course, German sausage.

FLORIDA MUSTARD

This mild mustard, also called champagne mustard, is made with wine from the Champagne region. Like Bordeaux mustards, it is best with spicy food.

Vinegars and Oils

WINE VINEGAR

The finest wine vinegars are made in oak vats by a slow process which encourages a higher concentration of aromatic qualities. There are several kinds: red, white, rosé and sherry. White wine vinegar is best for mayonnaise, Hollandaise and similar sauces. Red wine vinegar should be used in a *sauce hachée* and *sauce à la diable*.

DISTILLED MALT VINEGAR

Although any vinegar can be distilled, malt vinegar is usually used. Distilled vinegars are colorless and very strong – simply because the distillation process has increased the percentage of acetic acid which they contain. It is because of their strength and their extreme slowness to deteriorate that they are used extensively for pickling (particularly onions). Manufacturers also use them in bottled sauces.

FLAVORED VINEGARS

These usually consist of herbs steeped in wine vinegar, and may include tarragon, basil, lemons, savory, thyme, shallots, sugar, salt, horseradish, bay leaves and rosemary. Tarragon vinegar, good for Béarnaise sauce and salad dressing, is the most popular. Most can be made at home.

RICE VINEGAR

Chinese vinegar can be red, white or black. There is also a Japanese variety called *su*. As a general rule, the white is most used, especially as a flavoring in soups, and in sweet-and-sour dishes. Cider or wine vinegar are the best substitutes.

SPIRIT VINEGAR

The liquid (often molasses or sugar beet alcohol) is distilled before all the alcohol has been converted to acetic acid. It is colorless, and is used mainly for pickling purposes.

MALT VINEGAR

Malted barley is mashed, heated with water and fermented into a crude type of beer, which is then fed into steel or plastic vats filled with beech shavings. The acetobacters are introduced and left for several weeks until acetic acid is formed. The vinegar is then filtered, matured and colored with caramel. Malt vinegar is used for pickling (particularly walnuts) and is an ingredient in the well-known Worcestershire sauce.

CIDER VINEGAR

The sugar in apple pulp is converted to alcohol and then to acetic acid in the usual way. Home-produced cider vinegar is cloudy, while commercial types are crystal clear, due to filtering. It is used a great deal for general cooking purposes, and also makes an excellent substitute for rice vinegar in Chinese and Japanese cooking. It also makes good salad dressings.

White wine vinegar with rosemary
Garlic vinegar
White wine vinegar with green peppercorns
Dill vinegar
Distilled malt vinegar
Chile vinegar
Red wine vinegar
White wine vinegar with tarragon
White wine vinegar
Spirit vinegar with lemon
Cider vinegar
Malt vinegar

WALNUT OIL

The kernels of the walnut, native to south-eastern Europe and Asia, contain oil with a pleasant nutty taste which is used mainly for salads. France and Italy are the main producers.

OLIVE OIL WITH HERBS

This oil has been extracted from black olives; the herbs make it suitable for use in salads and sauces.

AVOCADO OIL

The pulp of the avocado fruit contains an oil which is used mainly for cooking. The oil is probably extracted only from damaged fruit because of the popularity of avocados as a fruit.

SESAME SEED OIL

Probably of African origin, the sesame plant *(Sesamum indicum)* yields an oil that is used for cooking and in salads. It is also popular in Chinese cooking.

SUNFLOWER OIL

The seed of the sunflower, native to North America, contains a tasteless oil excellent as both a cooking and a salad oil. It is also used for making margarine.

OLIVE OIL

This popular oil is produced mainly in Greece, France, Italy and Spain. Two types are sold: virgin oil and pure olive oil. Virgin oil is obtained only from the pulp of high-grade fruit; pure olive oil has been pressed from the pulp and kernels of lower-grade olives. Good olive oil (pressed cold from fresh ripe fruit) is a clear green color and odorless; yellow oil (from secondary pressings under heat) is not usually of such good quality. Olive oil can be used in salads or for cooking.

GRAPE SEED OIL

Grape seeds contain an oil used for salads and making margarine.

CORN OIL

This oil, from corn kernels, is a favorite with cooks. It is a good frying oil, and is used to make margarine.

PEANUT OIL

Peanuts contain about 50 per cent oil, which is excellent for salads and for frying. It is also used in margarine and canned fish.

OTHER OILS

ALMOND OIL
Sweet almond nuts contain oil used in baking and confectionery.

COCONUT OIL
An oil from the dried copra which is excellent for frying.

PALM OIL
Oil from the palm fruit seed used in margarine and cooking.

POPPYSEED OIL
The seeds contain an oil used in salads or for cooking.

RAPE OIL
Produced from the seeds of the rape plant *(Brassica napus)*, this is used for cooking.

SAFFLOWER OIL
This is used in special diet mayonnaise and salad dressings.

SOYBEAN OIL
The seeds of the soybean contain an oil used in salads, for cooking, and in margarine.

Walnut oil

Olive oil with herbs

Sesame seed oil

Avocado oil

Grape seed oil

Sunflower oil

Corn oil

Olive oil

Peanut oil

Fruit

ATTEMPTS AT THE cultivation of fruit date back over 8000 years. Evidence of carbonized apples was found by archaeologists in ancient dwellings in Turkey; and neolithic sites in Denmark and Switzerland have yielded the fossilized remains of fruits such as sloes, blackberries, raspberries, strawberries, bilberries and crab apples. These apples were larger than the wild types found today, and assumed to be at an early stage of cultivation.

Apricots and peaches were grown in China some 3000 years ago. Their cultivation gradually spread westwards, the apricot becoming so well established in Armenia that the Romans called it *armeniacum*, "the Armenian apple".

Armenia, northern Persia and the foothills of the Caucasus contained the finest orchards of the ancient world. Here was the home of the vine, the quince, the medlar, pomegranate, and probably also the plum and the bullace. It is thought that the Phoenicians took the vine from Armenia to Greece and Rome, and that the Romans in turn planted vines in southern France and along the steep banks of the Rhine. The cultivation of fruit also spread southwards to the "fertile crescent" of Mesopotamia, where farmers grew crops of pomegranates, apples, cherries, peaches, mulberries and figs.

Oranges, native to China, are thought to have appeared in India during the first century AD, and from there went first to the east coast of Africa, then to the Levant. Roman horticulturists planted orange groves in Italy and may have introduced the orange to Spain, although the Spanish orange is also ascribed to the Moslem invaders who introduced the lemon. Oranges made their way to the New World in the sixteenth century, and were finally established in California in 1769. Bananas followed a similar route, though somewhat earlier; they reached India in about 500 BC, and from there migrated to the Canary Isles and the West Indies via Africa.

By the seventeenth and eighteenth centuries there was considerable exchange of fruits between Europe and America. The American cultivated strawberry was first introduced in 1660, and American apples were being sold in London's markets in the 1770s, along with bananas from the West Indies and a new, bright pink plant that nobody knew how to cook. It had come from Central Asia, where it was, and still is, eaten raw. This sour and acid-flavoured fruit was called rhubarb, and eventually became popular in America and Britain, where it is eaten stewed with sugar.

The pineapple was the only fruit from Central America to gain international status, until the recent popularity of the avocado. The pineapple had been cultivated in Brazil and Peru at least a thousand years earlier, sharing its domestication with the guava, papaya, avocado, star apple and sour sop. All these fruits spread to the Caribbean islands, to mingle with those that were indigenous.

Southeast Asia has a bounty of interesting and succulent fruits such as the banana, mango, carambola, durian, rambutan and mangosteen. The rambutan is unlikely to be found outside its native Malaysia, but the mango, which was transported to the Caribbean in the seventeenth century, has since become known throughout the world.

Varieties and hybrids

The willingness of some fruits to "marry" with others and to respond to selective crossbreeding has inspired horticulturists ever since the Romans first tried grafting plum trees. The development of fruits has come about by way of two botanical systems: variation and hybridization. Variations are produced by two parent plants of the same species that have different characteristics or qualities. Crossing two varieties of apple such as Worcester and McIntosh Red produces a third – "Tydeman's Early Worcester", which combines the best qualities of both parents.

Crossbreeding between parents that are genetically unalike, or distinctly different, results in a hybrid. Crossing a grapefruit with a tangerine produces a fruit which bears some of the characteristics of both species, in this case the tangelo. Of all fruits, the citrus family has responded best to hybridization. A few examples are the ugli fruit, also a cross between a tangerine and a grapefruit; the clementine, a hybrid of the tangerine and the sweet orange; and the citrange, resulting from a cross between a citron and an orange.

Many of these hybrids may turn out to be mere botanical curiosities with little commercial application, but some are becoming popular in the world market. The Jamaican ortanique, a cross between the orange and one of the tangerine varieties, probably the satsuma, is an example of this.

Some seasonal varieties of fruit have an attractive quality or unusual appeal; examples are blood oranges, pink grapefruit and red bananas with pink flesh.

Commercial uses of fruit

All citrus fruits have aromatic oils in their skins – oils which are used in cooking, in liqueur-making and which are also essential to the perfume industry. Lemon oil is widely used as a flavoring agent, and the skin of bitter oranges, such as the bergamot orange and the Seville or bigarade, produces oil of neroli and oil of bergamot for use in scents. Countless fruits are used as a flavoring for liqueurs and brandies, some of the more famous being curaçao, based on the orange, and kirsch, based on the cherry.

Citric acid, found mainly in the pulp of the fruit, is a useful by-product of lemons. Prepared in crystalline form it is used for flavoring cordial drinks and confectionery. Enzymes of papaya and pineapple are used in meat tenderizers because they help to break down protein.

Many fruit flavors, such as bananas, pears and pineapples, have been synthesized for the food industry. They are particularly useful in the manufacture of ice cream and soft drinks.

Buying and storing fruit

When buying fruit, watch out for soft spots or bruises. If possible, buy produce that is displayed openly, rather than depending on prepackaged fruit; also, buy in season for reasons of both flavor and economy. Methods of testing for ripeness, however, vary with each individual fruit.

Unless you plan on eating the fruit immediately, it is best to buy produce that is slightly underripe and let it ripen at home over a two- to three-day period. Most ripe fruit should be stored in the refrigerator, while under-ripe fruit can be stored at room temperature. All fruits have individual characteristics and it is impossible to give an overall rule on when fruit is ready to be eaten.

Fruit in the kitchen

Fresh, canned or dried fruit can be put to a variety of uses in the kitchen. It can be eaten raw in salads, as a dessert or with cheese, or can be cooked with meat or on its own.

The sugars and acids in fruit contribute greatly to the flavor and ultimate purpose to which the fruit will be put – whether for cooking or as fresh, dessert fruit. The plantain, for example, contains a lot of starch and is less sweet than its close relative, the banana, so is used mainly as a vegetable. Cooking apples are also lacking in sugar, but are high in malic acid; they pulp easily when cooked, while dessert apples remain firm.

Citrus fruits as part of a salad or compote should be peeled with a knife to remove the white "pith". Ideally, the inner core, seeds and segment membranes should also be removed. When removing the zest from the skin of citrus fruits, use a potato peeler and take off the top layer only. If you need a large amount to flavor a dessert, take off the whole peel, string the pieces together and blanch them several times; then dry them and leave them in syrup to sweeten. If you want to use citrus peel as a sweetener, rub a sugar cube over the peel.

Don't sugar strawberries in advance, as the sugar absorbs the water content and the fruit goes mushy. Red currants, blackcurrants and the rarer white variety will need to be destalked, a tedious job but less so if a fork is used to strip the fruit from the stems. Most berries yield a fair amount of water; add sugar and cook briefly to keep them whole.

Melons should be prepared just before serving; otherwise they lose some of their fine aroma and flavor. Bananas, apples and pears all darken on exposure to air when peeled, and should be dipped in acidulated water (water with a squeeze of lemon juice, or a teaspoonful of tartaric acid or ascorbic acid). It is best to use slightly under-ripe fresh fruit for canning, as the pectin content will be at its highest.

Stone Fruit

PEACH (*Prunus,* spp.)

Probably of Chinese origin, this fruit has over 2000 varieties. The velvety soft skin encloses firm, juicy flesh with one large stone. Peaches are normally classified as being either freestone or clingstone, and can be eaten fresh, canned or dried in desserts, or used in preserves and liqueurs.

CHERRY (*Prunus,* spp.)

Cherries, both dark-skinned and light-skinned, are available for a short time in summer. The best variety for cooking is the Morello, which is excellent for pies and jams. Cherries are also available canned and may be used in various types of liqueurs and brandies.

DATE (*Phoenix,* spp.)

Principally cultivated in the desert oases of southern Algeria and Tunisia, dates are also grown in South Carolina and Arizona. The most popular date varieties now cultivated – Medjool and Deglet Noor, among others – are all, as their names imply, of Arab origin. Dates can be bought fresh or dried all year round, and may be served as a garnish for a fruit tray or may be stuffed with cream cheese. Dates also freeze well and so may be kept for an extended period.

Cherries

Peach

Dates

NECTARINE (*Prunus,* spp.)

A smooth-skinned member of the peach family, nectarines have sweet, juicy flesh and are usually served as a dessert fruit. They are normally sold ripe and therefore should be eaten on the day of purchase. Nectarines can also be made into preserves.

Californian nectarine

Nectarine

APRICOT (*Prunus armeniaca*)

Native to China, apricots are in season through late spring and summer. The sweet flesh encloses a single stone and is covered by a tender skin. Available fresh, dried or canned, apricots can be eaten raw or used in desserts, or to make wines, brandies, preserves.

Apricot

PLUM (*Prunus,* spp.)

A late summer to early autumn fruit, plums can be served for dessert or for baking. Both types can be eaten raw, although cooking plums are more acidic and rather dry in comparison to the juicy, richer-tasting dessert plum. Many different varieties are available. The damson is a European plum which, unlike other varieties, is not suitable for eating raw. It is very dark and tart with a thick skin and makes excellent preserves. The greengage (known as the Reine Claude) is a plum with a yellowish green skin. It is one of the sweetest and best-flavored plum varieties. The mirabelle is a small golden-yellow plum; it is eaten stewed, made into jam, and is also made into a liqueur of the same name. Small and dark blue, the sloe is a very sour variety of plum used to make sloe gin and jam. Most plums can be eaten fresh and all can be used in jam-making and for compotes to be served as desserts. They are available fresh, dried and canned.

UNUSUAL STONE FRUIT

LOQUAT
(*Eriobotrya japonica*)
The loquat or Japanese medlar belongs to the same botanical family as the apple. A native of China and Japan, it has been quite widely cultivated in Mediterranean countries. The yellow pear-shaped fruit is the size of a crab apple. It can be eaten fresh or stewed and is also made into jam.

LYCHEE (*Litchi chinensis*)
Although normally considered a fruit, lychees can be used as nuts. They are eaten fresh, canned or preserved in syrup, or the fruit may be dried, in which case the pulp acquires a nutty, raisinlike taste.

MEDLAR
(*Mespilus germanica*)
A fruit the size of a small apple with a brown skin and firm flesh, it is thought to be native to oriental countries and often grows wild in Europe. It is generally eaten fresh but can also be used to make preserves.

Red Ace plum

*Damson;
prune plum*

Italian plum

Greengage

Burbank plum

*Californian
Santa Rosa plum*

Berries

BLACK CURRANT
(*Ribes nigrum*)
Usually sold stripped from their stalks, these summer fruits are always served cooked, as a filling for pies and puddings. They also make excellent preserves, and form the basis of the famous French liqueur, *cassis*. They are thought to have therapeutic properties in cases of arthritis.

Black currant

CRANBERRY
(*Vaccinium oxycoccus*)
Grown almost exclusively in America, but also harvested in Finland, cranberries are too acid to be eaten raw, but are usually used as cranberry sauce, a traditional accompaniment to turkey. They are also used in pies, ices, liqueurs and jellies. Available fresh in winter, they can also be bought frozen.

Cranberry

RED CURRANT (*Ribes rubrum*)
Rather tart for eating raw, these summer fruits have many other uses: they make a sparkling jelly, excellent with roast lamb, poultry and game; a delicious summer salad tossed with grated raw vegetables; and, dipped by the bunch in lightly beaten egg white, then "frosted" with fine sugar, they make a simple but dramatic table decoration. They are also used in jams, syrups and wine.

Red currant

BLUEBERRY
(*Vaccinium corymbosum*)
Originally wild, this somewhat tart fruit is now grown commercially. Blueberries are eaten raw with sugar and cream, stewed, made into soups, preserves, and jams or used in muffins and pies. They are in season in midsummer.

Blueberry

WILD STRAWBERRY
(*Fragaria*, spp.)
The wild strawberry or *fraise du bois* is smaller and more aromatic than the ordinary cultivated variety. It is usually eaten fresh and does not need to be hulled before eating.

Wild strawberry

GOOSEBERRY
(*Ribes grossularia*)
Enjoyed in Europe since the Middle Ages, these are summer fruits with a very short season. Sweet varieties are delicious eaten raw; tart ones make excellent preserves and desserts and can be made into wine.

Gooseberry

LOGANBERRY
(*Rubus loganobaccus*)
A cross between the raspberry and the blackberry, the loganberry embodies the best of each. It is available fresh in the midsummer months, or canned.

Loganberry

RASPBERRY (*Rubus idaeus*)
Raspberries often appear in two crops, one summer, one autumn; the latter are often smaller but juicier. Raspberries can be eaten on their own with cream and sugar or made into drinks, soups, fine preserves, sorbets and other desserts. Available fresh or frozen, they are considered to have excellent diuretic properties.

Raspberry

BLACKBERRY
(*Rubus fruticosus*)
This nutritious black fruit is picked wild around the country in late summer and early autumn, and has also been cultivated commercially for over a hundred years in America. Eaten fresh, they make a refreshing dessert, or they can be made into preserves, pies and syrups, often combined with apples. Blackberries are also thought to aid infections of the mouth and throat.

Blackberry

STRAWBERRY
(*Fragaria × ananassa*)
A native of America, strawberries are available fresh, frozen and canned, and are delicious eaten alone or with cream. They can be made into preserves, soups, pies and desserts. Their peak season is in late spring and early summer, though they are available all year.

Strawberry

OTHER BERRIES

ARBUTUS (*Arbutus unedo*)
This rather tasteless berry is the fruit of the strawberry tree. It is mainly used in preserves, for the extraction of alcohol, and in a drink similar to cider.

BOYSENBERRY
(*Rubus*, spp.)
Similar in appearance to the loganberry, this fruit can be eaten fresh or are frequently used to make preserves.

BUFFALO BERRY
(*Shepherdia argentea*)
A tart yellow fruit the size of a currant and containing one seed, the buffalo berry or buffalo currant is used in making pies and preserves. It is native to North America.

CAPE GOOSEBERRY
(*Physalis peruviana*)
Similar in appearance to a ground cherry, this yellow berry can be eaten raw or made into preserves.

CLOUDBERRY
(*Rubus chamaemorus*)
A small golden fruit which grows in Europe in large areas of open moorland, the cloudberry can be used in desserts or jams.

GROUND CHERRY
(*Physalis pruinosa*)
Also known as the strawberry tomato and dwarf Cape gooseberry, this is a sweet, but slightly-acid tasting, fruit enclosed in a lantern-shaped husk. It is usually made into preserves, but can also be eaten raw when ripe.

HAWTHORN
(*Crataegus*, spp.)
The haws (berries) of this plant are used in the making of jams and jellies. A wine can be made using the haws and flowers of the plant.

HONEY BERRY
(*Rubus*, spp.)
A relative of the raspberry, the honey berry can be eaten raw or can be cooked for use in desserts and preserves.

HUCKLEBERRY
(*Vaccinium myrtillus*)
Acid-tasting when raw, this berry (also known as whortleberry and bilberry) is used mainly in desserts, preserves and confectionery. It is also made into a wine in central Europe, used both for drinking and for medicinal purposes. Huckleberries are available in summer.

MULBERRY (*Morus*, spp.)
There are various species of this fruit, but the white mulberry (*Morus alba*) and the black mulberry (*Morus nigra*) are the most common. They are mostly eaten fresh or used in jams and wines, but can also be used to make a mildly astringent syrup.

NASEBERRY
(*Achras sapota*)
The pulp of this brown fruit is embedded with inedible black seeds and is palatable only when ripe. The flavor, however, is delicious, resembling the taste of brown sugar. It is also called sapodilla or chickoo.

PHENOMENAL BERRY
(*Rubus*, spp.)
Similar to the loganberry in both parentage and appearance, this fruit is usually cooked in jams and preserves, but can also be eaten raw.

SALMONBERRY
(*Ribes spectabilis*)
The salmonberry is an American wild raspberry or bramble. The name derives from the large berries that are salmon-red or wine-red when fully ripe. They can be eaten fresh or cooked in pies and desserts, and are sometimes made into preserves.

TANGLEBERRY
(*Gaylusacia frondosa*)
This is a type of bilberry that grows wild in some parts of America. The sweet-tasting berry may be eaten fresh or cooked in pies and desserts.

VEITCHBERRY
(*Rubus*, spp.)
A close relative of the loganberry, this fruit can be used in similar ways.

WHITE CURRANT
(*Ribes sativum*)
Less acid-tasting than the red currant, this berry can be eaten on its own or used in preserves or desserts.

WORCESTERBERRY
(*Ribes divaricatum*)
This is actually an American species of the gooseberry. The small black fruit was first sold in Worcester, USA when it was thought to be a hybrid of a gooseberry and a blackcurrant. It can be used in similar ways to the gooseberry.

Citrus Fruit

ORANGE (*Citrus,* spp.)

The best known of the citrus fruits, this, like other members of the citrus family, is native to China and Southeast Asia. There are both bitter and sweet oranges. The two main varieties of bitter orange are Bergamot (*Citrus bergamia*), used mainly for perfumery and essential oils, and the Seville orange (*C. aurantium*), which bears bitter-tasting fruits unsuitable for eating raw. The fruit itself is used in marmalades, though the rind is used for its oil which is extracted and used in liqueurs such as curaçao, or in orange flower water. Seville oranges are sometimes added to meat and fish dishes for piquancy.

Sweet oranges (*Citrus sinensis*) are available all year round and may be used in a multitude of ways: the fruit is served plain, cut up in salads or sliced for drinks or as a garnish; its juice is drunk plain or used in sauces and batters; its rind is grated for baking and using whole as a shell for salads and ices, or sliced and candied. They are extensively grown in the South, Israel, South Arrica, and in Australia and are usually classified as normal, blood and navel. Common types of normal orange are Spanish and Jaffas – good for juicing and slicing for use in salads and fruit salads. Navel oranges, so-called because they have a circular mark at the stem end resembling a navel, are also good in salads. Blood oranges are small, with slightly rough skin, and have sweet, juicy flesh with flecks of red. They are usually eaten on their own, though they too can be used in salads. The Ortanique is another variety of orange, but flatter in shape.

TANGERINE (*Citrus reticulata*)

Native to southern China and Laos, the tangerine is a small, sweet orange containing numerous pips. Generally thought of as being the same thing as a mandarin (although biologists are still confused by their nomenclature), these fruits have very loose skin which is easy to remove. They are available fresh or canned, and can be eaten on their own or used in fruit salads. They are also sometimes candied and glazed, or used to make liqueurs and marmalades.

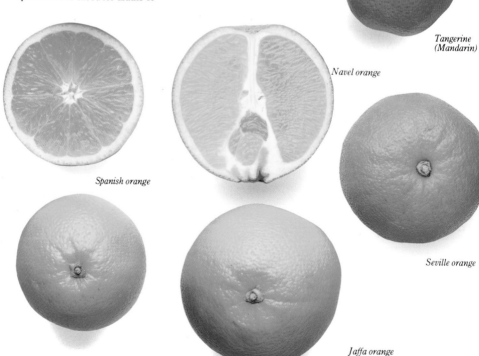

Tangerine (Mandarin)

Navel orange

Spanish orange

Seville orange

Jaffa orange

KUMQUAT (*Fortunella japonica*)

Of Chinese origin and no bigger than a large olive, the kumquat has sweet skin and juicy, slightly bitter flesh. It can be served fresh and eaten with the skin, but is also available bottled in syrups. Kumquats may be included in mixed fruit salads, or used in marmalades and other preserves.

Kumquat

CLEMENTINE (*Citrus*, spp.)

This is regarded by some as a variety of tangerine, and by others as a cross between the tangerine and sweet orange. Mainly produced in northern Africa, it is practically seedless. The skin is easily removed.

SATSUMA (*Citrus*, spp.)

The satsuma (or seedless mandarin) is similar to the tangerine in taste and appearance, with loose, smooth skin and pale orange flesh. Usually eaten fresh, it can be used in preserves.

GRAPEFRUIT (*Citrus paradiis*)

A popular species of the citrus family, it is native to the West Indies, but is now grown in many hot climates. Often served as a breakfast appetizer, it is thought to contain an enzyme which stimulates the metabolism, hence its frequent use in slimming diets. Available all year round, there are two basic varieties: white, which is particularly good for juicing, and pink, so sweet that it can be eaten without additional sugar. Often available in the form of canned segments, grapefruit can be eaten raw or grilled with brown sugar. It is also used in fruit drinks, juices and marmalades.

OTHER CITRUS FRUIT

POMELO (*Citrus glandis*)
The largest of the citrus fruits, the pomelo or shaddock has a thick skin and a bitter fibrous pulp similar to the grapefruit. It is usually eaten on its own.

TANGELO (*Citrus*, spp.)
A cross between the tangerine and the grapefruit, this tapers slightly at the stem end. It is good for juicing, eating as a fresh fruit, or in salads.

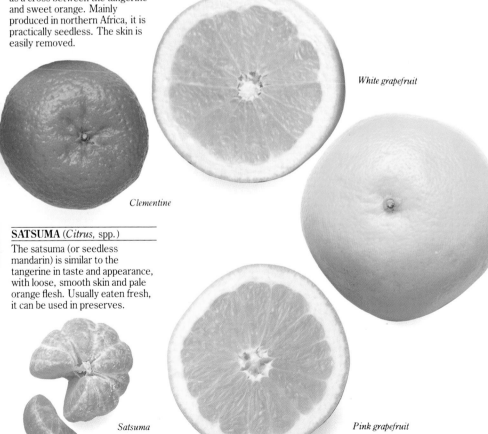

White grapefruit

Clementine

Satsuma

Pink grapefruit

LIME (*Citrus aurantifolia*)

This small, thin-skinned fruit of Indian origin is closely related to the lemon and is, in fact, often used as a lemon substitute. It is used in juices, cocktails, pickles, preserves and curries. Its grated zest or peel is often used in sherbets and ice cream.

LEMON (*Citrus limon*)

Of Indian origin, and now grown worldwide, the lemon is easily the most versatile of all the citrus fruits. Its acid taste makes it unpleasant to eat as a fruit, but it has many culinary uses, particularly in baking and confectionery and in the preparation of lemon juice and sugar for lemonade. A few drops of lemon juice will enhance delicate fish or poultry dishes, creams and pies. The acid can also be used to prevent cut fruit from turning brown when exposed to the air.

CITRON (*Citrus medica*)

Native to China, the citron, unlike other members of the citrus family, is not cultivated for its flesh or juice but for its thick, fragrant rind, which is candied and used in cakes and confections, and in the preparation of candied fruits and liqueurs. It is an important part of the Jewish festival of Succoth.

Lemon

Lime

Citron

UGLI (*Citrus,* spp.)

Native to the East Indies, the ugli is a hybrid between the tangerine and the grapefruit. It is similar in appearance to the latter, but is slightly smaller with thick, rough skin, sweeter-tasting flesh and few pips. Uglis have the same uses as grapefruit, and are often substituted for them.

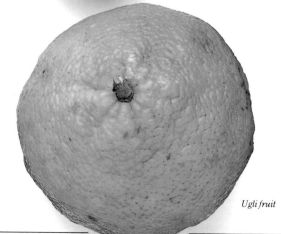

Ugli fruit

Pears

PEARS (*Pyrus communis*)

Today there are over 5000 varieties of pear in existence throughout the world. Dessert pears (illustrated) have a juicy, white flesh that is slightly acid-tasting but also sweet. They have a strong but pleasant scent. Stewing pears are rather hard and tasteless, with little juice. Pears ripen and are harvested during an extremely short period and, once ripe, go bad very quickly. The stewing varieties keep for a slightly longer period than the dessert pears. Varieties for eating fresh are Bartletts and Williams' which are in season in late summer. Comice and Bosc are excellent pears to use for cooking and pickling. Pears are also available dried (page 96) and canned, and can be served as a dessert with cream or other fruits. Eaten fresh, they may be served whole with cheese or cut up and added to fruit salads. They can be stewed and puréed, or used in preserves and confectionery.

Bosc

Bartlett

Williams'

Comice

Sliced Comice

Apples

The many varieties of apple (*Malus domestica*) can be divided into two groups: dessert and cooking. Dessert apples (those that are eaten fresh) include McIntosh, Jonathan, Red Delicious and Golden Delicious. Some varieties which are good for eating raw and also for most cooking purposes (for example, in purées, or pies, or simply baked whole) are Granny Smith, Greenings, Cortland and Rome.

GRANNY SMITH

Originally grown from a pip in nineteenth-century Australia, this apple's crunchy hard flesh, sharp distinctive taste and bright green skin have made it popular and easily recognizable. A worldwide choice both for cooking and eating.

Granny Smith

BRAMLEY

This is the main British cooking apple. Large and green, sometimes flushed with red, its flesh is sharp and juicy and is not usually eaten raw. It can be used in apple pies, or for making apple chutney, or cored, peeled and sautéed in butter to serve with bacon and sausage at breakfast.

GOLDEN DELICIOUS

One of the major varieties of dessert apples in America, South Africa and England, the Golden Delicious or Yellow Delicious is firm and crisp when the skin is greenish, or less crisp but sweeter when completely golden. It is a good contrast, both in flavor and texture, to blue cheese.

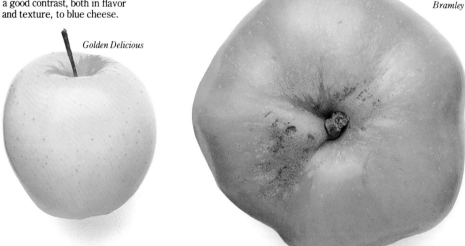

Golden Delicious

Bramley

STARKING

From France, a crisp dessert apple with red-streaked skin and very white, sweet flesh. Also called Starking Delicious, it is best served early in the season on its own at the end of a meal, with cheese, or made into a dessert by being cored, sliced in rounds and fried in a sweet batter as fritters.

CRAB APPLE

Available briefly in autumn, this small, acidic, applelike fruit can be red or yellow. High in pectin, it is widely used in making jellies and preserves, and for other food accompaniments.

RED DELICIOUS

An American variety, this is one of the world's best eating apples. Firm, sweet and long-lasting, its red skin makes it look attractive in a fruit bowl as well as served baked with roast meat.

Red Delicious

Starking

Crab apple

SPARTAN

The Danes developed this firm apple with a custardlike taste that is popular for eating and cooking. It goes well in a cold salad with onions and cured meats.

McINTOSH

Slightly tart, best freshly picked, this all-purpose American apple is good on its own, in salads, or with meat, and takes less cooking time than other varieties.

ROME

Crisp, firm and juicy, this is America's most popular cooking apple. It is also good to eat.

McIntosh

Spartan

Rome

Grapes

Cyprus Gold

GRAPES (*Vitis vinifera*)

There are either green or black
grapes available, and different
varieties of both are grown in
many parts of the world for eating
fresh, for wine-making and for
drying. Most likely originating in
western Asia, they are one of the
oldest cultivated plants. Grapes
are a vinous fruit, growing in
clusters, and have digestive and
therapeutic properties which are
rare in other types of fruit. They
are normally classified as being
either table grapes, which would
include all the varieties shown
here, or wine-making grapes (such
as Pinot Noir, Chardonnay,
Riesling and Cabernet Sauvignon),
both of which are good for eating
raw. They are available all year
long. They can be eaten on their
own or in fruit salads, and are
often used as a garnish in
desserts. Dried grapes are
known as raisins, currants and
sultanas (page 98).

Superior

Emperor

Thompson

Benhanna

Melons

There are several types of melon, but broadly speaking there are three groups defined by form and color. There are musk or netted melons, with a "network" pattern on the skin, winter melons, which are quite smooth-skinned, and cantaloupe melons (rockmelons), which have a warty exterior. There is also the watermelon (*Cucumis citrullus*), with a dark green skin and bright red flesh. Musk melons have flesh of a yellowish green color; the flesh of winter melons is green-tinged – the best-known types are Casaba and Honeydew. The flesh of the cantelope is orange colored. A new melon in this category is the Ogen, which has greenish flesh.

Melon is eaten in its natural state either at the beginning of a meal as an hors d'œuvre or at the end as a dessert.

OGEN (*Cucumis melo*)

A small, round hybrid variety named after the kibbutz in Israel where it was first cultivated, this is widely sought after for the sweet succulence of its flesh. It is available from spring to midwinter; one melon should be allowed per person.

WATERMELON
(*Cucumis citrullus*)

Indigenous to Africa, the rich red, occasionally yellow, flesh of the watermelon is especially refreshing as it is 91 per cent water. Grown in tropical countries and in warmer parts of America and Europe, it is available from summer to early autumn. Round or oblong, when ripe the skin should be a rich deep green or green variegated with dark gray, sometimes with a yellow underside, and its thin surface should come away easily when scraped with a fingernail. For vine-ripened sweetness, the stem end should be slightly sunken and calloused. Mostly eaten as a thirst-quencher in very hot weather, it can also be eaten in fruit salads or, sliced, with vinaigrette dressing.

Ogen

Watermelon

CHARENTAIS (*Cucumis melo*)

The Charentais's orange, sugary and fragrant flesh make this fruit popular both as a dessert or first course. Available all year round in many places, it keeps well when stored in a cool, dry place and ripens after several days in a warm room. When ripe, it is fragrant even before being cut. Although at its best when freshly cut, it can be stored in the refrigerator for up to two days if covered in plastic wrap.

Charentais

CANTALOPE (*Cucumis melo*)

Thought to have originated in Asia, also known as rockmelons, cantaloupes are widely available during summer. When ripe, it is extremely fragrant and its flesh sweet. It can be served with ice cream.

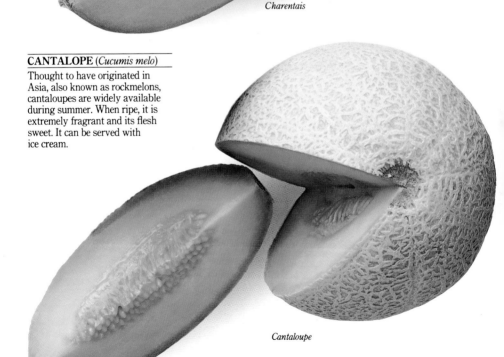

Cantaloupe

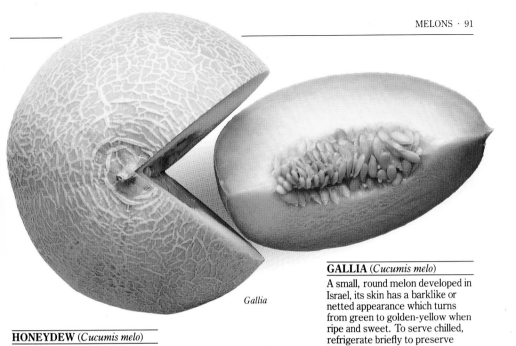

Gallia

GALLIA (*Cucumis melo*)

A small, round melon developed in Israel, its skin has a barklike or netted appearance which turns from green to golden-yellow when ripe and sweet. To serve chilled, refrigerate briefly to preserve its taste.

HONEYDEW (*Cucumis melo*)

An oval melon available all year round in most places, its delicate taste and pale-green flesh contrasts well with a thin slice of raw, cured ham or sweet wine such as muscatel or port.

Honeydew

Tropical Fruit

GUAVA (*Psidium guajava*)

This fruit of the guayaba tree is probably native to Haiti, but is now found in most tropical and subtropical countries. It varies in size from that of a walnut to an apple, and is one of the most commonly planted tropical fruits. When ripe, the skins are light yellow in color, the pulp is juicy and contains small seeds. The flesh varies in color from white to yellow to pale pink. Available in the spring and summer, the fruit has a sharp taste, and is therefore usually used for stewing and making tarts and preserves. It can be bought fresh (as shown) or canned (in slices). Guavas are noted for their high vitamin C content; in some varieties it is higher than that of citrus fruits.

*Papaya
(Pawpaw)*

Guava

Kiwifruit

Passionfruit

PASSIONFRUIT
(*Passiflora edulis*)

The fruit of a perennial climbing plant native to Brazil, passionfruit (or purple granadilla) can be eaten fresh when the skins are deeply wrinkled and the fruit is juicy, or used to make preserves and ice cream. It is most readily available in the summer.

KIWIFRUIT (*Actinidia sinensis*)

A native of China, the kiwifruit or Chinese gooseberry is now grown in many countries, especially New Zealand. It has a sweetish taste and a hairy skin, which should be removed before eating. It may be poached and sprinkled with lemon juice, but more commonly is eaten fresh, either on its own or in fruit salads and desserts. It is available from midsummer to winter.

PAPAYA (*Carica papaya*)

Native to Central America, but widely cultivated in all tropical countries, the papaya or pawpaw is a large berry with a yellowish rind and yellow to salmon-colored flesh with a large central cavity containing many seeds. It has a fairly sweet taste when ripe (similar to apricots and ginger) and, like melon, makes a good dessert or breakfast fruit. It can also be cooked as a vegetable before it is ripe, and is often used to make preserves and pickles. When served raw, papayas should be chilled and sprinkled with lemon or lime juice. They are most readily available in the spring and summer months.

MANGO (*Mangifera indica*)

This fruit, native to India, can be green or yellow-red (as shown), and contains a pit surrounded by a sweet and sticky pulp, tasting like nectar and peaches, which can be eaten on its own or used in preserves and chutneys. It is an important source of vitamin A. At its best in summer, it can be bought fresh or canned. India is the biggest producer, although mangoes are grown in many tropical climates.

Mango

Feijoa

Pineapple

FEIJOA (*Feijoa sellowiana*)

Now grown mainly in New Zealand, the feijoa is native to Brazil and Uruguay. The white flesh tastes like a combination of pineapple and strawberry and is delicious in fruit salads, but is principally used for jams and other preserves. It is available in late spring and summer.

PINEAPPLE (*Ananas comosus*)

The pineapple is really a cluster of fruits of the ananas tree, which all combine to form one "multiple fruit". Native to South America, it is now grown in most tropical and subtropical countries. It has a high sugar content and is one of the finest table fruits. Attractive and tasty, they are available all year round and make an excellent dessert fruit. Pineapples can be bought fresh (as shown), canned (in chunks, slices and crushed), or candied (page 125).

OTHER TROPICAL FRUIT

BABACO (*Carica pentagona*)
Native to Central and South America, but now grown extensively in New Zealand, this is a five-sided relative of the papaya, and resembles it and the pineapple in its delicate flavor. It may be eaten raw or stewed, used in salads, pickles and chutneys.

CUSTARD APPLE
(*Annona*, spp.)
A term covering a group of fruits which includes the cherimoya (also known as sherbet fruit), sweet sop, sour sop and bullock's heart. They are tropical fruits which rarely appear in temperate zone markets. The cherimoya has a pineapple flavor while the sweet sop, or sugar apple, has a sweet, custardlike flesh. The flesh of the sour sop is white and more acid than the others. The flesh of the

bullock's heart is more solid and sweet; it gets its name from its shape and dark brown color.

DURIAN (*Durio zibethinus*)
A fruit native to Southeast Asia and much enjoyed there. Its main characteristic is a highly unpleasant smell which probably accounts for the fact that it has never attained a wider popularity. It has a dull yellow skin when ripe and its pulp, eaten raw, is creamy.

MANGOSTEEN
(*Garcinia mangostana*)
Similar in appearance to the lychee (page 79), but not related to it or the mango, despite the name, this slow-growing tree fruit is originally from Southeast Asia. The thick rind and deep pink pith should be removed to reveal the delicately scented and

flavored white flesh. Mangosteens may be eaten on their own or in fruit salads.

CARAMBOLA
(*Averrhoa carambola*)
Native to Southeast Asia, but also grown in South America, the carambola or star fruit gets its name from the five-pointed star shape of the slices when the fruit is cut across. With its sour-sweet taste, it is refreshing in fruit salads or as a drink, and may also be used as a garnish.

TAMARILLO
(*Cyphomandra betacea*)
Indigenous to Peru, the tamarillo or tree tomato is related to the tomato. Rich in vitamin C, it has a strong sweet flavor and may be eaten raw, stewed, baked or broiled, or used in savory dishes and preserves.

Other Fruits

QUINCE
(Cydonia vulgaris/oblonga)

There are many varieties of this hard and acid Asiatic fruit which, although one of the earliest known fruits, is not one that has a widely popular appeal. Rarely eaten uncooked, it is used principally in preserves and baking and turns pink when cooked. Japonicas are the flowering variety of quince but have less flavor.

PRICKLY PEAR
(Opuntia ficus indica)

Native to America, and now found in all temperate regions, the prickly pear or Indian fig is available from midsummer to midwinter. A member of the cactus family, it has a thorny skin which must be removed before eating. It can be eaten raw or stewed and is used in preserves.

FIG *(Ficus carica)*

There are several varieties of white, purple and red figs and their cultivation today is extensive, particularly in the Mediterranean countries. They are very good eaten fresh, some are canned or used in relishes and many are dried (page 96). Figs are excellent in baking and desserts and are also good when stewed.

Japonica

Quince

Prickly pear

Fig

PERSIMMON *(Diospyros kaki)*

There are several varieties of the persimmon – also called kaki fruit or Sharon fruit – which is native to China and Japan. It can be eaten fresh or cooked and is often candied. It is available from midsummer to midwinter.

BANANA *(Musa nana)*

Native to tropical countries, bananas are sweet-tasting and are usually eaten raw – often on their own or incorporated in fruit salads – although they can also be gently baked or flambéed with brown sugar, brandy or rum. The skin of the fruit is green when unripe changing to yellow when ready for eating. Available all year round, they are nutritious and rich in vitamin A.

Persimmon

Banana

POMEGRANATE
(Punica granatum)

The pomegranate, indigenous to Persia, is among the most ancient of fruits. It is available in the autumn months, and usually eaten as a raw fruit, though its juice is often extracted and used in drinks. In parts of the Middle East it is included in soups, and in the West Indies it is used widely in cooking and in preserves. Pomegranate seeds are used to make grenadine syrup (page 63).

PLANTAIN *(Musa paradisiaca)*

Native to the tropics, the plantain is a type of cooking banana, larger than dessert bananas and with a lower sugar content. Unsuitable for eating raw, it is cooked in a wide range of savory dishes and is popular in West Indian, Latin and African cooking. It is available all year round.

RHUBARB
(Rheum rhaponticum)

The stem of a large perennial plant thought to be native to Tibet, rhubarb is, technically, a vegetable, though it is used as a fruit. Available from midwinter to midsummer, it can be bought fresh or canned, and is used in sauces, pies, preserves and wines.

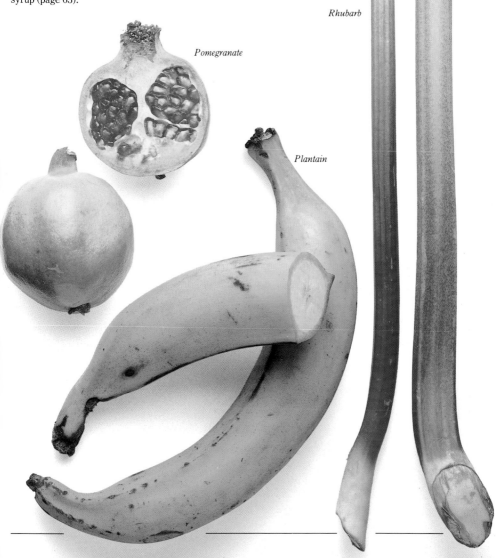

Rhubarb

Pomegranate

Plantain

DRIED FRUITS

IF A RIPE FRUIT IS dried it loses most of its moisture, accumulates natural sugars, and keeps almost indefinitely. This fact has been known to Middle Eastern people for over 5000 years. They have always preserved dates, figs and apricots by sun-drying, which is still the most favored technique, although some fruits are now artificially dried. Medieval Europeans put their apples into warm ovens, then peeled, cored and threaded them onto strings, and suspended them from the kitchen ceiling. In the monasteries, however, monks dried their plums, grapes and apples on straw-covered stone floors.

Dried fruit was introduced to America by the settlers, who also brought with them apples, nectarines, grapes, peaches, quinces and apricots, to add to the indigenous plums, cherries and persimmons. Today, California is the main producer of dried fruit.

Methods of processing

Six pounds of fresh fruit produce only one pound of dried fruit. The fruits are harvested by hand, the stalks and pits removed. They are then fumigated and graded before being spread out in the sun to dry. While sun-drying gives fruit a golden, translucent appearance which

cannot be achieved mechanically, it has many disadvantages, principally that of cost, which makes mechanical driers more popular. Most fruits are picked when ripe (except pears, which are picked while still green and left to ripen on trays). They are then chemically treated with either sulphur smoke or an alkali dip, depending on the fruit. Both of these methods accelerate drying, but the alkali dip is preferred for whole fruits, such as prunes or grapes.

Dried fruit in the kitchen

Dried fruit is sweeter and richer than fresh fruit, which makes it invaluable in baking and desserts. It is most often used in fruit cakes and cookies and occasionally in stuffings. It can be eaten on its own, candied as a confectionery item, mixed with cereals, or topped with yogurt or whipped cream.

Packets of ready-mixed dried fruit can be bought in most supermarkets and health food stores, but the fruit can also be bought separately. Currants, raisins and sultanas are usually sold washed and ready to use; other dried fruits may need washing and soaking, preferably overnight. Keep the liquid in which they were soaked and use it to cook the fruit.

FIGS

California and the Mediterranean countries (particularly Turkey) are the world's main producers of figs, which are usually sun-dried. They can be eaten as they are, reconstituted with water in compotes, or chopped and used for baking and confections.

PEARS

Dried pears are now available in many health food stores and some supermarkets. They are used for making compotes and the famous Swiss *birnenbrot* (pear bread).

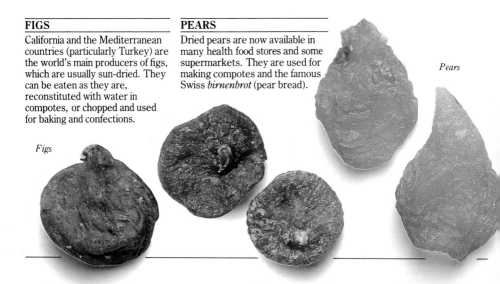

Pears

Figs

PEACHES

Although peaches are usually preserved by canning, a small part of the crop is halved and dried for use in fruit compotes, baking, jams and other preserves.

Peaches

PRUNES

Like dates, prunes (dried plums) vary widely in quality. Long enjoyed as a breakfast compote with great digestive qualities, they can be eaten on their own or used in cakes, puddings, sauces, the Arab stew *tadjub ahmar,* and also as a filling for dumplings and fritters. They can be canned or preserved in brandy or vinegar, and are sold pitted and unpitted. Prunes also make a fine brandy.

Prunes

APRICOTS

Dried apricots are almost preferable to the fresh fruit, unless the latter is very ripe and sweet. They vary in form from the withered yellow strips, with must be soaked and cooked with sugar to make them palatable, to plump, sun-dried sweet fruit which can be eaten as it is.

Apricots

DATES

Dried dates vary in quality and form from the large, plump table dates, pitted or unpitted, to pressed slab dates, which are considerably cheaper. They are classified into dry, semi-dry and soft types, of which the soft is the most popular. Dried dates can be eaten as they are or used in baking and confections.

BANANAS

Drying concentrates the elusive taste of the banana to produce a deliciously chewy and highly nutritious snack. The fruits are usually cut and dried in the sun. Dried bananas are also used in baking, and the vacuum-dried purée of the ripe fruit produces a type of flour.

Bananas

Dates

CURRANTS

The dried fruit of the small, seedless grape of Corinth in Greece, from which they take their name, currants are used mainly for baking.

RAISINS

A type of dried grape and one of the most popular of all dried fruits, raisins are mainly produced in California and the Middle East. They make a good snack, especially if mixed with nuts, and are also used in all kinds of baking.

GOLDEN RAISINS

Also called sultanas or white raisins, these are another type of dried grape. These are larger and sweeter than raisins, and are used when the color of raisins and currants is not desired.

Currants

Raisins

Sultanas

Apples

APPLES

Dried apples have been a winter standby of country housewives since ancient times, when cold storage and other modern methods of preservation were unknown. They attract moisture, however, and so have a shorter shelf life than other dried fruits. They can be eaten on their own or used in baking.

OTHER DRIED FRUIT

RED DATES

Although called "dates", these are in fact jujubes (native to China but also cultivated in the Mediterranean area). Usually sun-dried, they are used in Oriental and Indian cooking as flavorings for both sweet and savory dishes.

NUTS

BOTANICALLY, NUTS ARE single-seeded, dry, hard-shelled fruits that have to be cracked to open them, such as chestnuts and hazelnuts (filberts). However, the term is also used for any seed or fruit with an edible kernel in a hard or brittle shell; for example peanuts – strictly speaking a legume – walnuts and coconuts. Since the earliest times, nuts have been used as source of food and oil. They were collected by food-gathering peoples before the birth of agriculture, were used extensively by the Greeks, and there is evidence that they were cultivated by the Romans.

Nuts are also an important feature of Middle Eastern cookery. In fact, medieval Europe learned the use of nuts in cooking from the Arabs, who not only used them in sauces with meat and poultry, but in marzipan, nougat and other sweetmeats. Spain, occupied for almost eight centuries by the Moors, also adopted the use of nuts in cooking, and took the technique to the Americas after the Conquest. They found the Aztecs already using pumpkin seeds and peanuts, and probably pecans, as thickeners for poultry and fish and shellfish sauces. Almonds are used extensively in Scandinavian cooking, and they are also important in Indonesian, Far Eastern and African cooking. In fact, the use of nuts is universal: they are present in every aspect of cooking from hors d'oeuvres through to desserts.

Using nuts
Some nuts, such as pecans and Brazil nuts, can be shelled more easily if they are allowed to stand in boiling water for 15 to 20 minutes. To blanch (remove the thin inner lining of) shelled nuts such as almonds, pistachios and walnuts, pour boiling water over them and then rinse immediately with cold water. Hazelnuts (filberts) need to be put under the broiler for a few minutes before peeling. Nuts are more easily chopped if they are warm and moist. Roasting nuts brings out their flavor. Once shelled and skinned (if desired), they can be placed in a medium oven – 350°F – for 10 to 20 minutes.

Storing nuts
The length of time nuts will keep varies according to the type: unshelled nuts are protected from heat, air, light and moisture, and therefore will keep almost indefinitely anywhere; but shelled nuts do not keep as well, and should be stored tightly covered in a cool, dark, dry place or freezer. Both salted and unsalted nuts should be refrigerated although, of the two, unsalted nuts last longer.

WALNUT (Juglans regia)
Also known as the English walnut and Persian walnut, this is available in the shell, shelled, ground or chopped. It can be used when immature or ripe, and dried or toasted. Young green nuts are pickled in vinegar (page 68); immature walnuts are an important ingredient in the Mexican national dish, *chiles en nogada* (peppers in walnut sauce); ripe walnut as are eaten as a snack nut and are used in stuffings, confectionery, baking, salads, and vegetarian cooking. A liqueur, *brou*, is made from the shucks or casings of the nuts. Walnut oil (page 75), which has a pronounced flavor, is used for salad dressings. Black or American walnuts (*Juglans nigra*) have thick, hard shells and are usually larger than European walnuts. Stronger-tasting than the latter, they are used in baking and ice creams. Butternut (*Juglans cinera*), also known as white walnut, has a rich and pleasant flavor and is often used in confectionery.

Whole walnut

Shelled walnut

Ground walnut   *Chopped walnut*

BRAZIL NUT
(Bertholletia excelsa)

The seeds of a tall forest tree of South America, Brazil nuts are sold whole and shelled. They can be eaten on their own, and are also used in confectionery and cakes.

Whole brazil nut

Shelled brazil nut

PECAN (Carya illinoensis)

The pecan nut, indigenous to North America, is related to the walnut. It is eaten in large quantities as a dessert nut, plain or salted, and used to make nutbreads, confectionery, ice creams and in vegetarian dishes. Its best known use is in the popular American dessert, pecan pie.

Whole pecan

Chopped pecan

Shelled pecan

CASHEW
(Anacardium occidentale)

The fruit of a tropical tree native to America, the cashew grows as a single, hard protuberance beneath a fleshy fruit. The nuts are used in baking, in cashew butter, or are eaten as a cocktail nut. They are usually sold shelled and salted.

Whole cashew

HAZELNUT
FILBERT (Corylus maxima)

These are both fruits of the hazelnut or cobnut bush. Native to the Mediterranean region, they are now grown widely and are readily available throughout the world. Both hazelnuts and filberts are rich in oil (which can be used for salads and cooking) and the nuts may be eaten on their own or used in butters, confections and desserts.

Whole hazelnut   *Shelled hazelnut*

Chopped hazelnut   *Ground hazelnut*

ALMOND (Prunus dulcis)

The seeds of a Mediterranean tree of the peach family, almonds, when growing, are covered with a green outer skin which is later removed. One of the most popular nuts worldwide, there are two types, sweet and bitter. The latter contains prussic acid and is never eaten raw, but its essence can be distilled and used as a flavoring. Sweet almonds are used whole for baking and confectionery, ground into a paste for butters, pralines, fillings, and nougat, chopped, diced and shredded for cooking and garnishing, roasted, salted or sugared. Sugared almonds may be covered in sugar, syrup or honey.

Whole almond   *Ground almond*

Chopped almond

PEANUT (Arachis hypogaea)

Native to South America, the peanut (or groundnut or monkey nut) is not, strictly speaking, a nut but a highly nutritious legume. Its outer "shell" is the dried fibrous pod of the plant, and contains the seeds or "nuts". It can be eaten raw or roasted and is used primarily for peanut butter (page 69) and peanut oil (page 75).

Whole peanut

Shelled peanut

TIGERNUT (Cyperus esculenta)

Always referred to, and thought of, as nuts, tigernuts or earth almonds are really the starchy rhizomes of a plant native to Africa. Usually sold dried, they have an almondy taste and can be eaten on their own, like peanuts, or cooked or made into a flour.

Tigernut

Shelled bitter almond   *Shelled almond*

Blanched almond   *Flaked almond*

CHESTNUT (*Castanea sativa*)

Native to southern Europe, the sweet chestnut has been grown for many centuries and used in soups, cereals, stews and stuffings. It is the only nut which is treated as a vegetable – because it contains more starch and less oil than other nuts it can be cooked differently. It can be eaten whole, either roasted, boiled, or steamed. Once shelled, they are preserved whole in sugar or syrup as marrons glacés (page 124), dried, used chopped in stuffings or with vegetables, or ground into a flour.

There are two types of water chestnut. *Trapa natans* has an edible seed and a floury texture and is eaten raw, roasted or boiled in central Europe and Asia. A related aquatic plant, ling (*Trapa bicornis*), is grown in China, Korea and Japan. Its seeds are eaten boiled, or preserved in honey and sugar or used for making flour.

The Chinese water chestnut or *pi tsi* is a tuber which is cultivated in the East Indies, China and Japan. It is used sliced as a vegetable and, outside Asia, is usually bought canned.

Shelled chestnut

Whole chestnut

PISTACHIO NUT (*Pistacia vera*)

The fruit of a small tree native to the Middle East and central Asia, pistachios are prized for their pleasant, mild flavor and ornamental color. They may be used in stuffings, sauces, confectionery, baking and ice creams, but are commonly eaten salted as a cocktail or dessert nut. To preserve their brilliant color, shell them and boil in water for a few minutes, then remove their skins.

CHUFA NUT (*Cyperus esculenta*)

Related to the tigernut, this is fairly popular in Europe. When ground it is used in the Spanish drink *horchata de chufa*.

Chufa nut

COCONUT (*Cocos nucifera*)

All parts of the fruit are used, but only the milk and meat as food. Coconut milk is a refreshing and nutritious drink, and can be used in curry sauces. Coconut meat can be eaten fresh, or dried and used in baking and confectionery (page 124). Most coconut meat, however, is dried to form copra, from which coconut oil (page 75) is extracted. The sap of the coconut palm can be fermented to produce a palm tree wine, *arrack*.

MACADAMIA NUT (*Macadamia ternifolia*)

Native to Australia and now also grown in Hawaii, macadamia nuts are usually sold shelled and roasted in countries where they are not grown.

Macadamia nut

PINE NUTS (*Pinu pinea*)

The seed of the stone pine, native to the Mediterranean, pine nuts, or kernels are eaten raw or roasted and salted like peanuts. In Italy they are used to make soups and sauces, such as the famous *pesto* sauce, in the Middle East they are popular in *dolmas*, and they can be eaten raw in salads.

Pine nut

Coconut

Pistachios

GRAINS

G rains are the seeds of food, or the cereal, grasses and other plants. They include such staples as wheat, oats and corn. When agriculture first began in the Middle East, Central and South America in about 7000 BC, grains figured prominently – wheat and barley are Middle Eastern crops, and corn is Mexican.

The starchy carbohydrates which are provided by grains are essential in human nutrition. Rice is a staple food for half the world's population, the remaining half cultivating wheat, oats, corn, barley, millet and so on, depending on soil and climate. There are starchy dishes in every cuisine in the world, including Mexico's corn tortillas, Italy's many pastas, and Brazil's farofas, made from cassava (manioc) meal.

Most grains come from the cultivated grasses (*Graminaceae*) wheat, corn, rice, oats, barley and rye. In addition, there are other crops that are good starch-providers, including tapioca and cassava meal from the root of the cassava plant and sago from the sago palm. Fecula or "flour" products also come from the roots of such plants as the lotus, arum lily, bracken, potato, and other tubers. From the "cereal grasses" we harvest the valuable grains – how we use these grains depends on their individual structure and their behaviour as foodstuffs.

RICE

There are about 7000 varieties of rice (*Oryza sativa*). Probably native to India and Indo-China, it comes in many forms. Brown rice is simply the rice with its bran, which is removed during the secondary stage of milling (or "pearling") to give us the familiar white polished grain. The bran in brown rice offers additional protein, plus traces of iron, calcium and vitamin B, but takes longer to cook. Not all rice varieties are white when polished: Carolina and some Italian rices are amber.

Rice is divided into three groups: long-, short- and medium-grain. Long-grain rice is four to five times as long as it is wide and, when cooked, the grains are separate and fluffy. It is used in salads, curries, stews, chicken or meat dishes. Short- and medium-grain rice have short, plump grains which become tender and moist when cooked with the grains clinging together. Each type of rice is suited to traditional cooking styles: Indian cooks prefer a dry rice, especially for pilaus; Japanese and Chinese cooks use short-grain rice which can be shaped by the fingers, and is easily handled with chopsticks.

Under the general classification of long-grain rice are the American Carolina and the delicate Basmati from Pakistan. The short-grain rices include Japan's kome, and the stubby round Italian rice. There is also wild rice, which, despite its name, is a water grass, not a grain. Native to North America and known to botanists as *Zizania aquatica*, it is long-grained and gray-brown in color, with a "nutty" flavor. Wild rice is used mainly for stuffing game and poultry. Converted, precooked or prefluffed brand-name rice is a commercial product that has been parboiled then dried, and though its cooking results are more easily determined, there is some loss of flavor.

Rice in the kitchen

Rice will keep almost indefinitely, a fact only important to western households that do not use rice as a staple food. In cooking, long-grain rice will absorb one and a half times its bulk in liquid, depending on the type of grain. Basmati, for example, will absorb less water than Patna or Carolina. Short-grain rice will absorb over four times its bulk in liquid.

Rice can be cooked separately or processed to make rice flour, flaked rice and ground rice, for use in puddings, cakes and as a thickening agent for sauces, soups and stews. Fermented rice makes some potent Chinese spirits, and the famous Japanese *sake*.

WHEAT AND FLOUR

Wheat is a cereal grass, and was probably first cultivated in Mesopotamia. There are two main varieties, bread wheat (*Triticum aestivum*) and hard wheat (*T. durum*), used for making pasta (page 108), and semolina.

Bread wheat is the world's most important cereal crop; its unique quality is due to the high gluten content of the wheat berry. Gluten is a muscular substance of great elasticity that strengthens the cellular structure of bread. When yeast liberates carbon dioxide gas during "proving", and water releases steam during baking, the gluten helps the bread to expand – without gluten, bread would be flat and heavy.

The wheat berry, and the way it is milled, gives us our flours in different varieties and grades. The berry consists of the outer husk or bran, the endosperm, containing most of the starch to make flour, and the inner core or wheat germ embryo. When the entire grain is milled we obtain a brown flour rich in nutrients and protein called Graham or whole-wheat flour. The "brownness" of the flour depends on the amount of bran included, white flour containing the endosperm only.

Strong, hard or bread flour is milled from certain varieties of bread wheats, while plain, all-purpose, soft or cake flour has less gluten, and comes from soft types of flour. Self-raising flour contains an aerating agent.

Flour in the kitchen

Flour provides the basic structure of bread, cakes, batters and pastry, but the structure is further dependent upon the type of flour and the raising agent. Bread flour must be aerated by yeast, although brown flour can be leavened either with yeast or with baking soda. Bread also requires kneading to strengthen the gluten. The soft flour in cakes is raised by the dispersal of air or gas by baking powder and or whisked eggs. Steam is liberated in oven-cooked batters by whisked eggs, while pastry owes its texture to the plasticity of fat, and steam released by water in the dough, depending on the type of pastry. Soft flours produce a softer, spongier texture – you cannot beat air into bread flour, but soft flours are more easily leavened by thorough beating which introduces aerating.

Grains

RYE (Secale cereale)

Probably of southwest Asian origin, rye is similar in composition to wheat. In Europe it is used mainly for making rye bread and crispbread (particularly in Scandinavia). It is also used in the manufacture of drinks such as whiskey in America, gin in Holland and beer in Russia.

Rye

MILLET (Panicum miliaceum)

Native to Asia, millet was once the principal cereal of Europe, rivalling barley. It is the seed of an annual gluten-free grass which is widely eaten as a cereal in Africa and Asia, and is also used as a source of starch in Russia. Millet has as high a protein content as wheat, but its lack of gluten makes it inferior for baking. Millet flour is used for flat breads and griddle cakes. The grains can be mixed with beans and vegetables, and used in soups and stews.

Millet

CORN (Zea mays)

Indigenous to Mexico, corn (also known as Indian corn or maize) has been cultivated for thousands of years, both as a vegetable (page 36) and a source of flour. It is one of the most important foods in its whole form, cornmeal. It is used in many American recipes such as cornbread and hominy, and is also an important source of starch, corn syrup and cooking oil. The fermented grains are used to make Bourbon.

Corn

Grains and Grain Products

BUCKWHEAT
(*Fagopyrum esculentum*)

An annual grain plant thought to be native to China, its seeds are roasted and made into flour used for pancakes, crisp thin cakes, and noodles called *soba* in the Far East. Buckwheat groats, or "kasha", are used in soups.

Buckwheat

BARLEY (*Hordeum vulgare*)

Barley is native to Mesopotamia, where it was milled to make bread and fermented to make beer. Malting barley is used in the production of whiskey, gin and beer. In countries where barley and rye crops flourish, you will find barley cereals and barley bread. It is not, however, usually used to make bread flour.

Barley

GLUTINOUS RICE
(*Oryza sativa*, spp.)

Despite its name, this rice, widely used in Chinese cooking, is completely gluten-free. When boiled it becomes sweet and sticky and is thus used mainly in baking and confectionery, and also for making beer. Two varieties are shown: black and white. The white variety is dehulled in processing.

Black glutinous rice

OATS (*Avena sativa*)

Native to central Europe, oats are a Scottish staple, and are milled to varying degrees of fineness. Cooked with water, oats become oatmeal is often added to cakes, cookies, muffins, yeast and quickbreads and is also a popular breakfast cereal.

Oats

WHEAT
(*Triticum aestivum, durum*)

Thought to have first been cultivated in the Nile region, it is the source of the highest quality bread and baking flours. There are many different varieties: the durum wheat type is best known for making pasta and semolina.

Wheat

White glutinous rice

CONVERTED RICE
(*Oryza sativa*, spp.)

This rice is parboiled to remove its surface starch, thus leaving most of the nutrients and vitamins in the grains, unlike other white rice varieties. It provides the best of all possible options, since it has the nutritional value of brown rice, without its chewy texture and longer cooking methods.

Converted rice

BASMATI RICE
(*Oryza sativa*, spp.)

Grown in the foothills of the Himalayas, this narrow long-grain rice is one of the finest. It should be washed and soaked before cooking and is the best rice to eat with Indian food.

Basmati rice

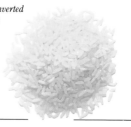

ITALIAN RICE
(*Oryza sativa*, spp.)

Also called arborio, this large, round-grained rice is used for the classic Italian rice dish, *risotto*. Brown and white varieties, shown here, are available.

Brown Italian rice

White Italian rice

BROWN RICE
(*Oryza sativa*, spp.)

This is the whole natural grain of the rice before it is processed. It needs more water and longer cooking than white rice.

Brown rice

COUSCOUS

A cereal processed from semolina into tiny pellets, this is best known for its use in the traditional North African dish of the same name.

Couscous

LONG-GRAIN RICE
(*Oryza sativa*, spp.)

Grown all over the world, Carolina (long-grain) or Patna rice is the most versatile and popular of all. The grains, which are hulled and polished, remain firm, fluffy and separate when cooked.

Long-grain rice

SHORT-GRAIN RICE
(*Oryza sativa*, spp.)

A short-grain strain of polished rice that becomes tender and moist when cooked; it is suitable for puddings and molded salads.

Short-grain rice

PEARL BARLEY

Dehulled and polished barley grains which may be added to soups, stews and vegetables or served as a pilaf in place of potatoes.

Pearl barley

SEMOLINA

The hard part of durum wheat sifted out of flour and used for pasta, which would be difficult to make with "soft" flour. It is also used in desserts.

Semolina

OTHER GRAINS

SORGHUM
(*Sorghum vulgare*, spp.)
A type of millet cultivated in in Africa and Asia, the seeds when ground are made into bread, cookies and cakes and are used in soups. Another variety of sorghum, *Holcus sorghum* var. *saccara*, produces a smooth sweet syrup.

WILD RICE
(*Zizania aquatica*)
Native to North America, wild rice looks like rice and is used in the same way, although it is in fact a water grass The dark brown grains are longer and thinner, and turn slightly purple when they are cooked.

Flour and other Grain Products

MATZOH MEAL

Ground *matzohs* (unleavened crispbreads), made of wheat flour and water, are used in place of leavened breadcrumbs during the Jewish Passover.

Matzoh meal

POLENTA

A type of meal ground from corn or maize, cornmeal, or polenta, can be eaten on its own as a breakfast cereal or used to garnish meat and fish dishes.

Polenta

TAPIOCA

These are pellets made of manioc flour, a starch extracted from the root of the manioc or cassava plant (*Manihot esculenta*). They are used in baby food and to thicken soups and stews.

Tapioca

SAGO

The dried, starchy granules obtained from the sago palm (*Metroxylou sagu*) grown in the Far East, sago is used in desserts, puddings, and as an ingredient, particularly in Scandinavian recipes, such as the Danish dish *sagosuppe*.

Sago

CRACKED WHEAT

Also known as burghul or bulgur, this processed wheat is popular throughout the eastern Mediterranean and the Middle East. It may be baked, cooked as a pilaf, soaked and served as a raw salad (Lebanese *tabbouleh*) or pounded into a paste with lamb to make the Lebanese *kibbi*.

Cracked wheat

OATMEAL

Dehulled oats ground to make oatmeal of varying degrees of fineness (as shown), or softened and rolled to make rolled oats.

Coarse oatmeal

WHEATGERM

The germ or "embryo" of the wheat grain, from which new wheat plants can be grown, wheatgerm is usually extracted from the grain during flour-making. Although it only forms a small part of the grain it is considered to be high in nutritional value, and can be eaten on its own or used to make the basis of a flour. It is used in soups and stews and as a thickening agent.

Wheatgerm

BARLEY FLOUR

Once the main ingredient of bread, this is now usually combined with wheat flour to increase its gluten content (bread made exclusively from barley flour tends to go dry very quickly).

Barley flour

Fine oatmeal

CORN MEAL

A gluten-free flour that must be reinforced with wheat flour for bread-making. It is also used to make cakes.

Corn meal

LOTUS ROOT FLOUR

A gluten-free flour milled from dried and powdered lotus root, it is used in Chinese and Japanese cooking as a thickener for sauces.

Lotus root flour

RICE FLOUR

A gluten-free flour milled from both ordinary polished white and brown rice grains, this is widely used as a thickening agent, both alone or in conjunction with other flours for cakes and cookies, and in the Chinese kitchen for making a variety of noodles called *fun*.

Rice flour

RYE FLOUR

Frequently used in combination with wheat flour because of its unsuitable gluten content, rye flour makes the characteristic "black" breads of northern and eastern Europe.

Rye flour

BRAN

The brown outer layer of any grain, usually separated from the heart during flour-making, this is a valuable source of fiber in the diet, and can be used to make a flour in its own right.

Bran

WHOLE-WHEAT FLOUR

Whole-wheat flour, milled from the whole grain of the wheat, includes the bran and wheatgerm which are removed in ordinary flours.

Graham flour

SOY FLOUR

This is not a flour in the conventional sense, but a highly nutritious food supplement which can be added to soups and cakes.

Soy flour

WHEAT FLOUR

There are many varieties of wheat flour, ranging from the all-purpose (as shown) to fine cake flour.

Wheat flour

POTATO FLOUR

Made from cooked potatoes that have been dried and ground, this flour is often used as a subtle thickening agent.

Potato flour

BUCKWHEAT FLOUR

A type of pancake flour particularly popular in America, France and eastern Europe.

Buckwheat flour

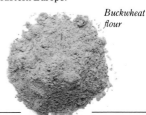

PASTA, NOODLES AND DUMPLINGS

PASTA – THE WORD SIMPLY means "dough" – is the staple diet of Italy, essential to the Italian kitchen and far more popular than its rivals, bread, polenta (cornmeal) and rice. Pasta, or to give it its official title, *pasta alimentari*, falls into two main types: the factory-made flour and water paste, called *pasta secca*, "dry" pasta, as sold in packages, and the fresh paste made with flour and eggs called *pasta all'uovo*, or *pasta fatta in casa*, "home-made" pasta.

Pasta secca begins as a springy dough of flour, salt and water which is then cut, pressed or moulded into a variety of shapes, sizes and designs which include tubes, ribbons, spirals, shells, bows and wheels, to provide a versatile foundation for an equally bewildering number of sauces. Even the Italians find the study of pasta confusing, since names and shapes vary from province to province.

Pasta uses the flour milled from the hard, translucent *Triticum durum* wheat, although there is also a type which is made with buckwheat. Durum produces fine, gritty particles of amber-colored semolina flour (page 105), which is more durable than bread flour. When mixed to a dough with water this makes a nutritious paste that can be dried and kept indefinitely; you can test for good-quality pasta by running your finger along the surface – it should be silky smooth and quite pliant.

Strictly speaking, home-made *pasta all'uovo* should also be made with semolina flour, but plain flour is a good substitute, and with the addition of eggs, salt, and perhaps a little water or oil to soften the dough, makes a good-quality *sfoglia*, as the rolled-out sheet of finished pasta is called.

Some pasta-makers, especially from the region of Emilia-Romagna, color their paste with spinach purée which, not unnaturally, turns the pasta green – *lasagne verdi* or *tagliatelle verdi* are examples. There are also whole wheat versions.

Pasta's origins and development
Historians will always argue over the provenance of pasta. It is probably indigenous to Italy, having been developed by the Etruscans from a Greek recipe, a dough cake cut into strips and called *laganon*, from which the word *lasagne* is ultimately derived. Yet one of the earliest words for pasta was *tri*, from the Arabic *itriyah*, "string", which, as a description of spaghetti (literally "little threads"), hints at an Arabic origin.

By the fifteenth century, pasta was known as *vermicelli*, or "little worms", and in Sicily as *maccheroni*, a word of disputed origin. Today, macaroni is a generic term for all types of *pasta secca*, and recipes and sauces have swollen the ranks of pasta into a confused legion of nearly 600 different shapes.

The Italians, artists in the kitchen, found that some shapes were particularly suited to certain sauces; that *spaghetti* from Naples complemented the meat *ragù* of Bologna; that delicate *fettucine* noodles went best with a cream and mushroom sauce; and that the ribbons of pasta called *trenette* were the life partner to the Ligurian *pesto* made with basil and pine nuts. The majority of pasta shapes are, however, successfully interchangeable with the infinite variety of sauces – the spirals of pasta called *fusilli* or *archimede* are just as companionable to *vongole* (clams) as is the traditional *spaghettini*.

Some shapes are particularly well suited to baking and to stuffing. The tubes of *cannelloni* and *rigatoni* are filled with meat, or chopped vegetables, covered with a cheese-flavored béchamel sauce and finally baked *al forno*. *Lasagne*, the large sheets of pasta, are alternately layered with ground meat and sauce, and then baked as before. Smaller shapes, such as *ravioli*, hats (*cappelletti*) or half-moons (*tortellini*) are stuffed and may be cooked *in brodo* (broth) or water.

Pasta in the kitchen
The basic types of pasta, dry or fresh, can be further divided into categories according to their use: *pasta asciutta* and *pasta in brodo* or *pastina*. Briefly, the term *pasta asciutta* describes all those substantial daily dishes such as the familiar spaghetti or macaroni served with a sauce; pasta stuffed with meat, cheese or puréed vegetables, such as *ravioli* or

cannelloni (*pasta ripieni*, meaning "stuffed"); pasta dishes baked in the oven – *al forno* – such as *lasagne*.

Pasta in brodo, the second category, is pasta in miniature; tiny shapes of pasta (*pastina*) that find their natural element in soup – *in brodo* – such as wheels (*ruote*), shells (*conchiglie*), butterflies (*farfalle*), and a host of other motifs. Thrifty cooks sometimes employ broken scraps of *pasta secca*, that have dropped to the bottom of the grocer's bin or sack, to make a rustic dish of pasta, cheese and tomatoes called *tuoni e lampo* or "thunder and lightning".

Whereas opinions might vary about which pasta goes best with which sauce, everyone is united on the topic of how pasta should be cooked. *Pasta asciutta* needs plenty of salted boiling water, roughly 4 quarts of salted water to each pound of pasta, otherwise the pasta gets sticky since the water cannot cope with the excess starch. Some experts demand that salt be added after the pasta, otherwise a slight aroma of phenol is liberated, but the majority of cooks usually ignore such finesse, merely insisting that pasta should be cooked to a precise minute – give or take a second or two.

Cooking times vary according to the pasta, but the end result should be *al dente* – in other words, not soft but with firmness to the bite. Some people like their pasta firmer, even hard; the term for this is *fil de ferro* ("wire"). Pasta should not be drained too thoroughly, otherwise you will find that it sticks together, especially lasagne. As a further precaution, cooks may add a teaspoon of oil to the water while it is still boiling to prevent the pasta from sticking together.

NOODLES AND DUMPLINGS

The Chinese, pioneer inventors that they were, must have discovered the value of starch pastes early in history, and celebrated noodle reports followed Marco Polo's visit to China in 1270. We may assume that pasta was an independent invention: *vermicelli* was a staple in the Italian diet long before the thirteenth century.

Since there has been domestication of grains for over 8000 years it can be assumed that the production of noodles is quite ancient.

Familiarity with grains led to the grinding of flour, and flour plus water produces a pliable paste that can be cut and dried and kept.

The word "noodle" derives from the German, Bavarian and Austrian words for dumplings – *nudeln*, *knödl* and *knödel* – and dumplings seem to have originated from the practice of nipping off pieces of uncooked dough or bread (*croûtons*), and dropping them into soups or stews; variations on this theme exist from Hungary across Europe to Britain.

Types of noodles

While noodles and pasta have much in common they fall into different categories. Noodles are defined as a food paste made of flour, water and eggs which may be sold and used either dried or fresh. Most Italian pasta, when made commercially, contains no eggs. In many western countries, particularly in Germany and America, noodles must include eggs, unless sold as "plain noodles". Noodles are also referred to as *vermicelli*, regardless of whether they come from Italy or Hong Kong, and the main areas of production are central Europe, America and the Far East.

The Germans are credited with being the first to make a noodle dough with eggs, and in the familiar ribbon-shape of commercial noodles. This type of egg noodle paste is also popular with the Italians and the Chinese. Asian noodles, however, may be based on a number of different flour pastes, with or without eggs, including the flour of mung beans, soy-beans, buckwheat, seaweed, corn, chick-peas, rice and durum wheat, and sold in skeins of fine threads that are typically Eastern. The Japanese have an impressive range of *menrui* (noodles) made of white wheat or golden buckwheat such as *soba*, *somen*, and *udon*. Japan shares with China a fondness for bean-gelatine or cellophane noodles, called, in Japan, *harusame*. Another popular Japanese noodle is *shirataki*, made from *konnyaku* (devil's tongue or snake palm plant), a member of the arum family.

Noodles in the kitchen

Commercially made noodles will last almost indefinitely, kept in a cool, airy place. Noodles should be cooked according to the recipe or instructions on the package. Presoaked noodles need less cooking than dried ones, and they are usually soaked to facilitate cooking in stir-fried dishes – 5 minutes should be sufficient. *Harusame* noodles and Chinese cellophane noodles may need presoaking for 30 minutes. Straight from the package, *soba* noodles need about 7 minutes, *somen* 7 minutes, and *udon* 20 minutes. Unlike *vermicelli*, they are preferred soft, and not *al dente* in the Italian style.

Pasta

Capellini

CAPELLINI
(pasta asciutta; secca)

The finest ribbon pasta, *capellini* (or *vermicelli* or *capolnevere*) can be home-made or bought ready-made in a shop. *Capelli d'angelo*, meaning "angel's hair", is the thinnest variety.

LASAGNETTE
(pasta asciutta; secca)

A smaller version of *lasagne*, this is a flat, ribbon pasta about ¾ inch wide, with a ruffled edge.

SPAGHETTI
(pasta asciutta; secca)

Known as *vermicelli* in southern Italy, the word *spaghetti* means "little strings". It remains the most popular type of pasta and is available fresh or dried.

FEDELI *(pasta asciutta; secca)*

This is a very fine, cylindrical pasta, similar to *vermicelli*. It is available fresh or dried. *Fedelini* is even finer.

Fedeli

Lasagnette

Buckwheat spaghetti

Whole-wheat spaghetti

Extra-long spaghetti

Tagliatelle verdi

Tagliarini verdi

Tagliatelle

Tagliarini

Spaghetti

TAGLIATELLE
(*pasta asciutta; all'uovo*)

Tagliatelle or *fettucini* is the pasta specialty of Bologna. These flat, ¹/₄-inch wide ribbon noodles are, like all pasta, made from durum wheat and can easily be made at home or bought fresh or dried. They are served with a variety of sauces, ranging from a simple milk and butter mixture to one with a rich meat, fish or poultry base. *Tagliatelle verdi* (top) has puréed spinach added to the basic dough.

TAGLIARINI
(*pasta asciutta; all'uovo*)

A flat, ribbon-like pasta, similar to *tagliatelle*, but slightly smaller in width. It can be home-made, obtained fresh in a pasta shop, or bought ready-made. Also available as *tagliarini verdi* (top), this pasta is usually served with a sauce as for *tagliatelle*.

CASARECCIA
(pasta asciutta; secca)

Pasta lengths that are curled into shape, with a twist at one end.

Casareccia

BOZZOLI *(pasta asciutta; secca)*

This pasta is named for its cocoon-like shape.

Bozzoli

CRESTI DI GALLO
(pasta asciutta; secca)

This is named for its ridged mane that looks like a cock's comb.

Cresti di gallo

LUNGO-VERMICELLI COUPE *(pasta asciutta; secca)*

This name describes the pasta accurately as long *vermicelli*, cut into pieces.

Lungo-vermicelli coupe

RICCINI *(pasta asciutta; secca)*

This ridged, shell-like pasta takes its name from the Italian word *riccio*, meaning "curl".

Riccini

GRAMIGNA
(pasta asciutta; secca)

This has small, grasslike shapes. The name actually means "grass" or weed.

Gramigna

FESTONATI
(pasta asciutta; secca)

The word *festonati* means "festoon" or "garland".

Festonati

CAVATAPPI
(pasta asciutta; secca)

Ridged pasta in a twisted shape.

Cavatappi

FUSILLI BUCATI
(pasta asciutta; secca)

This pasta is made in the shape of tiny springs.

Fusilli bucati

GNOCCHI (*pasta asciutta; secca*)

These small dumplings, shown made from durum wheat, are also available made from potato or semolina flour.

ORECCHIETTE
(*pasta asciutta; secca*)

Pasta shaped like an ear. The name derives from the Italian word *orecchio*, meaning "ear".

GNOCCHETTI SARDI
(*pasta in brodo; secca*)

A smaller version of gnocchi, this is named for its sardinelike shape.

Gnocchetti sardi

Gnocchi

Orecchiette

PIPE RIGATE
(*pasta asciutta; secca*)

A ridged pasta made in the shape of a pipe.

SPIRALE (*pasta asciutta; secca*)

Pasta lengths twisted together to form a spiral.

ANELLI (*pasta asciutta; secca*)

Anelli, meaning "ring", is an appropriate title for these pasta shapes, shown made from whole-wheat flour (brown) or durum wheat (pale).

Pipe rigate

Spirale

Anelli (whole-wheat)

LUMACHE MEDIE
(*pasta in brodo; secca*)

These shapes resemble snails' shells, thus the name *lumache*, which means "snail".

VEGETABLE-DYED MACARONI
(*pasta in brodo; secca*)

Made from durum wheat, this may be dyed green with spinach or red with tomatoes.

Anelli (durum wheat)

Lumache medie

Vegetable-dyed macaroni

FARFALLE
(pasta asciutta; secca)

The name means "butterfly".
Farfallini (pasta in brodo) are the
same, but smaller.

CAPPELLETTI
(pasta asciutta; secca)

Little pastry hats made, like most
pasta, from durum wheat.

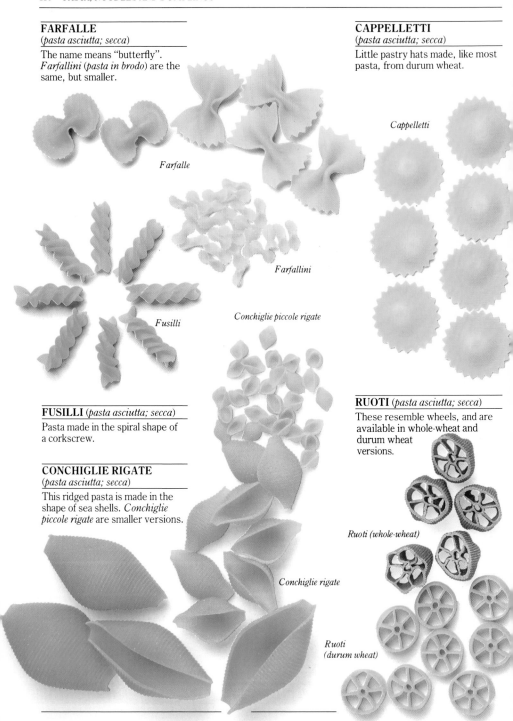

Farfalle

Cappelletti

Farfallini

Fusilli

Conchiglie piccole rigate

FUSILLI *(pasta asciutta; secca)*

Pasta made in the spiral shape of
a corkscrew.

CONCHIGLIE RIGATE
(pasta asciutta; secca)

This ridged pasta is made in the
shape of sea shells. *Conchiglie
piccole rigate* are smaller versions.

RUOTI *(pasta asciutta; secca)*

These resemble wheels, and are
available in whole-wheat and
durum wheat
versions.

Ruoti (whole-wheat)

Conchiglie rigate

*Ruoti
(durum wheat)*

TUBETTI LUNGHI
(pasta asciutta; secca)

Known as elbow macaroni, this pasta is made in short lengths with a slight bend resembling an elbow joint. Whole-wheat and durum wheat variations are illustrated.

Ditali

Tubetti lunghi (whole-wheat)

Ditalini

Tubetti lunghi (durum wheat)

MACARONI
(pasta asciutta; secca)

This is a generic term for all types of *pasta secca*, but is commonly used to describe this wider hollow version of spaghetti.

SMALL MACARONI
(pasta asciutta; secca)

This is also known as *bucatini*.

DITALI *(pasta asciutta; secca)*
The Italian word *ditali* means finger of a glove, or thimble. *Ditalini (pasta in brodo)* are merely smaller versions of *ditali*.

Macaroni

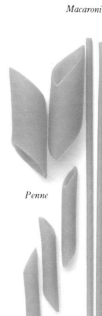

PENNE *(pasta asciutta; secca)*
Small or large sizes and ribbed versions of this pasta shape are easily obtained.

Penne

Rigatoni

RIGATONI *(pasta asciutta; secca)*
This name is derived from the Italian word *riga*, meaning "line".

Elicoidali

Ziti

ELICOIDALI
(pasta asciutta; secca)

This is similar to *rigatoni*, but is smaller in size with a spiral (helical) line pattern.

ZITI *(pasta asciutta; secca)*
Another version of macaroni, but cut into short lengths.

Small macaroni

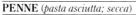

LASAGNE (*pasta asciutta*)

Often home-made, but widely available dried, this is the broadest of the ribbon pasta. *Lasagne* can be bought smooth, ridged or with a ruffled edge and can be made with whole-wheat dough or with the addition of puréed spinach.

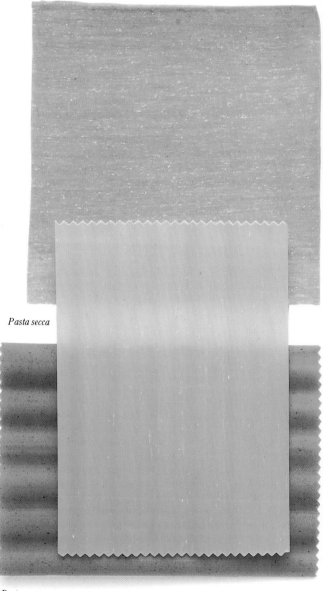

Pasta all'uovo

Pasta secca

Pasta secca

Pasta secca

Whole-wheat lasagne
(pasta secca)

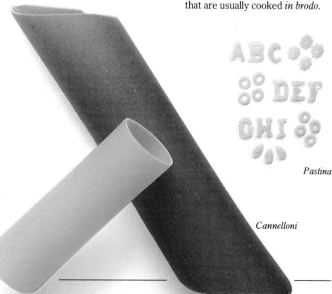

TORTELLINI
(pasta asciutta; all'uovo)

A small, stuffed pasta dumpling which, according to legend, was modelled on Venus's navel. It is usually stuffed with a variety of the following: chopped chicken breast, pork, mortadella or Bologna sausage, cheese and nutmeg. Tortellini is widely available ready-made, either dried or fresh.

RAVIOLI
(pasta asciutta; all'uovo)

This is the most well-known pasta dumpling. Square in shape, it is traditionally stuffed with spinach and ricotta cheese or herbs, but can be filled with a savory meat mixture. Cooked in boiling water, it is often served with a gravy or sauce, or small *ravioli* may be cooked *in brodo* (in soups). *Ravioli* is usually served fresh, but can be bought ready-cooked in a can.

CANNELLONI
(pasta asciutta; secca)

The word *cannelloni*, meaning "big pipes", describes this hollow, cylindrical pasta shape, which is stuffed and baked *al forno*.

Tortellini

Ravioli

PASTINA *(pasta in brodo; secca)*

Pastina is the general term for the wide variety of tiny pasta shapes that are usually cooked *in brodo*.

Pastina

Cannelloni

Egg Noodles and Dumplings

Egg noodles

All of these noodles are made with eggs, the darker yellow ones containing more egg than the others. These noodles are normally sold in compressed bundles of varying size and have usually been pre-cooked by steaming so they require only a minimal amount of preparation at home. The main difference between noodles and Italian pasta lies in the way they are prepared rather than their substance or shape. Most of the noodles shown are dried.

Commercial noodles are made from about 1 lb fresh eggs to every 8 lbs semolina flour. The dough is mixed, kneaded, rolled, laminated, cut and dried, all by machine.

European noodles may have ultimately derived from the *spätzle* (little sparrows) of Württemberg, where egg dough is forced through the holes of a colander into boiling water. They accompany veal, cabbage, or are mixed with chopped meat or herbs and served as a salad.

Fresh egg noodles

Dried egg noodles

Dried egg noodles

Chinese noodles

CHINESE NOODLES

Dried egg noodles

These vary considerably, but typically they are about ¹⁄₈ inch wide, dried and sold like loosely tangled balls of wool. Noodles are *mein* and *mee* in Chinese cooking, and feature in many dishes, incorporated with meat and vegetables.

Dried egg noodles

Dried egg noodles

EGG DUMPLINGS

CSIPETKE
These Hungarian egg-flour dumplings are scraps of dough dropped into boiling water and served with soups and goulash.

KASNUDLN
From Austria, these are a variety of Uszka, made either with a savory filling such as cheese or meat, or with a sweet filling such as fruit and spices.

USZKA
This is a type of *ravioli* from Poland. It is an egg-flour dough which is stuffed with mushrooms, then dropped into soup. *Uszka* means "little ears" and describes the shape of the dumplings.

Rice, Bean and Wheat Noodles

RICE NOODLES

Noodles are a symbol of longevity in China and are often served at birthday parties as a wish for long life. These rice noodles are made in long strands before being folded over and packaged.

Rice noodles

RICE NOODLES

These flat, ribbonlike rice noodles are made in long strands and are often called rice sticks.

Rice noodles

Rice noodles

Rice noodles

RICE NOODLES

Noodles made from rice are more commonly eaten in southern China, where more rice is grown. The curled pad of noodles illustrated here is commonly known as "rice vermicelli".

WHEAT NOODLES

These flat, sticklike wheat noodles are available in different widths, and are interchangeable with rice noodles according to taste.

TRANSPARENT NOODLES

Chinese and Japanese transparent noodles are made with mung bean paste (shown here), pea starch or wheat flour. In Japan they are known as *harusame* ("spring rain"), and feature in *yosenabe*, a kind of chop suey of fish and vegetables in broth. In India, transparent noodles are called *sevian* or "China grass" and are used to make sweet dishes.

Wheat noodles

Transparent noodles

OTHER NOODLES AND DUMPLINGS

BIJON

These noodles are produced commercially in Southeast Asia from corn kernels. The kernels are steeped in water for 4–7 days to encourage the fermentation of butyric acid, then mashed and formed into "dumplings" with cornstarch. The dough is extruded into long strands, parboiled for 2 minutes, then sun-dried for about 4 hours.

Other noodle types from the same area include Canton noodles made from wheat flour, duck eggs, salt and vegetable oil, *miki*, made with wheat flour, eggs and soda, ash and *misua*, which are fine wheat noodles like the Japanese *udon sotanghon*, a version of transparent noodles. These noodles would

be served with such typical dishes as *laksa*, a fish and coconut milk soup.

BREAD DUMPLINGS

Bavarian *knödl*, Austrian *knödl*, and Czech *knedliky* are all made with stale bread or yeast dough, and may be sweet or savory. Pennsylvania Dutch *rivels* fall into this category, being a boiled yeast dough that accompanies chicken-corn soups and meat stews.

SHIRATAKI

These are noodles made from the starch of the devil's tongue plant (*Amorphopallus rivieri*), cultivated in China and Japan. The tubers are dried to make *konnyaku* flour, used to make

shirataki ("white waterfall"). They feature in the well-known *sukiyaki* dish.

SOBA

These are the most popular type of noodle in Japan, made with golden buckwheat, and served in the many *sobo-ya* restaurants. The noodles may be presented in *zaru* bowls, accompanied by *nori* (a kind of seaweed) and horseradish.

SOMEN

These are thin, very fine, white wheat noodles which are often served cold.

UDON

Very narrow, ribbonlike white wheat noodles, these are served in hot soups and mixed meat and vegetable dishes.

BAKING INGREDIENTS

SOME INGREDIENTS, though unobtrusive, play a vital role in baking; others are more decorative. In the first category are the raising and thickening agents – the ingredients responsible for the "inside" chemical changes in baking. In the second are those that provide the additional touches, the colorings and the decorations.

Uses in the kitchen

Yeast is used to raise the strong gluten flour of bread doughs, and baking powder is used for most cakes and some breads. Fresh yeast should be grayish-brown and crumble easily. When old, the brownish shade darkens. It should be dissolved in warm water before being combined with other ingredients. Dry yeast should be sprinkled on the water and greater heat and more moisture are needed than with fresh.

Many thickeners, such as arrowroot and cornstarch – so important in gravies and sauces – are used in baking as well, while gelatin, sold in powder and in sheets, is used to set both aspics and gelatin-based desserts. Generally, dried baking goods, such as yeast, baking powder and cornstarch, will keep indefinitely, stored in tins in a cool dry place.

There is a wide range of edible decorations and colorings for the pastry cook to call upon. Many of the traditional coloring dyes, such as chlorophyll and cochineal, are being replaced and augmented by synthetic colors which give a huge range. There are also many commerical products available in hard and soft candy as well as candied fruits.

FRESH YEAST

Yeast is a plant with active living cells which feed on sugars and produce alcohol and carbon dioxide. One of the main raising agents used in bread, fresh compressed yeast should be bought in small quantities, as it loses its potency quickly once broken.

Fresh yeast

YEAST CAKES

This is another form of fresh yeast, compressed into a rounded shape rather than being sold in a block. It can be bought in Oriental food stores.

Yeast cakes

BREWERS' YEAST

This yeast is not a raising agent, but is used mainly for brewing wines and beers, as its name implies. It is available dried, powdered or in tablets.

Dried brewers' yeast

Powdered brewers' yeast

RED YEAST

A type of wild yeast, red yeast is sold dried and used mainly for fermenting purposes, in particular to make Oriental vinegars.

Red yeast

DRIED BAKERS' YEAST

Today, dried bakers' yeast is manufactured only in factories and is almost always based on a solution of molasses and water. It is used for the same purposes as fresh yeast, but it will keep for much longer. It is also available in an instant form.

Dried bakers' yeast

PECTIN

A carbohydrate that occurs naturally in certain fruits, pectin is used mainly in jams and jellies to help them set. Pectin extracts can be bought commercially or can be made at home.

Pectin

BAKING SODA

Baking soda (also known as bicarbonate of soda and sodium bicarbonate) has no leavening properties, but can be used as a raising agent when combined with an acid such as sour milk.

Baking soda

CREAM OF TARTAR

This substance is found in the juice of grapes, after they have been fermented in wine-making. It reacts with baking soda to produce carbon dioxide to leaven batters.

Cream of tartar

BAKING POWDER

There are several kinds of this leavening agent, but basically they are composed of baking soda plus various acids or acid salts. It can be bought commercially or made at home from cream of tartar, baking soda and salt. When water is added to baking powder, carbon dioxide is given off and the mixture to which the baking powder has been added is areated. Too much baking powder can spoil the texture and flavor of a cake, so it is important to use only the amount stated in a recipe.

Baking powder

CORNSTARCH

A fine, white flour obtained from corn, used for thickening gravies and sauces and for baking cakes.

Cornstarch

ARROWROOT

This delicate nutritive starch is obtained mainly from the West Indian plant of the same name (*Maranta arundinacea*). It is most often used as a thickening agent.

Arrowroot

KUZU

The tuberous roots of the Kuzu vine, when boiled and mashed, are often used as a thickener in Chinese and Japanese cooking. It is commonly sold as a powder.

Kuzu

AGAR-AGAR

A neutral-tasting gelatinous product obtained from various Far Eastern seaweeds, agar-agar has a variety of names: Bengal isinglass, Ceylon moss, Japanese moss and Macassar gum. It is used mainly in the making of jellies, and gelatinlike desserts. Sold in threads, flakes or powder form, it is only partially soluble in water, unless boiled.

Agar-agar

GELATIN

Extracted from boiled beef bones and tendons, gelatin is available as powder or in transparent sheets. It is a jelling agent, most often used in the making of desserts and prepared meats.

Powdered gelatin

Sheet gelatin

OTHER BAKING GOODS

AMMONIUM BICARBONATE

The predecessor of modern leaveners, this renders non-fermented dough spongy.

GUM ARABIC

A product obtained from the *Acacia senegal* tree, gum arabic prevents the crystallization of sugar and is used to glaze marzipan fruits.

GUM TRAGACANTH

A gum used in making gum paste for sugar flowers and cake decorations. It comes from a plant found in the Middle East.

Coloring Agents and Decorations

MARZIPAN FRUITS

Almond paste is shaped and then tinted with food dyes to resemble fruits. These are used as cake decorations or often are boxed as gift sets.

COCONUT

Dried (desiccated) coconut in flaked or finely shredded form is often used plain or toasted as a garnish, or it may be included in baking recipes such as macaroons.

GUMDROP DIAMONDS

Soft and chewy in texture, these sugar decorations, also known as diamond jellies, are particularly useful for making patterns on cakes and desserts.

SPRINKLES AND NON PAREILS

Available in tiny tube (non pareils) and ball (sprinkles) shapes, these hard sugar treats are quick and easy to apply as dessert and cake decorations.

FOOD COLORING

These are sold in a powdered form or, more commonly, as a liquid. They may be of artificial or natural origin and should be used sparingly as too much can give food a vivid tint. Natural food dyes include alkannet (a red or blue coloring from the root of *Anchusa tinctoria*), annatto (an orange dye from the seeds of the West Indian *Bixa orellana*), carotene (a yellow pigment linked to vitamin A, found in carrots), chlorophyll (green pigment from leaves, such as spinach and nettles), and cochineal (a pink pigment obtained from the female of an insect species, *Dactylopius coccus*, found in Mexico and Iran).

Marshmallow

Almond paste fruits

Coconut

(flaked)

(finely shredded)

Chestnut purée

Gumdrop diamonds

Dragees

Sprinkles (non pareils)

Sugar drops

Sprinkles

Candy violets and rose petals

Powdered food coloring

Crystallized violets, rose petals and mint leaves

Liquid food coloring

MARSHMALLOW

A soft white confection that is eaten plain or toasted. It is made of sugar, egg white and gelatin and coated in powdered sugar. Originally made from the roots of the marshmallow plant.

CHESTNUT PUREE

Cooked shelled chestnuts are puréed (sometimes with cream) and added to smooth-textured desserts or may be used in poultry stuffing.

DRAGEES

Shiny and smooth-coated hard sugar balls are often used on cakes for special occasions.

SUGAR DROPS

Sugary sprinkles, available in different shades, are useful for small and large cakes.

CANDY VIOLETS and ROSE PETALS

These hard sugar flowers, popular cake decorations, are available in different sizes and shades.

CRYSTALLIZED VIOLETS, ROSE PETALS and MINT LEAVES

Dipped in egg white and granulated sugar, these flowers and leaves are used to decorate small cakes and ice creams.

MARRONS GLACES

Often boxed as a gift confection these chestnuts are first preserved – a lengthy process – and then glazed with syrup.

Marrons glacé

GLACE CHERRY

Cherries, coated in a sugar and glucose syrup mixture, are used as ingredients in fruit cakes and chocolates and as decorations.

MIXED PEEL

A mixture of citrus fruit peel, sugar and glucose syrup, mixed peel is included in rich fruit cakes and Christmas puddings.

CRYSTALLIZED PINEAPPLE

Pineapple with a sugary coating can be eaten as a confection or used chopped as a decoration.

CANDIED ORANGES and LEMONS

Simulated fruit slices made of sugar and gelatin make decorative finishes.

BAKING CHOCOLATE

This slab chocolate is produced when crushed cacao bean liquid is cooled and shaped into blocks. It is also known as cooking or unsweetened chocolate. Sweet and semi-sweet chocolates, which contain more sweetening and cocoa butter, are also available and used for baking and making sauces.

ALMOND PASTE

Crushed, blanched almonds mixed with vanilla and sugar. Also known as almond icing or marzipan, the mixture is rolled out and used to cover fruit cakes before they are frosted. It is believed to have originated in the Middle East.

CHOCOLATE BARK

Served whole or crumbled, it is used on vanilla ice cream or cakes.

ANGELICA

The stalk of the herb angelica (page 55) is coated in sugar and used chopped or cut into slivers as a cake decoration.

Glacé cherry

Sugar-coated cumin seeds and mimosa balls

Mixed peel

Strawberry and chocolate crunch

Chocolate chips

Crystallized pineapple

Crystallized ginger

Candy oranges and lemons

Baking chocolate

Almond paste

Chocolate bark

Angelica

SUGAR-COATED CUMIN SEEDS and MIMOSA BALLS

These are seeds with a coating of tinted sugar. Hard and crunchy, they provide a contrasting texture to a creamy dessert.

STRAWBERRY and CHOCOLATE CRUNCH

Sugar topping for cakes and ices.

CHOCOLATE CHIPS

Tiny chocolate chips used in cakes and cookies and for decoration.

CRYSTALLIZED GINGER

Stem ginger with a sugary coating that can be eaten as a confection or used chopped as a decoration.

RICE PAPER

A very fine wafer used to coat the undersides of certain confections.

Rice paper

OTHER USEFUL CONFECTIONS

NOUGAT
Originally from Europe, nougat is made of sugar, syrup, egg whites, and often nuts and glacé cherries.

PASTILLAGE
A gum paste used on cakes, this is prepared with icing sugar, gum tragacanth or gelatine and cornstarch. It may be colored.

COFFEE

COFFEE ORIGINATED IN Ethiopia, where *Coffea arabica*, one of the three main species, grows wild. The others, *C. robusta* and *C. liberica*, come from the Congo and Liberia respectively. The coffee tree requires a hot, moist climate and a rich soil.

The word "coffee" comes from the Arabic *quwah*. *C. arabica* was first cultivated about 575 AD but it was not until the fifteenth century that the plant was extensively grown in southern Arabia. From there it spread to countries bordering the Indian Ocean and the Mediterranean. By the mid-seventeenth century it had reached all of Europe, where innumerable coffee-houses, sprang up. It reached North America by 1668. Early in the eighteenth century it was taken to the French West Indies and from there was introduced to Brazil and the rest of South and Central America. Today, coffee is grown in the West Indies, Mexico, Central America, tropical South America, Africa, India and Indonesia. *C arabica*, *C. robusta* and *C. liberica* are all grown commercially and each has its own varieties.

The green coffee beans are extracted from the ripe red berries of the tree. Each of the berries contains two beans or two seeds. Approximately 4000 berries produce 2 lbs of coffee.

Extracting the brew

Coffee beans are classified into three main types. The finest coffee comes from *C. arabica* and has a low caffeine content. *C. robusta* is a strong, high-caffeine type, but of inferior quality. Finally, there is *C. liberica*, which is very productive but mediocre in taste.

Taste and aroma are induced by roasting the raw green beans. The beans turn a pale yellow at around 212°F and on reaching 450°F swell to almost double their size, turn dark brown, and sweat oil on the surface, giving them an attractive glossy appearance.

There are four main types of roast. The high or double roast has a strong, bitter taste and should always be drunk black. The full roast has a slightly bitter taste but lacks the "burnt" taste of a high roasted bean. Medium roast produces a strong-tasting coffee without the

bitter taste, while the light or pale roast allows the milder beans to develop a full, delicate taste and aroma which is good with milk.

Strong, black coffees, especially those from *C. robusta*, tend to be more stimulating on account of the caffeine present. Decaffeinated coffees are made in one of two ways: naturally by washing out the caffeine alkaloid, and chemically by the use of a solvent. Other plants used to flavor coffee or as coffee substitutes include the dried roots of the dandelion (*Taraxacum officinale*), a relative of chicory.

Instant coffees are available in powder form or granules, and have been in use since the 1930s, heralding the era of convenience foods. They are produced by brewing freshly roasted and ground coffee to obtain a strong concentrate. This is then passed through an atomizing spray into a stream of hot air which evaporates the water and leaves behind a fine residue powder.

Freeze-dried coffee is the most successful method of making an aromatic instant coffee. The coffee is brewed, frozen into slabs and ground into particles which are then put into a vacuum with a small amount of heat. This turns the ice directly into steam, leaving the ground particles dry, chunky and ready to use.

Coffee in the kitchen

Raw coffee beans will keep indefinitely in a cool, dry place. Once roasted and ground, the coffee should be used as soon as possible; the finer the grind, the more rapid the loss of taste.

Brewing coffee is merely a matter of infusion or boiling. Boiling coffee gives it a strong, bitter taste, as much of the aroma is steam-distilled from the brew and the bitter components are dissolved into it.

Coffee used in recipes should be made very strong and concentrated, or you can use instant coffee powder, with excellent results. Any recipe that includes the term "mocha" will have a distinctive coffee taste. Coffee also features in several alcoholic drinks, for example Irish coffee and such liqueurs as Tia Maria, kahlua, crème de café, crème de mokka, and Bahia, mostly made from the pulp of the coffee berry.

HIGH ROAST BEANS

Shown here is an Algerian *C. arabica* bean. Like all high or dark roasts it has a rather bitter taste as the oil, which sustains a coffee's sweetness, has come out.

REGULAR GRINDS

Coarse grinds are better for percolating. Use high roasts, which are stronger, at dinner; light ones at breakfast.

DRIP GRINDS

The best texture to preserve the delicate taste and aroma. Medium grinds are suitable for percolator, drip pots and carafes.

FINE GRINDS

Ideal for infusion, espresso machines and electric coffee makers that use paper filters.

DANDELION COFFEE

Extracted from the root, it can be brewed as a caffeine-free substitute for coffee.

DECAFFEINATED

When ground, treated with solvent and dried, coffee loses most of its caffeine.

INSTANT FREEZE-DRIED

Made by freezing a brew of good coffee, grinding it to particles and removing the water in a vacuum.

High roast beans

High roast regular grind

High roast drip grind

High roast fine grind

Dandelion coffee

Decaffeinated

Instant freeze-dried

Light roast beans

Full roast beans

Medium-light roast beans

Costa Rican unroasted beans

Costa Rican roasted beans

Instant

LIGHT ROAST BEANS

Shown here is a Kenyan *C. arabica* bean. The light roasts have a delicate taste and can be drunk with milk.

FULL ROAST BEANS

Shown here is the Mocha bean. Highly regarded, it has a strong distinctive taste on its own but blends well with milder beans.

MEDIUM-LIGHT ROAST BEANS

Shown here is a bean from Turkey, where the unique style of brewing strong coffee from powdered beans originated.

COSTA RICAN UNROASTED BEANS

Beans can be stored for two to three years before roasting which gives them aroma and caramelizes them. All coffee is best when freshly roasted.

COSTA RICAN ROASTED BEANS

A fine, mild and rich-bodied *C. arabica* bean, it has a slightly acid taste. Always medium or lightly roasted, it is good unblended.

INSTANT COFFEE

Usally made by heat-drying coffee, it's not as rich but is more convenient.

OTHER COFFEES

COLOMBIAN
A full-bodied coffee bean that has little acidity.

JAMAICAN
A large yellow bean *C. arabica* coffee with a delicate flavor.

KENYAN
The pale green African

C. arabica beans give a rich liquor with a sharp taste when roasted.

MOCHA
A *C. arabica* type, originally from the old port of Mocha in Yemen, this is one of the world's finest coffees.

MYSORE
East Indian bluish gray *C. arabica* beans, giving a liquor with a fine, strong taste.

SANTOS
Santos and Rio, both from Brazil, have green-yellow beans which give a smooth, mellow liquor.

TEA

TEA IS THE WORLD'S most popular drink. It is the name given to the leaves of the tea plant *Thea sinensis*, an evergreen tree or shrub which grows in damp tropical or sub-tropical regions at altitudes of up to 7000 feet. Though the plant may have originated in India it had reached China (where as *cha* it is the national drink), by 200 AD and Japan (where it was not only a popular drink but had reached great ritual significance in the *cha-no-yu* – tea ceremony) by the eighth century. It was brought to Europe by the Dutch in 1610, reached England in 1644, and America at the beginning of the eighteenth century. It has subsequently spread throughout the world. It is grown principally in China, Taiwan, Japan, India, Sri Lanka and Southeast Asia, and, to a lesser extent, in Africa.

There are two main types of tea, black and green, produced from different treatments of the leaves after they are picked. For black tea, which is amber-colored and strongly flavored, the leaves are fermented. For green tea, greenish yellow in color and rather bitter in taste, this step is omitted. There is another category of tea: Oolong, grown in China, Taiwan and Japan, which is partly fermented with a subtle flavor combining the characteristics of both black and green tea. Oolong is often perfumed and flavored with jasmine flowers.

The prime part of the tea shrub is the bud, enclosed by two downy leaves (*pekoe* in Chinese means "downy"). Tea planters refer to the "two leaves and a bud", while the word "pekoe" is employed to describe leaf sizes and grades. The leaves are plucked from the shrub by hand, and it takes about 4 lbs of leaves to produce 1 lb of black tea.

Processing the leaves
The plucked leaves are swiftly transported to the factory, where they are spread on racks to dry, losing about 50 per cent of their moisture content. After this "withering" process, the leaves are machine-rolled to break up the cellular structure, which releases the fermenting enzymes and encourages absorption of oxygen; the rolling technique was also designed to give a decorative twist to the leaf, imitating the original hand-twisted leaves of China. After rolling, the pulped leaves are left to ferment at about 82°F, and they gradually assume a coppery hue; fermentation is necessary to produce the characteristic taste and strength of tea. The fermentation is checked by "firing" in chambers, that is, passing a current of hot air over the leaves for about 30 minutes, at a carefully regulated temperature.

Once fired, the black and broken leaves are sifted by machine to be sorted into two main grades – "broken and small leaf" teas, and "leaf" teas. Usually, the larger the leaf size, the better the taste of the brew, while smaller leaves give stronger and darker brews.

Broken leaf teas are separated from the leaf teas by sifting, then further graded into broken orange pekoe, flowery broken orange pekoe, broken pekoe, and so on down to "fannings" and "dust", while leaf grades are flowery orange pekoe, orange pekoe, and pekoe.

These orthodox grades apply to both China and India teas, but in recent years, Indian manufacturers have gone over to machine-cutting, called "legge-cut" leaves. Such teas are quick to infuse and thus are particularly suitable for use in the tea-bag industry.

Tea in the kitchen
Tea is used as a hot beverage, as iced tea or tea punch. Ceylon tea is best for making iced tea or tea punch, since it is the only type that does not cloud. Black tea may be served with lemon and sugar or with milk, green tea with lemon and sugar or plain. In North Africa, tea is infused with mint leaves and a great deal of sugar added; in the Himalayas a kind of tea soup is concocted with yak butter and salt.

Tea is rarely used as an ingredient in recipes, but tea ice cream and tea soufflé are examples. The habit of taking soothing or stimulating beverages by infusion is universal; tea, coffee, Paraguayan maté (*Ilex pape*), Yapon tea (*L. cassine*) and guarana bread (*Paullinia sorbilis*) all contain tannin, theine or caffeine, but the majority of infusions, the tisanes or herbal teas, are free from stimulants. Tea should be kept in airtight containers.

KEEMUN

Keemun tea

A black tea from China with a large black leaf that makes a light infusion with a smoky taste and a special bouquet – "the fragrance of an orchid". Good to serve with food, it is best without milk.

ORANGE PEKOE

Orange pekoe tea

The finest grade of black Indian tea, it is picked from the buds and top leaves of the plant. Sometimes scented, it has a jasmine taste and is sometimes used in blends.

LAPSANG SOUCHONG

Lapsang souchong tea

A black China tea with large leaves and a rich smoky taste. Lapsang souchong needs slow brewing, is best without milk or lemon, and is often used in blends.

ASSAM

A high-quality, full-bodied, all-purpose black tea from Assam in northeast India. Usually drunk unblended, it makes a reddish brew with a full, malty taste. It is good with milk or on its own. Shown here is new season Assam.

Assam tea

GREEN

Green tea

A greenish gray China tea made in China, Taiwan and Japan, the leaves of green or gunpowder tea are characteristically rolled in pellets. Unfermented, it has a delicate taste and fine aroma, and is best drunk on its own.

FAN YONG

Fan yong tea

This is an unscented tea from China. Its black leaves make a mild, light infusion, low in tannin. It is best without milk and good with food.

JASMINE

Jasmine tea

A green tea from China with a distinctive fragrance, it is delicately scented with dried jasmine blossoms. A tea to enjoy on its own, never with milk.

Kanoy tea

Formosa Oolong tea

Darjeeling tea

Hibiscus tea

Rose hip tea

Bamboo tea

KANOY

This is a black, unscented tea with tiny black leaves from the island of Sri Lanka, once called Ceylon. It makes a bright golden infusion.

FORMOSA OOLONG

A black semifermented tea from Taiwan, it has the biggest leaf, but makes quite a light infusion tasting of ripe peaches.

DARJEELING

A black, slow-brewing Indian tea with a rich, rather fruity taste. Considered the best and most delicate of all the Indian teas, it is grown around Darjeeling.

HIBISCUS

Made from hibiscus flowers, the brew is red, tart and fruity.

ROSE HIP

Made from the fruit of the wild rose plant crushed with the seeds, it makes a tart brew.

BAMBOO

A strong-tasting, bitter black tea from China, so-called because it is encased in dried bamboo leaves.

OTHER TEAS

CEYLON
Delicate and fragrant high quality teas grown in altitudes of over 4000 feet.

CHAMOMILE
This herbal tea, made from the flowers only, has a delicate flavor. Other herbal teas include spearmint, peppermint and many blends with excellent flavor.

EARL GREY
A well-known blended tea scented with bee balm to give it a distinctive taste.

SUGARS, SYRUPS AND HONEYS

UNTIL THE SIXTEENTH century, when cane sugar from the West Indies became readily available and inexpensive, the world depended mainly on honey as its sweetener. Like honey, sugar cane is of ancient origin. It was first cultivated in India 2500 years ago and called, in Sanskrit, *karkara*. Sugar derives from the Arabic form of the word *sakkara* (*sukkur*), and appeared in the thirteenth century in England. The recorded history of cane sugar begins when a member of Alexander's army mentions it in 325 BC. It reached China by 100 BC but the Japanese did not get it until 700 AD, though by 400 AD it was being widely cultivated in the Middle East. Pliny the Elder called it a kind of honey made from reeds. So did the Crusaders, who encountered it in the eleventh century and introduced it to Europe. It remained expensive until Columbus introduced the canes into Hispaniola, now Haiti-Dominican Republic, in the West Indies in 1493. Its cultivation spread throughout the islands and cane sugar became, and still is, a main source of sweetness.

There are several types of sugar. The white crystalline product used in the kitchen or found on the table as "sugar" is a purified chemical, a carbohydrate consisting of almost pure sucrose or cane sugar, which in its turn contains glucose (dextrose or grape sugar) and fructose (fruit sugar).

Sugar is created in green plants by photosynthesis. The plants convert carbon dioxide and water into carbohydrates, using the energy provided by the sun. The carbohydrates are synthesized in the leaves and converted to sugar – sugar is the main source of the plant's energy and is important to its metabolism. Some plants have an additional reserve of sucrose, and these sugar-rich varieties are used by the sugar industry. They are the sugar cane, sugar beet, the maple, and several varieties of palm tree.

Sugar from canes

Sugar cane (*Saccharum officinarum*) is the world's principal source of sugar. The cane is harvested mechanically; only in a few places is it still gathered by the traditional method of hand-cutting. The cut cane is fed into a crushing machine to extract the juice, which is then chemically treated to precipitate the impurities, and boiled to give a saturated solution. This syrup must then be processed to allow the "cropping out" of sugar crystals. The technique is progressive, so that the residue mother liquor, or molasses, may yield a further crop of crystals.

Brown sugar is produced when cane juice is boiled to provide the first crop of sugar crystals and molasses. The crystals are brown simply because they are coated with liquid molasses. Washed, the crystals would be almost white, with a faint golden tint.

During the cropping out process in the refinery, sugar crystals are produced that leave a residue of syrup. These syrups are variable in quality – a secondary syrup is bound to be more concentrated than a primary one. Such syrups also vary in color from very light to dark brown, almost black. The final, non-yielding syrup is blackstrap molasses, a concentrate of about 50 per cent sugars with minerals and organic materials. Molasses may be a blend of syrups from different varieties of cane, and marketed in grades according to quality, or a blend of refinery syrups obtained during the refining of white sugar.

Sugar from roots and trees

The sucrose obtained from the sugar beet (*Beta vulgaris*) is identical to the sugar processed from the cane, both in strength and quality. It is extracted by pulping or slicing the washed roots, which are soaked in hot water to provide a sugar solution, processed in the same fashion as cane sugar. Sugar beets will not, however, produce brown sugars, though a bitter-tasting molasses is obtained from them.

American settlers learned from the Indians to exploit the maple tree as a source of sugar. Straight from the tree, the sap is sweet but without color or flavor, and it must be boiled to produce the dark syrup with its characteristic maple taste.

Palm sugar comes from the date, coconut, toddy and palmyra palms. The sap is collected by tapping the trunk or top of the tree, and reducing it to syrup, a clear and transparent product which is then allowed to crystallize.

Sugar in the kitchen

Brown sugars are used for their characteristic taste and for the fact that they add moistness to the finished product; brown sugars are often specified in recipes for bread and cakes. Confectioners sugar is used to make candies and replaces superfine sugar in some cake recipes. Typically it is used for frostings. Treacle, molasses, corn syrup and maple syrup all have important applications: they are used in baking and confectionery and as toppings.

Frostings and syrups may need boiling, as will many types of confectionery, jams and jellies, reaching temperatures that are critical to the success of the recipe. Temperatures can be checked with a sugar thermometer, and the density of the syrup with a saccherometer. Boiling sugar syrups are inclined to crystallize or grain if the crystals are not entirely dissolved before bringing to the boil. Any stray crystals clinging to the side of the pan may precipitate graining and should be brushed down into the syrup with a brush dipped in water. The addition of a little cream of tartar and glucose will help to prevent graining, and scum forming on the syrup.

HONEY

Honey is the oldest sweetening substance; it was used long before sugar. Ancient brewers used it to make the fermented drink, mead (from the Sanskrit *madhu*, a honey drink), which sustained Beowulf and lesser mortals during the Age of Heroes. Its traditional use, however, has been in baking. The ancient Greeks used honey in a bread called *melitutes*, which the Romans subsequently borrowed, and called *panis melitus*, and also baked a sacrificial honey cake known as *libum*.

The practice of sweetening bread with honey led in turn to a wealth of spice-honey cakes, such as the French *pain d'épices*, the German *lebkuchen* and the English gingerbread. Eastern confectioners discovered the happy marriage of almonds with honey, and the recipes spread far and wide – to Italy, where the candy *torrone* was fashioned, to France, where nougat was produced at Montélimar, and to Spain in the form of *turrón*. The Maya made a liqueur, *Ixtalseutun*, out of it; the Aztecs sweetened their chocolate with it.

Although honey can be made artificially, it is the natural product made by the bees which is normally used. The honey-combs are uncapped by machine and the honey extracted from the combs by a centrifugal force which spins it out, or by heat extraction. The honey is then strained, filtered and packed.

Types of honey

Honey is produced by the bee from nectar taken from a variety of flowers and trees. It is the true essence of flowers, and each species of flower in different parts of the world will produce a honey or characteristic flavor. For example, the famous Hymetus honey of Greece is produced as a result of bees visiting sage, marjoram, thyme and savory; and, as you might expect, combinations of orange blossom, lemon and lime produce citric lemony tasting honeys.

There are many types of honey, and they can vary a great deal in flavor and appearance. Apart from the fact that they are available in wax combs or as liquid in jars, the actual liquids can differ greatly, ranging from very thin to almost hard, and may be white, golden, amber, varnish-brown, and even black.

The difference in the consistency of honeys is due to a variety of factors: plant sources, water content and temperature while processing. Flavors too, are easy to analyse, but it is not known why honeys each develop a particular color.

Honey in the kitchen

Honey can be eaten on its own or used as an ingredient. Its main use is still in baking: it is the sweetener for many Oriental and Arab cakes, also for the Turkish *baklava*, the Greek *pasteli* and the popular *halva*, as well as for those sweetmeats already mentioned. It is used for curing ham, making honey butter, coating breakfast cereals, and is delicious cooked with chicken and almonds.

When cooking with honey, bear in mind that its sugars tend to caramelize when heated, and that some of its delicate aroma may also be driven off. Also, all honeys tend to crystallize and harden with age.

Sugars and Syrups

SUPERFINE SUGAR

Much finer than granulated sugar, superfine sugar is used generally for baking in cakes and pastries. Because of its texture, it dissolves quickly and so is also popular for use with fruits and cereals.

Superfine sugar

GRANULATED SUGAR

Several textures of white refined sugar are available. The most common is granulated, a general-purpose sugar used both for the table and in cooking.

Granulated sugar

PRESERVING SUGAR

Also known as coarse sugar, this is boiled in the refinery to obtain a large grain or crystal, which helps to eliminate scum forming when making preserves.

Preserving sugar

CONFECTIONERS' SUGAR

This is powdered sugar with the addition of tricalcium phosphate or cornstarch as a conditioner against damp, which may cause the sugar to get lumpy or to solidify. It is used to make meringues, cakes, frostings and confectionery.

Confectioners' sugar

GLUCOSE

Natural glucose occurs in large quantities in grapes and honey. Commercial glucose is available as a powder, a syrup and in chips. Used in jam and confectionery, it is also useful to athletes as a quick source of energy because it is easily absorbed.

Glucose

RAINBOW SUGAR CRYSTALS

Vegetable dyes are added to white sugar to produce pastel-shaded crystals. They may be served with coffee for an attractive table presentation and are often used for decorating cakes and other baked goods and confections.

Rainbow sugar crystals

CANDY CRYSTALS

These fairly large brownish crystals are particularly popular with coffee drinkers because they dissolve slowly. The coffee retains some of its bitter taste and is sweetened gradually as it is drunk.

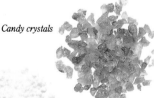

Candy crystals

DEMERARA SUGAR

Raw brown sugars – such as Demerara and Barbados – go through a preliminary cleaning process in their country of origin and are exported already packaged. They vary in taste and appearance and are used mainly in rich, dark fruit cakes.

Demerara sugar

BROWN SUGAR

Several manufacturers produce a variety of brown sugars which differ in shade and texture. These are refined sugars with cane molasses added. The refining process leaves a coating around the crystals (which is soluble in water) whereas with Demerara sugar the molasses is in the crystals. Both the light and dark types shown here are used with cereals and coffee and also in fruit and spice cakes. There are other brown sugars on the market which do not contain cane molasses. These consist of white sugar with a vegetable dye added, and this will be stated on the packet.

Dark brown sugar

Light brown sugar

CUBE SUGAR

This is refined and crystallized sugar that has been moistened and compressed into square or rectangular blocks. Brown varieties are also made in Europe. Cube sugar is used for the table to sweeten hot drinks.

Cube sugar

MOLASSES SUGAR

The darker the sugar, the more molasses it contains. This lightly processed brown sugar is moist and soft in texture. It is generally used in rich, dark fruit cakes.

Molasses sugar

MUSCOVADO SUGAR

A lighter brown than molasses sugar, muscovado is also soft and moist. It is used in fruit cakes and a variety of it is an important ingredient in many Indian dishes.

Muscovado sugar

LUMP SUGAR

The large golden crystals of yellow lump sugar, popular with Chinese cooks, are also used in desserts and drinks. Dark brown concentrated lump sugar is used in many Chinese and Indian dishes.

GOLDEN SYRUP

This is molasses residue that has been clarified. It is specially processed to obtain the golden color, hydrolized to reduce the water content, and stabilized microbiologically to prevent fermentation in the jar.

Golden syrup

MAPLE SYRUP

The processed sap of the maple tree, this syrup has a distinctive taste. Its best known use is for pouring over pancakes and waffles but it is also used in maple butter, maple sugar cake, cookies, frostings, in baked beans, ice cream, baked ham, candied sweet potatoes, baked apples. Enthusiasts claim there is no substitute.

Maple syrup

CANE SYRUP

The concentrated sap of sugar cane, it is sometimes substituted for molasses.

Cane syrup

Yellow lump sugar

Dark brown lump sugar

FRUIT SYRUPS

These simple preparations of white sugar, fruit and water, are especially popular in the Middle East. They are prepared from fruit pulp, such as rosehips (rosehip syrup) or blackcurrants (cassis syrup), or from the petals of flowers treated with a pectin enzyme that destroys natural yeasts, boiled, bottled and sterilized. Fruit syrups are used as a base for drinks, and to top ice creams and desserts.

Cassis syrup

Rose hip syrup

BLACK TREACLE

A darker and heavier version of golden syrup, this is used in rich fruit cakes and spicy sauces.

Molasses

Black treacle

MOLASSES

A by-product of sugar-making, dark or blackstrap molasses (shown here) improves the keeping qualities of breads and cakes and is rich in iron. Light molasses has a milder flavor and is used as a table syrup.

OTHER SYRUPS

CORN SYRUP

A by-product of corn (*Zea mays*) cultivation, corn syrup is converted from cornstarch. It is used for a great variety of products, including beverages, canned fruits, ice cream, baked goods and preserves.

SUGAR SYRUP

This is granulated sugar which is dissolved in either hot or cold water.

Honeys

COMB

The natural form in which all honey is found, comb honey is eaten wax and all. Normally the wax combs are cut by hand to remove the honey; when commercially processed they are uncapped by machine.

HONEY CONTAINING COMB

This luxury item – also known as chunk comb honey – contains a section of the comb in a jar filled with clear honey.

ENGLISH

This is a blend of honeys gathered from a variety of English blossoms. Also available creamed, it is often thought essential for a "proper" afternoon tea.

PURE ORANGE BLOSSOM

This comes from *Citrus aurantium*, and is produced mostly in Spain, but also California, Mexico, South Africa and Israel. It is a light, delicately citrus-tasting honey, especially good in custards.

MANUKA

This thick dark honey comes from the prolific "ti" or tea tree of New Zealand (*Leptospermum scorparium*). Its rich taste is good in cooking.

JAMAICAN

Clear and dark with an exotic tropical flower taste, this thick honey is good to use in cooking.

HUNGARIAN ACACIA

A thin, very pale honey from *Robinia pseudocacia*, Romania, France and Italy also produce this mild variety which tends always to remain liquid.

Honey containing comb

Comb honey

English

Pure orange blossom

Manuka

Hungarian acacia

Jamaican

OTHER HONEYS

ALCAHUAL

This amber-colored honey with a fine flavor is exported from Mexico. Also from Mexico are Campanilla, Morning Glory and Aguinaldo.

BARBERRY

Another amber-colored honey, this is derived from the flowers of *Berberidacae*.

BUCKWHEAT

Wild buckwheat honey is mainly produced in California as "Californian sage honey". Cultivated buckwheat makes a very dark brown honey with a strong flavor. It is the main type used for making honey cakes and Jewish honey wine.

ILEX

This honey comes from the holly tree and is mild and light-colored. It is popular in Europe.

LAVENDER

A popular European honey, especially in the south of France, it is amber-colored, often with a greenish cast and a butter-smooth texture.

HEATHER

Heather-covered heaths produce a creamy honey which liquefies when stirred. It is extremely popular in Britain and Europe, coming either from ling (*Calluna vulgaris*) or from bell heather (*Erica cinera*).

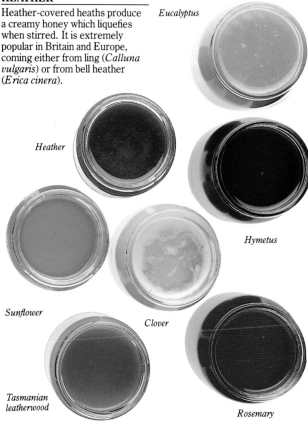

Eucalyptus

Heather

Hymetus

Sunflower

Clover

Tasmanian leatherwood

Rosemary

EUCALYPTUS

There are about 500 varieties of this creamy honey, all native to Australia. Some honeys are light to medium amber, others quite dark. Flavors range from the delicate *Eucalyptus albaros* to the extra-light but sweet and cloying *E. melliodora* and the dark strong *E. tereticorius*.

HYMETUS

From thyme, marjoram and other herbal blossoms growing on Mt Hymetus in Greece, this dark, clear and slightly thick aromatic honey is considered to be one of the best in the world. It is a perfect complement to tart natural yogurt and is excellent used in the confection *baklava*.

CLOVER

This is perhaps the most common and most popular honey in America and Europe. It comes from the red or white *Trifolium repens*, is thick and pale amber. Also available clear, its mild taste is best for general cooking.

SUNFLOWER

Produced mainly in Greece, Turkey, southern Russia and Argentina, sunflower honey loses its excellent fragrance in cooking.

LOGWOOD

This honey, produced mainly in Jamaica, is made for export and is usually light in color.

MANGO

This amber-colored honey is dense in body.

POHUTAKAWA

A rare honey from New Zealand, this has a unique and salty flavor and comes from the tree *Metrosideros excelsa*.

SWEET BASIL

A honey of very light color,
with a characteristic herbal flavor, popular in Europe.

TULIP TREE

This honey is dark brown with a heavy body and delicate, quincelike flavor.

TASMANIAN LEATHERWOOD

From Australia, this rich, creamy honey has a distinctive taste and is high in glucose. If necessary, it can be put in warm water for 30 minutes to make it clear. It can be used for general cooking.

ROSEMARY

This strong, aromatic herb honey is produced mainly in the countries around the Mediterranean from the small blue flowers (once associated with the Virgin Mary) of *Rosmarinus officinalis*.

Eggs

GGS, ONE OF THE most essential and versatile foods used in cooking, have been eaten and enjoyed since the beginnings of civilization. Often venerated as a symbol of life and fertility, many ancient philosophers saw eggs as a symbol of the world and the four elements, since they held that the shell represented earth; the white, water; the yolk, fire; and air was found under the shell at the round end of the egg. To early Christians, eggs were a symbol of rebirth and were hard-boiled, decorated and given as presents at Easter.

The eggs most often used today come from the domestic hen – either the farmyard or "free-range" variety, or the modern "battery" variety. There is no nutritional difference between free-range and battery eggs and none between brown and white eggs, since the shell color is related purely to the breed of hen. As far as culinary purposes are concerned, free-range eggs deteriorate more quickly.

Composition of the egg

The egg is made up of the outer shell (about 12 per cent of its total weight); the albumen, or white (about 58 per cent) and the yolk (about 30 per cent), which is held in place by a twisted strand of material called "chalaza", which is usable. (As is the tiny dark fleck often present. This should be removed only if the eggs are being used in a light-colored sauce.) There is also an air chamber at the rounded end of the egg. This gradually expands as the egg loses its freshness.

Egg white proteins, when whipped, break and expand, forming elastic-walled cells that trap air, which in turn expands when subjected to heat (as in the oven). This is what makes egg whites such a valuable leavening agent. Yolk proteins, on the other hand, bind and thicken. They are less stable than those of egg whites, and, when exposed to excessive heat, harden and separate from the yolk's fat and water molecules, and the yolk curdles. This is why egg yolk mixtures should be heated gently.

Fresh egg white should be firm, thick and support the yolk. A less than fresh egg has a thin white that spreads away from the yolk and a yolk which breaks easily.

Eggs in the kitchen

Eggs are extremely versatile. Apart from their endless uses in main dishes, soufflés and baking, they can be used for a number of general culinary purposes: to thicken, emulsify, coat, bind or glaze other foods and to provide a foamy base. They can be boiled, poached, baked, fried or pickled, though some, because of their size, may be less suited to general cooking. Unless a recipe specifies otherwise use a large egg; two small ones can always be substituted.

Egg whites are more easily foamed when the eggs are at room temperature and at least three days old. Fat, even the merest trace from the yolk or any grease on the beater or bowl, will prevent foaming; salt acts similarly. A tiny amount of acid (such as cream of tartar) will make the whites stiffer and give greater bulk, while sugar keeps the proteins supple. Sugar or acid should be added when the egg white is just beginning to foam, otherwise it will remain as gritty particles. For cakes, soufflés, mousses and soft meringues, beat the whites until glossy peaks form a slight bend when the beater is removed. For hard meringues and chiffon cakes, the foam should be very white and glossy and form peaks that stand straight up. Do not over-beat or the whites will become dry and lose air.

Storing eggs

Refrigerated eggs keep fresh for three to four weeks, but should be kept away from strong-smelling foods since they absorb odors. Eggs spread less while still cold so, unless separating or frying them, it is best to bring them to room temperature before cooking. Store eggs with the pointed end downwards so that the yolk rests on the white rather than on the air chamber. Do not freeze eggs unless separated as their shells crack at low temperatures. Eggs can be frozen for up to nine months, but allow them to thaw completely in unopened containers before use.

CHICKEN

Both brown and white eggs have the same nutritional value and it is a matter of personal taste which you choose to buy. Chicken or hen eggs are the only eggs to be produced on a large commercial scale and are the familiar standard by which other eggs are compared, the average weight being about 2 ounces. They are used in all aspects of cooking.

Chicken eggs

GOOSE

The goose egg has a slightly richer taste and should always be used very fresh and cooked lightly. These eggs weigh 8–10 ounces – four to five times the size of a chicken's egg.

Goose egg

QUAIL

Considered a delicacy, these small eggs are usually eaten medium- or hard-boiled, shelled and used in salads, pickled, or poached and set in aspic.

Quail egg

PHEASANT and PARTRIDGE

Rarely available, these eggs are usually solid white, buff or olive, although some species nest in open areas and their eggs are blotched with brown or black for protection against predators. They can be served hard-boiled, shelled and used in salads, may be pickled or set in aspic and served as an hors d'oeuvre.

Pheasant egg

Partridge egg

1,000-YEAR-OLD

Raw duck eggs preserved in lime, pine ash and salt for between 50 and 100 days, these emerge translucent blue and green, looking much older than they are – hence the name. Firm in texture, they are rich with a slightly fishy taste. They are a Chinese delicacy, usually shelled, sliced, steamed and served cold.

DUCK

These eggs are richer tasting then chicken eggs and can acquire a harmful bacteria as they are usually laid in a dirty spot. However, they are still suitable for eating if they are boiled for 15 minutes or used in baking. The white turns bluish and the yolk a reddish-orange after boiling. They should be eaten very fresh and are not suitable for meringues.

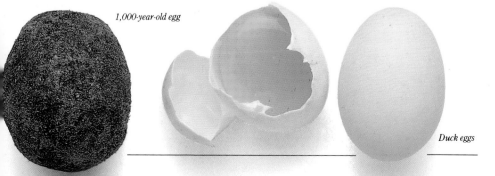

1,000-year-old egg

Duck eggs

GUINEA FOWL

Flecked with brown, this egg has a more delicate taste than a chicken's egg. It is best medium- or hard-boiled for 3 to 5 minutes, cooled, shelled and then tossed into green salads.

Guinea fowl egg

Gull egg

GULL

These eggs vary in size, depending on the species of gull, but are almost always camouflaged with dark blotches. They lack the strong fishy taste which is common to the eggs of most sea birds. They are usually hard-boiled for 5 minutes, cooled and eaten cold with a little celery salt.

OSTRICH

This egg is rarely available, but it is edible provided it hasn't been left to bake in the sun or been partially hatched. Up to twenty times the size of a chicken's egg and with a thicker shell, one egg can feed a family of four.

BANTAM

The bantam is a breed of chicken, and its eggs, similar in taste to chicken eggs although only about half the size, may be used in the same way. The difference in tints has no effect on the taste.

Bantam eggs

PULLET

Another type of chicken egg, laid by a chicken in her first year.

Pullet egg

OTHER EGGS

PLOVER

Like quail eggs, these are considered to be a delicacy. Plover eggs are usually served lightly boiled.

TURKEY

Cream-colored, speckled with brown and sometimes twice the size of a chicken's egg, turkey eggs are similar in flavor and may be used in their place.

TURTLE

Sea turtle eggs are exported to Europe from South America, the Caribbean, Africa and Australia. Rarely available, this soft-shelled delicacy is prized by connoisseurs for its mild rich flavor.

Ostrich egg

FATS AND MILK PRODUCTS

IN ADDITION TO MEAT, animals have been the main source of fat and dairy products since they were first domesticated. While westerners rely mainly on cattle, vast areas of the world use the milk of camels, sheep, goats and even yaks to produce foodstuffs.

Fats and milk products can be looked at in four categories: milks; creams; sour creams and yogurts; and butters, margarines, cooking and baking fats.

Milk is composed of water, calcium and albumen, milk protein (casein), milk sugar (lactose), milk fat and vitamins. The final product depends on how the milk is processed and how one or more of milk's main constituents is treated.

In many countries, the milk sold has, by law, to be pasteurized – that is, freed of any bacteria which could cause milk-borne disease. Usually the milk is heated to below boiling, held at this temperature for a few seconds, then cooled immediately.

As milk cools the fat rises to the surface and this is "creamed" off to make butter or cream. The fat content of cream varies considerably; common types are half-and-half, light cream and whipping cream (light or heavy).

Yogurt is made by inoculating fresh milk with a lactic acid culture, of which there are several types, while fermented milks are made when both a lactic and alcoholic fermentation takes place. Sour cream is produced by introducing a lactic acid culture such as *Streptococcus lactis* into a low-fat homogenized cream.

Cream can be collected and churned into butter, which should have a fat content of 80 per cent. The cream used in butter-making can be either fresh or sour although most of the butter produced is from the former. The residue that is left after butter-making is buttermilk, although nowadays buttermilk is often made from pasteurized skim milk.

Margarine was originally "invented" as a low-cost alternative to butter by a French chemist. Today's margarine consists of refined, purified and hydrogenated edible oils such as sunflower, corn, soy and coconut. An expensive technological process blends together the oil and a high proportion of water to create a low-cholesterol polyunsaturated spread. Some hard or stick margarines contain saturated or animal fats. All animal fats – suet, dripping, lard – need some processing before use.

Fats and milk products in the kitchen

Milk is a versatile ingredient that can be used in many beverages and foods, including puddings, baked goods, soups and ice cream. Pasteurized milk should keep for four or five days in a refrigerator. It spoils but does not sour, so that in recipes calling for sour milk, buttermilk is used. Condensed milk and powdered milk are used in cooking, powdered milk in baking.

Cream can be kept for two to three days in a refrigerator, but will harden if left uncovered. It enhances many dishes and can be added to soups and sauces or used as a garnish. Overwhipped cream becomes buttery.

Margarine and butter should be kept in the refrigerator. They have good keeping qualities in temperate climates and can be deep-frozen for at least six months. Refined lard, grated suet and reduced suet can be kept for months in a refrigerator covered in a suitable container or vacuum-wrapped. Butter burns at a fairly low temperature and is unsuitable for frying unless mixed with a vegetable oil which has the effect of raising the optimum temperature. Clarifying butter by melting it so that the solids can be drawn off means that foods may be lightly fried without fear of burning. Apart from this, butter has a great number of uses in cooking, including the making of pastry, and flavored butters which are mixed with fresh herbs, or other ingredients such as caviar, sardines, garlic and paprika. Some types of margarine are interchangeable with butter in baking, but, like butter, margarine is not suitable for deep-frying.

In many countries yogurt is regarded as a guard against disease and varieties are used as a refreshing drink, also in cooking. In India, yogurt is mixed with fruits and vegetables and served as *raita*. Sour cream gives sauces a slightly acid taste. It should be added at the end of cooking time and either off the heat or on a low heat, otherwise it will curdle.

WHOLE MILK

Milk is the basis of all dairy products. Pasteurized milk (shown here) has been subjected to heat treatment to destroy bacteria. It should keep for four or five days in the refrigerator. None of the fat is removed from whole milk. Homogenized milk has been processed so that the cream does not rise to the top. Whole milk is used for drinking, cooking and baking.

BUTTERMILK

Originally the sour milk left over from butter-making, today buttermilk is usually made from pasteurized skim milk with an added culture to thicken its consistency. It is used as a drink, in baking and cooking, and is a good sour milk substitute.

POWDERED MILK

A useful fresh milk substitute, powdered milk consists of pasteurized, air-dried milk particles, which should be reconstituted with water before use, although it can be included with the dry ingredients in baking.

CREAM

Cream is the fatty part of fresh milk which rises to the surface when milk is left to stand. Cream is used in a number of dishes, and as the basis for many sauces. There are several varieties: the one shown, light cream, is used in coffee and with desserts.

CLOTTED CREAM

Cream skimmed from scalded milk, warmed over a low heat, and then cooled, clotted cream is a speciality of south-west England.

LIGHT WHIPPING CREAM

This type of cream is halfway between light and heavy cream as regards butterfat content. It is used for whipping and cooking.

GHEE

A type of clarified butter used in India, which is made by heating ordinary butter to rid it of impurities. It has a higher burning point than most other oils, which makes it perfect for frying and sautéing. It can be used as a sauce for lobster, and also to make *beurre noire* (French butter sauce).

YOGURT

A product made from curdled milk with the addition of a lactic starter, *yogurt* is its Turkish name. It is eaten plain but often has fruit or honey added for extra flavor; commercial varieties use evaporated milk and often contain fruit. Yogurt can be added to savory dishes and is also used as a dressing for salads, particularly cucumber.

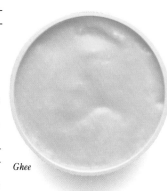

Ghee

BUTTER

A natural dairy product made from cream, butter can be unsalted or salted. The salted type shown here has better keeping qualities. It can be used for light sautéing or softened and flavored with herbs or other ingredients.

Milk

Yogurt

Powdered milk

Clotted cream

Cream

Buttermilk

Light whipping cream

Salted butter

Dripping

Lard

Margarine

Suet

DRIPPING

Fat that has separated from meat during cooking is strained or clarified and used as a cooking fat.

LARD

Melted, clarified and purified pork fat, this is used for deep-frying, roasting meats, and making pastry.

MARGARINE

A butter substitute made from animal or vegetable fats, or a combination of both, margarine can be bought in sticks or tubs.

SUET

The fat surrounding the kidneys of beef or sheep, suet is sold fresh for grating or already shredded and ready for use as shown. It is often used for steamed puddings.

OTHER MILK AND BUTTER SUBSTITUTES

SOFT MARGARINE

This variety is made from refined and purified vegetable oils only and contains polyunsaturates and emulsifiers. Not as fattening as butter, it is easier to spread than stick margarine.

SOY MILK

This is made from soybeans. Easily digested, it can be used as a substitute for dairy milk.

TOFU

Tofu, or bean curd, is soft and cheese-like with a bland taste. Available in soft, firm and silken forms, it is the staple of Japanese cooking. It may be eaten on its own or used in soups, sauces and dressings. Fermented tofu is a favorite Chinese snack, eaten deep fried and seasoned.

OTHER MILKS AND MILK PRODUCTS

CONDENSED MILK

Canned milk from which half of the water content has been removed and sugar added. It can be poured over fruit salads, and is useful for reconstituting and confectionery-making.

EVAPORATED MILK

This is canned milk with a large percentage of its water removed. It is similar to condensed milk but, because it has no added sugar, does not keep as well. Once opened, it should be stored and treated like fresh milk.

FORTIFIED MILK

Whole or skim milk enriched with vitamins (usually A and D) and minerals and proteins.

HEAVY CREAM

This contains a minimum of 36 per cent fat. Sugars and flavorings are sometimes added, as in *crème chantilly*, used in cakes and desserts.

LONGLIFE MILK

Milk that is pasteurized and vacuum-packed to render it sterile for long keeping.

LOW FAT MILK

This is milk with 1 per cent milk fat.

NON-HOMOGENIZED MILK

This is unprocessed whole milk. The cream rises to the top. It can be used for drinking, cooking and baking.

SKIM MILK

This is milk with less than 1/2 per cent milkfat but all the protein. It is usually fortified with vitamins A and D.

SOUR CREAM

Cream inoculated with a lactic acid culture, this is added to salad dressings and sauces to give a slightly acid flavor.

YOGHURT DRINKS or FERMENTED MILK

There are a number of sour milk drinks from different parts of Asia and the Middle East. These include *dough* from Iran, *kaelder milk* from Norway, *kefir* from Eastern Europe, *kumiss* from the USSR, *labar* from the Middle East, *mazoum* from Armenia and *skyr* from Iceland.

CHEESES

IT IS IMPOSSIBLE TO say where and when cheese was first produced, but the farmers in Mesopotamia, who first domesticated sheep and goats about 10,000 years ago, and wild cattle 2000 years later, certainly made cheese from milk, or enjoyed cheese which was accidentally precipitated. During the Middle Ages, monks furthered the development of cheese as a necessary meat substitute. Cheese-making differed from family to family and the methods passed from one generation to another. There are now, in fact, fewer cheese types than in former times, when cheeses were strictly local and every farmhouse produced its own supply.

The dairy cow provides the bulk of the world's milk and cheese, but a significant amount of goat's and sheep's milk cheeses are made throughout Europe and the Middle East. In addition, cheese is made from the milk of reindeer in Lapland, the yak and zebu in China and Tibet, the buffalo in the Philippines, India and Italy, and from the camel and, it is said, mares and donkeys, in Afghanistan and Iran.

Categorizing cheese

A cheese type is distinguished by its flavor and texture. Fresh cheese is unripened curd eaten shortly after it is made, while soft cheese is briefly ripened and easy to spread, and contains a high percentage of moisture and fat. Semi-hard cheese, matured with less moisture, is easy to cut. Hard cheese is long-matured with a low moisture content but may contain up to 50 per cent fat. It is a good grating cheese but difficult to cut.

Cheese may be identified partly by the formation of the rind. Rinds protect the cheeses' interiors and allow them to ripen properly. Apart from those with a manufactured wax coating, there are those with a dry or natural rind, or with a natural rind which is then dyed. Some cheeses are bathed in a brine solution. This hardens the rind and improves the flavor of the paste or body. White rind cheeses have a mold flora (usually *Penicillium candidum*). Washed rind cheeses, where the cheese is regularly wiped, washed or sprayed with water to encourage the

growth of bacteria molds, have a sharper, richer taste. Some cheese is distinguished by the absence of any rind, as with most fresh cheeses.

The paste further categorizes cheeses. In the early stages of cheese-making, the curd is a white flavorless mass. If the cheese-maker desires a soft cheese, the curd may simply be left to drain. With a firmer cheese, the curd is cooked, then pressed into molds. Some cheeses have a semi-hard body containing many holes of various sizes, caused by gas-producing bacteria during ripening. Blue-veined cheeses are those where the blueing is either induced by the application or inoculation of a bacteria culture, or occurs naturally.

There are several basic techniques in cheese-making recipes, where the consistency and flavor of the paste is determined by the cooking and treatment of the curd. Cheddar is heated to 86°F, cut, stirred and heated again to 104°F, the curd stacked to promote cohesion and acid formation, finely milled, salted and pressed. Gouda curds are cooked to 95°F, cut, stirred, molded and pressed, after which the cheeses are steeped in a brine bath. The curd of Caciocavallo cheese is toughened by immersion in hot whey and water; it is then kneaded and shaped. All these techniques are basic to cheese-making, but equally important are the infinite variety of traditional recipes, which may demand the addition of certain mold cultures or herbs, or the wrapping of cheeses in chestnut or vine leaves.

Finally, cheese is also categorized by the type of animal that produced the milk and by the shape of the finished product. Cheeses come in various shapes: wheels, loaves, pyramids, hearts, cylinders and squares.

Cheese in the kitchen

Cheese can be used in soups, soufflés, pastry, sandwiches, salads, pies, pizzas, tarts, on toast, as a garnish and for many other applications. The choice of the cheese may depend on the nationality of the dish, but also on the cheese's behaviour during cooking. Some cheeses, such as Emmenthal, are inclined to draw threads and become stringy, whereas Gruyère and Sbrinz cheeses do not. On the other hand, this stringiness is desirable in some dishes, such as Swiss fondue. Cheese is also chosen for its melting and spreading qualities: Cheddar or Dunlop cheese for Welsh and Scotch rarebit; or Gruyère for *fonduta*; firm or crumbly cheese, such as Greek Feta, Cheshire, and Roquefort, for salads and dressings. One of the most useful combinations for versatility is a mixture of grated Parmesan and Gruyère, the former giving the strong piquant flavor, the latter the smooth, binding qualities suitable for cheese sauces and for the base for soufflés and quiches.

Storing cheese

Storage can be a problem, if you need to keep your cheese for any length of time. A cool room or cellar is ideal, but the cheese should be wrapped in aluminum foil or waxed paper to prevent it from drying out. One good method is to wrap each piece in foil or paper, then in a plastic bag for storage in a temperate part of the refrigerator – the salad compartment, for instance. Remove the cheese to adjust to room temperature about 1 hour before serving, depending on the type of cheese and the size of the piece. Parmesan should be freshly grated and used at once. Grated cheese should be wrapped and stored as described above.

Fresh and Soft Cheeses

CREAM CHEESE

This is prepared in much the same way as cottage cheese, but with cream and milk. There are several types: double cream cheese and single cream cheese are two. American cream cheese is made with a hot cream/milk mix. French petit-suisse cheeses are small, paper-wrapped products; Demisel is salted, as its name suggests. There are, in addition, many other versions throughout the world. The *Kesong Puti* of the Philippines, and *Surati Panir* of India are both made with buffalo milk. Sheep's and goat's milk cheeses are made throughout the Middle East, and are sold as *Jupneh* (Saudi Arabia) and variously as *Lebbeneh* or *Labneh*, while Latin America has its *queso blanco* cheeses, made from cow's or goat's milk.

CURD CHEESE

"Curd" is the general name given to all unripened cheeses made from the separated curds of cow's or goat's milk. Curd cheese has a slightly acid taste, and is used in cheesecakes and in sweet and savory fillings. It is also a popular base for dips and spreads. It is sold in most countries.

Curd cheese

COTTAGE CHEESE

A lumpy, mild-tasting curd cheese, made from partially skimmed milk, this has a moist texture, and is usually sold in tubs. It is available in most countries, and is used in cheesecakes and salads. Pressed into solid curd and cut in cubes, it is eaten in India's *mattar pannir*.

Cottage cheese

Cream cheese

BRIE

Made by Briard farmers since the eighth century, Brie was served to Charlemagne in 774. It is a soft French cheese made from cow's milk, with a creamy, fruity taste that is delicious in snacks and as a filling for brioche. It is made in large, flat wheel shapes and there are many varieties. The thin crust, made in the same way as Camembert, is edible. Brie is ripened on straw mats for about four weeks at a controlled temperature.

Brie

Camembert

CAMEMBERT

This world-famous French cheese is made from cow's milk and there are several varieties. It has a distinctive taste which varies from mild to pungent as it ages. An excellent dessert and snack cheese, it is made in small cylinder or half-moon shapes, which means that it can be bought as an individual cheese. The cheese is sprayed with *Penicillium candidum*, and acquires a white crust of mold flora. It is brine-dipped and ripened for about three weeks.

COULOMMIERS

A French cheese made from cow's milk, this, like Brie and Camembert, has a white rind and a soft interior. It has a rich and creamy taste and is usually made in small wheel shapes. It is good for desserts and snacks.

BOURSIN AUX FINES HERBES

A soft French triple cream cheese (with a 75 per cent fat content), the variety shown contains rosemary, fennel and chives. It is most often served with crackers.

Coulommiers

Boursin aux fines herbes

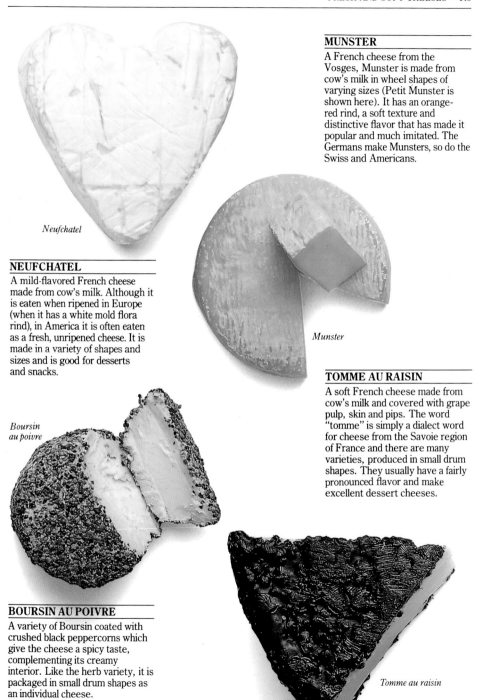

MUNSTER

A French cheese from the Vosges, Munster is made from cow's milk in wheel shapes of varying sizes (Petit Munster is shown here). It has an orange-red rind, a soft texture and distinctive flavor that has made it popular and much imitated. The Germans make Munsters, so do the Swiss and Americans.

Neufchatel

NEUFCHATEL

A mild-flavored French cheese made from cow's milk. Although it is eaten when ripened in Europe (when it has a white mold flora rind), in America it is often eaten as a fresh, unripened cheese. It is made in a variety of shapes and sizes and is good for desserts and snacks.

Boursin au poivre

Munster

TOMME AU RAISIN

A soft French cheese made from cow's milk and covered with grape pulp, skin and pips. The word "tomme" is simply a dialect word for cheese from the Savoie region of France and there are many varieties, produced in small drum shapes. They usually have a fairly pronounced flavor and make excellent dessert cheeses.

BOURSIN AU POIVRE

A variety of Boursin coated with crushed black peppercorns which give the cheese a spicy taste, complementing its creamy interior. Like the herb variety, it is packaged in small drum shapes as an individual cheese.

Tomme au raisin

MOZZARELLA

An Italian unripened curd cheese originally made from buffalo's milk, but now usually obtained from cow's milk. Made in various shapes, such as rounds and slabs, it is also packed shredded. It is a soft cheese with a rather moist texture. It has a mild, creamy taste and is widely used as a cooking cheese – in pizzas, lasagne and toasted sandwiches.

RICOTTA

An Italian fresh, unripened cheese made from the whey of cow's milk in Ricotta Piedmontese and Ricotta Vaccina, and sheep's milk in the regional types Ricotta Romana, Sarda and Siciliana. There is also a Maltese version, Rkotta, made from a mixture of cow's milk and sea water. It is smooth and milky-tasting and is used in a variety of sweet and savory dishes, including pizzas, and as a stuffing for ravioli, cannelloni and pancakes. It is packaged in various shapes and sizes.

Ricotta

Mozzarella

Caboc

COLWICK

A traditional cow's milk cheese from England. Usually made in cylinder shapes, the variety shown here has a dished center, which can be filled with cream and fruit. This cheese is usually sold unsalted to be served as a dessert, but can be salted and used as a savory cheese.

CABOC

A Scottish double cream cheese (with a 60 per cent fat content) made from cow's milk and rolled in oatmeal. It has a fairly sweet flavor and goes well with fresh fruit. It is made in small log or cylinder shapes.

FETA

A Greek cheese made variously with goat's and sheep's milk, or a mixture. Its roughly cut pressed curd is ripened in its own whey, salted beforehand. Feta is used in many Greek recipes; Greece has the distinction of being the world's leading consumer of cheese 34 lbs per person yearly.

Colwick

Feta

OTHER FRESH AND SOFT CHEESES

BARBEREY
A French cheese, Barberey or Fromage de Troyes is salted, molded and ripened for about three weeks. Sometimes it is sold unripened as a fresh cheese. Ripened cheeses resemble Camembert.

BEL PAESE
This is a relatively modern Italian cheese invented in 1929; its name means "beautiful country". It is a dessert type with a short ripening period. Bel Paese is a flat, round cheese with a slightly red rind flora.

BELI SIR
Both farmhouse and factory versions exist of this sourish Yugoslavian cheese, which is brine-ripened for about a month, and pressed in rectangular molds.

BRENZA
A soft and buttery cheese, Brenza or Bryndza is sometimes used as a basis for Liptauer spread. It is made in Hungary, Romania and the Carpathians from goat's or sheep's milk.

CHABICHOU
A goat's milk cheese from Poitou, France, this is made in the form of a cone or cylinder, with a natural dry rind.

CHAOURCE
This is an aromatic and slightly sour French cheese with a white mold flora rind. The cheeses are cylindrical and about 2½ inches high.

CHAUMES
A mild, tender cheese from the Atlantic Pyrenees region of France, this is factory-made from cow's milk and contains 50 per cent fat; Saint Albrey is similar. Circular and with a washed rind, it weighs 4½ lbs, and makes an excellent dessert cheese or may be used in Welsh rarebit.

EPOISSES
A small, cylindrical French cheese, this is a speciality of the Burgundy region, and the washed rind develops the orange smear of coryne bacteria. It may be spiced during manufacture, or dipped in marc de Bourgogne before sale.

LEIDERKRANZ
A Limburger-type rectangular American cheese with a very soft paste and mild flavor. The washed rind has the red smear of coryne bacteria.

LIPTAUER
A Hungarian cheese spread made from sheep's and cow's milk, Liptauer is a factory product based on a sheep's milk cheese, either Brenza or Liptó. Variations exist where butter, capers, onions, mustard and spices may be added.

LIVAROT
A strong, rectangular cheese from Normandy, France, with a red mould rind.

MASCARPONE
An Italian dessert cheese made from fresh cream and sold unripened, this may be flavored with liqueurs, and is sometimes sold mixed with candied fruits.

QUARK
This is a sharp, acidic skim milk cheese, usually found as a solid-packed mass. There are a variety of quark cheeses, which are widely employed in cooking, and to accompany other dishes. Quark is used in pastry, and in such recipes as *quarksahnetorte, quark-schnitten* and quark soufflé.

ROULE
A soft French cheese flavored with herbs, this is rolled up like a Swiss roll.

SCAMORZA
An old Italian cow's milk cheese related to Mozzarella, Scamorza was originally made from buffalo's milk. It is a drawn curd cheese of an oval shape, yellow in color with a firm but supple texture. It is used in pizzas.

STRACCHINO
There are several versions and types of this Italian cheese, originating in Lombardy. Taleggio and Robiolo are very soft, delicate cheeses, with a red-orange rind flora that results from their having been brined during ripening. They are uncut, unpressed cheeses. Stracchino Cresenza develops no rind flora.

Semi-Hard Cheeses

PORT SALUT

A mild French cheese with a firm paste and a washed rind. The small, round cheeses are made by Trappist monks from an ancient recipe. They are named "Port of Salvation" after the abbey, which itself was rechristened when the monks returned from exile after the French Revolution.

Port Salut

MANCHEGO

Spain's most famous cheese, this is made from sheep's milk and has a creamy, firmish textured interior, which sometimes has holes. Strong-tasting and ideal for snacks, Manchego is made in cylinder shapes.

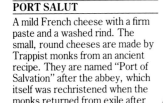

Colby

Manchego

COLBY

A popular American Cheddar-type cheese from Colby, Wisconsin. It is a washed-curd cheese (if the curds are washed thoroughly in cold water, the moisture content of the cheese is increased, making it mature more quickly). Made in various shapes, it is a mild cheese with a natural rind and slightly granular texture, which is popular in snacks and salads.

CANTAL

A cow's milk cheese from the Auvergne, it is often referred to as French Cheddar. It possesses a fine flavor and aroma and can be used in place of Cheddar for many recipes since it melts easily and does not tend to get stringy. Made in cylinder shapes, it is used in several regional dishes and is a good all-purpose table cheese.

Cantal

SAINT PAULIN

A rinded French cheese made from cow's milk, it can be bland or tangy, depending on its degree of ripeness, and is similar in taste to Port Salut. It is a good snack and dessert cheese and is made in small wheel shapes.

Saint Paulin

MONTEREY JACK

Monterey is a Cheddar-type cheese originating in Monterey, California, but now also made in other parts of America. It is derived from an old monastery recipe, and was first marketed in 1916. Made from cow's milk, it has a rather bland taste with a smooth, open texture, numerous holes and a natural rind. It is made in block shapes or large wheels and is used in snacks, sandwiches and in recipes. Monterey Jack, shown here, has an unmilled, lightly pressed curd with a high moisture content. There is also a grating-type Monterey, which is very useful for cooking.

Gjetost

Monterey Jack

FONTINA

A cow's milk cheese from the Piedmont region of Italy, it has a delicate nutty, slightly smoky taste and is much used for *fonduta*, a fondue of truffles, eggs and cheese. It is made in flat wheel shapes and has a natural rind.

GJETOST

A Norwegian whey cheese that can be made from either cow's milk (when it is also called Mysost) or goat's milk. Rather fudgelike in taste and appearance, it is made in cubes or rectangular blocks and is usually foil-wrapped. It is used in sauces, desserts and snacks.

CABRALES

Traditionally a goat's milk cheese (though there are now sheep's milk varieties) this is from the mountain regions of northern Spain. Made in cylinder shapes, it has a strong, pronounced taste and makes a good snack cheese.

Fontina

RACLETTE

A cow's milk cheese from Switzerland with a mild, nutty taste. Made in wheel shapes, it gives its name to a traditional melted cheese dish. There are several varieties, including Gomser, Bagnes and Orsières, all with a firm, texture.

Cabrales

Raclette

Cheshire

Double Gloucester

Dunlop

DOUBLE GLOUCESTER

This cow's milk cheese has a full flavor and is considered one of the great English cheeses. It is good for desserts and snacks and is made in cylinder shapes which weigh between 10 and 34 lbs.

CHESHIRE

A famous English cow's milk cheese from the county of Cheshire, dating back to the twelfth century, this has a crumbly texture and slightly salty tang. Usually fast-ripening, there are two types: red (shown), which is colored with annatto dye, and white. It is a good snack cheese.

LEICESTER

A firm-bodied English cow's milk cheese with a mild flavor, this is distinguished by its bright orange color, due to the addition of annatto dye. It is used like Lancashire as a melting and toasting cheese, and also makes a good snack cheese. It is made in cylinder shapes.

DUNLOP

A Scottish cheese made from cow's milk, this is a Cheddar-type cheese with a rather bland, buttery taste. It is a natural rind cheese said to have originated from an Irish recipe. In Scotland it is often eaten with buttered oatcakes; it makes a good snack cheese and is ideal for toasting. It is made in cylinder shapes.

EMMENTHAL

This world-famous Swiss cheese made from cow's milk has a fairly sweet, nutty taste and can be used as a basis for fondues and toasted snacks. Its name means "valley of Emme", the river which runs through central Switzerland. The 250-lb cartwheel, when cut open, reveals the large holes or "eyes" throughout the paste. The cheese has a natural rind and is softer and blander than Gruyère. Stringy when cooked.

Leicester

Emmenthal

Wensleydale

Lancashire

WENSLEYDALE

An English cheese from Yorkshire, this was once made from sheep's or goat's milk by Cistercian monks, but is now factory-made using cow's milk. White Wensleydale is a lightly pressed, salted type with a buttermilk flavor and a natural rind. There is also a blue-veined variety. White Wensleydale is a traditional accompaniment to apple pie and is made in cylinder and block shapes.

GRUYERE

Gruyère is a Swiss cheese, but variations are produced in France. France and Switzerland argued over the right to the name, which was finally granted to both by the Convention of Stresa in 1951. Made from cow's milk, Swiss Gruyère has a smooth, uniform paste with only a very few pea-sized holes, and a dark-brown natural rind. It is similar to Emmenthal in appearance and nut-like taste. Apart from being a good table cheese it is much used in fondues, sauces and quiches, since it does not get stringy. It is made in large wheel shapes.

LANCASHIRE

A mild-tasting cow's milk cheese from England, this is similar to white Cheshire. It melts well and thus lends itself well to cooking (particularly toasting). It is made in cylinder or block shapes and can be sold as wedges.

CHEDDAR

England's most famous cheese, this is made from cow's milk and varies from mild to very sharp. Cheddar cheeses are now made throughout the world, usually in a large, cylinder shape with a natural rind. A very versatile cooking cheese, since it doesn't get stringy. Cheddar can be used in sauces, soufflés, salads and pizzas. It is also good eaten on its own, or with apple pie.

CAERPHILLY

This is a cow's milk cheese from Wales with a mild, slightly sour taste. Usually made in cylinder shapes it is a good snack and dessert cheese. It hardly ripens at all.

Cheddar

Caerphilly

Gruyère

LEYDEN

A semi-hard Dutch cheese covered with a dark yellow rind and then with red wax. It is made from the whole or skim cow's milk and contains whole caraway and cumin seeds. Made in cylinder shapes, Leyden or Leiden goes well with cold cuts and make a good snack cheese.

EDAM

A mild, bland, buttery Dutch cheese with a thin natural rind and red wax coating, it is usually matured for three to four months. Made from cow's milk, it is a slightly harder cheese than Gouda due to its low fat content. Edam is sometimes spiced with cumin seed, and more mature versions are available. It is sold in ball shapes.

JARLSBERG

A Norwegian cheese originating in Oslo in 1959, this ranges from white to light yellow with large holes scattered throughout. It is made from cow's milk and has a firm, buttery interior and a mild, nutty taste. It is covered with a thick rind and then with a yellow wax. A good all-purpose cheese, it is used in the Norwegian *landgang*. Jarlsberg is made in wheel shapes.

Leyden *Gouda*

GOUDA

An excellent, mild Dutch cheese with a soft, buttery paste. Allowed to mature for over a year, Gouda develops an excellent flavor to become one of the world's great cheeses; it can also be eaten fresh. After brining, the cheese develops a natural rind. It is made in wheel shapes.

TILSIT

A firm-textured cow's milk cheese, first made by Dutch cheese-makers living in Tilsit, East Germany, but now produced all over Europe. It has a tangy taste, and is a good cheese for desserts and sandwiches. It can be made in wheel or block shapes.

Edam

Tilsit

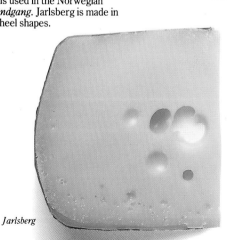

Jarlsberg

OTHER SEMI-HARD CHEESES

APPENZELLER
A Swiss cheese, cylindrical in form; its name originally derives from the Latin for "abbot's cell". These cheeses ripen in three to six months, during which time they are regularly turned, and washed with a mixture of white wine, water, and herbs.

BELLELAVE
A Swiss cylindrical cheese with a red rind flora. Also called Tête de Moine.

BRICK
A native American cheese first made in Wisconsin in the 1870s and named for its shape. It is a surface-molded cheese with a reddish brown rind which can be waxed. The interior contains small holes and is yellow-white. It is a mild, tangy cheese most often used in sandwiches and in toasting.

CHEVRE
Literally, the name means "goat" cheese, and there are many variations.

COON
A Cheddar-type cheese, this is made by a patent process which includes scalding.

DERBY
An English cheese from Derbyshire. It has a natural rind, firm paste, mild flavor, and comes in cartwheel shapes weighing about 35 lbs. Used as a toasting cheese, it is sometimes flavored with fresh sage leaves, which give green streaks to the cheese. Manufactured in this way, it is known as Sage Derby.

ESROM
A Danish cheese based on the French Port Salut, with a washed red flora rind. It is used in *smorgasbord* recipes.

GAMMELOST
A rapidly ripening Norwegian cheese that develops a unique mold growth on the rind. This is regularly pressed into the paste, and gives the cheese its characteristic sharp and tangy flavor. The paste is soft and dark brown in color.

HAVARTI
A Tilsit-type Danish cheese with an open, lacelike texture and a natural or washed rind – the dry rind gives Havarti a slightly sour taste, the flora on the washed rind makes it taste sharper. Havarti was the name of the farm of the cheese's developer, Mrs Hanne Nielson.

LIMBURGER
Once Belgian but now made in Germany, Limburger is a piquant, sometimes pungent, cheese. The rind is washed with coryne bacteria and the cheese is ripened for a period of about three to four weeks.

PONT L'EVEQUE
A square-shaped, soft cheese, this is one of the oldest from Normandy in France, with a fairly strong taste and aroma. Pont l'Evêque cheeses have a washed rind and are packed in small chipwood boxes in the manner of Camembert.

REBLOCHON
A French cheese from the Haute-Savoie, a mountainous region where the cheese is ripened in caves. Reblochon is a rich, creamy cheese with a mild flavor and washed rind. Its name means "second milking", because the French herdsmen who originally made it used milk from a second, illegal, milking.

SAMSO
Originally a Danish copy of the Swiss Emmenthal, this was named Samso from the island on which it was made. Related cheeses have the suffix "bo" added to the name of the island or town of manufacture: Danbo is a square-shaped cheese with a natural rind, and sometimes contains caraway seeds; Fynbo is similar to Samso, but smaller in size, and the paste has smaller holes; Elbo has a more regular, firm paste with few holes and a natural rind; Tybo is a smaller, quite solid cheese with the same fat content; Molbo shares characteristics with Dutch Edam, being shaped like a ball with a red rind; similarly, Maribo is like Dutch Gouda, but contains tiny holes and has a red wax rind.

SAUERMILCHKASE
A family of German cheeses made from low-fat milk, soured by a lactic acid starter, and without use of rennet. They vary considerably in shape, but all have a rind flora which gives them a color ranging from pale yellow to red-brown. The taste is sourish and sharp, and some cheeses have the addition of spices. Varieties include such cheeses as Mainzer, Harzer, Handkäse, Spitkäse and Strangenkäse.

Hard, Blue and Smoked Cheeses

PROVOLONE

Now made from cow's milk, but originally from buffalo's milk, this is a drawn curd cheese made in America, Italy and Australia. It is found in a variety of shapes such as pear, cone or cylinder and is hung by cords to mature and harden. All Provolones are smoked. The younger ones are milder and softer, and are used as table cheeses; the older, more robust and harder cheeses are used in cooking. Provolone is often used in cannelloni and ravioli.

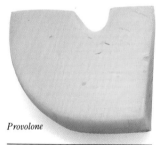

Provolone

PECORINO

A variety of hard *grana* cheese made from sheep's milk in central and southern Italy. Pecorino Romano is made by heating the milk, curdling with rennet, finely cutting the curd and pressing. The cheese matures in about eight months. Pecorino Sardo is made on the island of Sardinia, while Pecorino Pepato, made in Sicily, has added peppercorns. They are used both as table cheeses, and for grating.

Pecorino

PARMESAN

Parmesan cheese or, more correctly, Parmigiano Reggiano, is the noblest of a group of Italian cheeses known collectively as *formaggi di grana*, meaning hard cheeses with a grainy texture. The wheel-shaped, golden-colored cow's milk cheeses are made of finely cut, carefully separated curd, which is then stirred and scalded to 137°F before being pressed. The cheeses are salted over a period of weeks, after which they mature for two to three years, or even longer – they are categorized as *vecchio* (old), *stravecchio* (extra old), *tipico* (four or five years old), or *giovane* (less mature table cheese). Other *grana* cheeses include Grana Padano, made in considerable quantity throughout Lombardy, Grana Lodigiano, a low-fat cheese with an "eyed" paste of small holes, and Grana Lombardo from around Milan. Grana cheeses are widely used as a grating type for typically Italian recipes, such as minestrone, or pasta, and they may be incorporated in sauces.

Parmesan

SAPSAGO

A Swiss cheese made from soured skim milk, Sapsago is also known as green cheese because of its pale green color, due to the presence of clover which is added to the curd. It is a hard cheese which is normally grated before use, and makes a good all-purpose cooking cheese.

CACIOCAVALLO

An Italian cheese made from cow's milk, Caciocavallo is, like Provolone, one of the *pasta filata*, or "drawn curd" cheeses (in which the curds are softened by hot water, which means that they can be easily shaped by hand). Made by nomads, Caciocavallo means "cheese on horseback" since it is said to resemble saddle bags. It is an ancient Roman cheese. Made in gourdlike shapes, the young cheeses are used for snacks or desserts; older cheeses become hard and granular and are then used for grating and cooking.

Caciocavallo

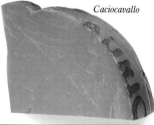

SBRINZ

A Swiss grating cheese, this is made from cow's milk by finely cutting the curd and scalding at temperatures above 130°F. The cheese is pressed to form a flat disc or wheel, then brined and "sweated" at 68°F for about four months, after which it is racked and left to mature for about two years. Sbrinz is a piquant, aromatic cheese, used as a table variety, and also for cooking, since it grates well, and is used for sauces and soufflés.

Sbrinz

Sapsago

Smoked cheese

SMOKED CHEESE

Traditionally made in long sausage shapes, this is used mainly as a snack cheese. The most commonly used cheeses are Emmenthal and Cheddar, but other cheeses may also be smoked and found in this form.

Mycella

GORGONZOLA

With Roquefort and Stilton, Gorgonzola is one of the three premier blue cheeses. In the manufacture of Gorgonzola, Italy's most famous blue cheese, the mould culture *Penicillium gorgonzola* is added to the curds with the starter. The curds are cut and packed into molds, then the unripe cheese is salted, pricked with needles and left for three months to develop the veining. It is used for stuffing pears, in *mousse au fromage*, and in salads. The cheese is pleasantly sharp in flavor, with a softish, white paste and greenish veins. It is fatter in texture than Roquefort and moister than Stilton.

Gorgonzola

MYCELLA

A Danish cheese made from cow's milk, Mycella has blue-green veins. It is usually made in tall, cylinder shapes, though smaller

ROQUEFORT

Considered by many to be the king of cheeses, Roquefort is a sheep's milk cheese from the Causes area of France. It is made in cylinder shapes and has a rich, strong taste. The success of Roquefort is due to the unique, very humid environment in the complex of local caves. The unripe Roqueforts are left to mature in the caves of Combalou mountain, where the moisture-laden air freely circulates spores of *Penicillium glaucum*, var. *roqueforti*, and in about six weeks the cheeses start to "blue". Roquefort is used for *tartelettes au Roquefort*, as a table cheese, and in salad dressing.

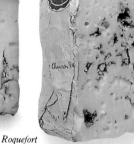

Roquefort

pieces are often sold foil-wrapped. It is used mainly as a table cheese, but can also be used to add a certain tang to both salads and salad dressings.

OTHER HARD CHEESES

ASIAGO
An Italian cow's milk cheese from the province of Vicenza in the north-west. There are two types: the Asiago d'Allevio made from a mixture of skim and whole milk, producing a fairly piquant, grating cheese, and the Asiago Grasso di Monte, with a smoother texture and a mellower flavor. Asiago is used in many recipes that

require a grating cheese, such as soups, pasta and meat dishes.

BERGKASE
This is a large, cartwheel-shaped Austrian cheese with a smooth, uniform texture and mild flavor, made from cow's milk. The curds are finely cut and the cheese hard-pressed until a natural rind develops.

KEFALOTYRI
A popular hard Greek cheese, meaning "head cheese", made by finely cutting and stirring the cow's milk curds, which are then heated before being pressed into molds – resulting shapes often resemble skulls or hats. They are then dry-salted, and left to mature for several months. The cheese is used as a grating type in several national dishes.

Blue Cheeses

BLUE CASTELLO
A Danish double cream soft-textured cheese made from cow's milk.

Blue Castello

DANISH BLUE
Lacking a national blue cheese, Danish cheese-makers in the early nineteenth century began experiments with mold cultures and came up with a selection of excellent blue cheeses, of which Danish Blue or Danablu is the most renowned. Made from homogenized cow's milk, it is soft-textured and creamy with a fairly strong taste, and makes a good dessert cheese. It is made in wheel shapes. Blucreme, another Danish blue cheese type, is an internal-mold cheese with added cream that is smoother and creamier than Danish Blue. It is made in 10 lb-loaves.

Bleu de Bresse

PIPO CREM'
A popular French blue-veined cow's milk cheese made in long cylinder shapes. Pipo Crem' is larger and creamier than Bleu de Bresse and comes from Ain in the same region.

Pipo Crem'

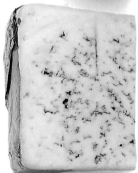

Danish Blue

BLEU DE BRESSE
A creamy French blue-veined cheese made from cow's milk, this is soft-textured and has a rich taste. It has a slightly higher fat content (50 per cent) than most blue cheeses, and weighs about 4½ lbs. Made in small cylinder shapes and often foil-wrapped, it is a good dessert cheese and is also used in *fromage cardinal* – a blend of cheese and paprika.

FOURME D'AMBERT
This is a strongly flavored, closely veined blue cow's milk cheese from the Haute-Savoie region of France. It is made in tall cylinder shapes.

Fourme d'Ambert

DOLCELATTE
Literally "sweet milk", this is an Italian blue cheese, made from cow's milk, with a very soft creamy texture, and greenish colored veining throughout. It is a factory-made version of the famous Gorgonzola. It is made in cylinder shapes.

Dolcelatte

Bavarian Blue

BLUE CHESHIRE

A worthy rival to Stilton, Blue Cheshire is a large, cylindrical blue version of the dyed Cheshire cheese, and one of the finest of all blues. Made from cow's milk, cheese ripens and "blues" only accidentally, although cheese-makers try and encourage the mold by pricking the cheese with needles and maturing it in a favorable atmosphere. It has a rich taste and is best served as a dessert cheese.

Blue Cheshire

BAVARIAN BLUE

A double cream, soft-textured blue-veined cheese with a mildly sour taste from West Germany, this is very rich and high in fat (70 per cent). Made from cow's milk, it has a creamy texture and spreads well, making it good for sandwiches. It has a molded surface and is made in small wheel shapes.

Stilton

BLUE SHROPSHIRE

A new arrival among blue cheeses, this is made not, as its name would suggest, in the English county of Shropshire, but in Scotland. It comes in cylinder shapes.

STILTON

Stilton is a relative newcomer to the great blue cheeses. Gorgonzola and Roquefort cheeses have been made for a thousand years or more, but Stilton first drew public attention in the early eighteenth century. Tradition has it that the cheese was first produced in Leicestershire, England, by a Mrs Paulet, and supplied to the Bell Inn at Stilton.

Stilton is a rich cow's milk cheese. White Stilton is sold when fairly young, but the Blue (shown here) requires about six months to develop. Steel needles are driven into the cheese, and it is left to ripen. It develops a natural rind, brown and crinkly. It is sold in tall cylinders which help to distinguish it from Gorgonzola and Roquefort.

Blue Shropshire

OTHER BLUE CHEESES

BLEU D'AUVERGNE
A small 4–5-lb cheese from the French Auvergne region, made by inoculating the curd, or sprinkling the surface, with *Penicillium glaucum* mold. The cheese is first washed, then dry-salt rubbed and pierced with needles to encourage the formation of mold.

BLEU DE CORSE
A white sheep's milk cheese produced on the Corsican plains, it develops interior mold to become "blue". Other cheeses of this type are sent to mature in the Roquefort caves.

BLEU DE GEX
A cheese from the Jura mountains with a firm paste, mild flavor and delicate blue veining; there is a very similar cheese from neighbouring Septmoncel, the Bleu de Septmoncel. Both weigh 12–15 lbs. Bleu de Sassenage, from the Isère, is also similar, but firmer in texture and much smaller.

BLEU DE LAQUEUILLE
This is a fairly modern French cheese from Puy-de-Dome, introduced in 1850. Like most French blue cheeses it is quite small, 5–6 lbs. It has a dry rind and mellow flavor.

BLEU DE L'AVEYRON
A French cheese matured in the natural caves of the Massif Central, a feature which it shares with Bleu de Causses and the famous Roquefort. This small, local blue cheese has a fine, delicate flavor and soft texture.

LYMESWOLD
This creamy, mild, blue-veined cheese was created in 1982 as an English rival to blue Brie. There are several varieties, all made in small wheel shapes. It is eaten on its own as a snack or dessert cheese.

FISH AND SEAFOOD

MARINE AND FRESHWATER fish were an important part of man's diet long before prehistoric societies learned to cultivate vegetables and domesticate animals. Fish provided protein and vitamins, and were easy to catch and prepare – it is even likely that a large proportion was eaten raw.

In Egypt, fish were abundant and cheap – cheaper than bread. Fish such as carp, barbel, bleak and loach were supplied by rivers and lakes, grey mullet and tuna by the sea. Even in early history the people of the Iberian peninsula were catching anchovies, sardines and cod, salting them, and exporting the resulting *bacalao* as far away as Asia Minor.

In Europe, pike provided both sport and feast, while in Scotland salmon was so common in the seventeenth century that a law was passed forbidding employers to give it to their servants more than three times a week. Carp – freshwater fish that often attained formidable proportions – were reared in ponds and lakes throughout Europe, the Middle East, and in China and Japan, where they provided inspiration for poets and cooks alike.

The most valuable fish of all time is the herring, which still supplies one-third of the world's catch – some 20 million tons. Today, cod, mackerel and tuna follow closely behind.

Fish in the kitchen
Fish are a good source of high-grade protein and most are low in fat. They contain a wide range of essential vitamins and minerals, together with certain fatty acids which seem to be valuable in preventing heart disease. They can be cooked in various ways, including frying, sautéeing, baking, broiling, steaming, poaching and barbecuing.

Choosing fish
Fish has a shorter storage life than most meats, so it is particularly important to select the freshest fish you can find. For this reason also, fish should always be cooked as soon as possible. Fresh fish have bulging eyes, firmly adhering scales and firm flesh; fish should never have an offensive odor. They can be kept refrigerated for no more than a day and should be frozen if they are not to be cooked within that time. Only freeze fish if you caught it yourself. *Never* freeze fish bought from a fishmonger as it may not be freshly caught, and may have been frozen before it reached the fishmonger.

Types of fish
There are more than 20,000 species of fish in the seas of the world, yet we exploit a mere fraction of this huge potential harvest. Admittedly, at least 50 per cent are commercially unacceptable, but of the remainder only about a dozen different fish regularly appear in the marketplace. The Portuguese and Japanese are exceptions. In the Tokyo market over 60 species are sold each day, and Japanese fishing boats scour the oceans to bring home the national daily average – about 7000 tons of fish – most of which will be eaten raw, as *sashimi*.

Elsewhere in the world tastes are more conservative. The bulk of the European catch consists mainly of cod, hake, herring, macherel, pilchard and anchovy, if only because they are so abundant; about a dozen species, out of a possible 160 types of fish inhabiting the Mediterranean and Altanic, are regularly in demand. Americans are fortunate in having a large number of saltwater fish available all year round. They include salmon, flounder, cod, halibut, trout, perch and bass.

It is not possible within the scope of this book to give a detailed list of the many fish eaten, but a selection of the most prominent ones are illustrated and described in the following pages. For a fully comprehensive list of fish and their uses, refer to the *Multilingual Dictionary of Fish and Fish Products* (United Nations).

SEAFOOD

Seafood consists largely of "shellfish" – the term includes edible freshwater and marine animals without backbones, the crustaceans and molluscs. Crustaceans, such as lobsters, prawns and crabs, have a hard, jointed exoskeleton or "crust" which they periodically shed and replace as they grow. Molluscs inhabit shells that are either hinged, like oysters and clams, or single, like the abalone, whelk, and winkle. For culinary purposes, other molluscs (such as land snails and the shell-less marine animals squid, cuttlefish and octopus), and edible frogs, have traditionally been considered as seafood.

Shellfish are prized for their tender, fine-textured flesh which can be prepared simply in a variety of decorative and delicious ways, but they are notorious for rapid spoilage. It is essential that they be extremely fresh or, if frozen, be consumed immediately on thawing, and come from unpolluted waters.

Fresh shellfish are available all year round, but their availability reflects seasonal and regional demands which, for most shellfish, reach a peak during the salad days of summer. Oysters are traditionally eaten in colder months when they are fatter and tastier.

Choosing seafood

To ensure freshness and the best flavor, it is preferable to choose live specimens and cook them yourself Freshwater crawfish, lobsters, rock lobsters and crabs should be very active and a rock lobster's or lobster's tail should curl up under its body when picked up. Fresh shrimps and prawns, usually only available in fish markets near the sea, should be crisp and dry; stale ones are limp.

Live mussel, clam, and oyster shells should be tightly closed. Any open ones which do not clamp shut when tapped sharply are stale or dead and should be discarded. Scallops may be alive when their shells are open – touch the inner membrane and it will move. Like snails, whelks and other gastropods will recede into their shell when touched. Once cooked, mussel, clam and oyster shells should open. If any do not, discard them. Some people think that bivalves, especially oysters, are best eaten raw when the shells have just been opened by hand (and the aid of a sharp oyster knife). It is sometimes possible to buy them like this on the half-shell or to buy them shucked in containers.

Crustaceans are often sold cooked and they should smell fresh and pleasant. A freshly boiled lobster or rock lobster should have a dry, bright shell with no cracks or holes in it and the tail will be tight and springy if the animal was alive when it was cooked. A stale-bodied lobster or rock lobster has a limp tail and legs which smell unpleasant. The same generally applies to crabs, which may also have a bleached appearance. Select a cooked crustacean that is heavy for its size.

When molluscs are not sold fresh, they are usually pickled in vinegar or brine, or canned. When pickled, they are often eaten raw with beer or other beverages, but if used in salads or similar preparations they should be rinsed first with cold water. Canned molluscs and crustaceans are already cooked. Commercially frozen ones may require cooking.

Preparing shellfish

A lobster or rock lobster should be prepared for broiling by being laid on its back and having a heavy, sharp knife inserted between the body and tail shell to sever the spinal column and kill the animal. The shell is split lengthways and the inedible bits removed. Lobster claws should be cracked. Lobster and rock lobster should be placed meat side up under the broiler (about 4 inches away from heat), cooked for 10 to 12 minutes, and basted frequently with melted butter. Crabs should be put into warm water, around 70°F for 30 minutes before boiling – a crab dropped straight into boiling water will shed its claws – covered tightly, simmered for 8 minutes per pound and left to cool in the water.

Raw or cooked shrimps, jumbo shrimps, and freshwater crawfish are prepared by having the head, upper shell (carapace), legs, tail section and dark intestinal vein running down the back removed. If raw, they are put into boiling water, steamed for 3 to 4 minutes or dipped in butter and deep-fried for 2 to 3 minutes or until golden. Every part of a lobster, rock lobster, and crab can be eaten except the grayish gill, aptly named "dead men's fingers", the hard stomach behind the eyes and, in the lobster, the black intestinal vein running through the body. The lobster's tan-colored liver or "tomally" (which turns green on cooking) can be left in the animal or removed and added to sauces.

The male lobster and rock lobster are slightly larger and have more meat than the female, but a female may contain the "berry" (coral or eggs), which is not only delicious to eat when cooked in the animal, but can also be used as a garnish for other dishes. Female crabs similarly have smaller claws than males and may contain brown eggs, also called berry.

All molluscs should be washed well and be left in several changes of fresh water (clams overnight) to help rid them of saltiness and sand before cooking. Scallops should have the membrane or mantle around the white meat discarded, but both the meat and red roe can be eaten. Oysters and scallops are shucked before cooking – oysters only need heating through, which takes about 1 minute; scallops are boiled, steamed or sautéed for 1 to 2 minutes, depending on size. Mussels should have the "beards" removed and may also need thorough scrubbing. Mussels and other molluscs are usually steamed or boiled in their shells for 1 to 2 minutes.

Freezing shellfish

Shellfish may be frozen if freshly caught, but they must be absolutely fresh and kept frozen only up to one month. To freeze, scrub and remove the molluscs from their shells, wash them in salted cold water, drain, pack in rigid containers with the strained juices (leaving room for expansion), cover, label and seal. Once thawed, they are best used in soups and sauces, added towards the end of cooking. Shrimps, jumbo shrimps, and freshwater crawfish may be frozen with their heads removed, either raw or lightly boiled and cooled, sealed in plastic bags, and labelled. Lobster and rock lobster should be cooked, cooled and frozen the same day they are caught. Crabs should be cooked and cooled and the meat removed from the shell and packed in containers.

Preparing squid, cuttlefish and octopus

Fresh squid (calamari) and cuttlefish are prepared by having their tentacles and head pulled from the tail, or body, section. Any intact ink sac is removed from the head and may be reserved for use in cooking. The head and inner organs are discarded. The thin cuttlebone is pulled from the tail section, the bone discarded and then the animal washed and rubbed under cool running water so that its reddish violet membrane is removed.

Once prepared, squid with tail sections less than 3 inches long can be poached, broiled, or sliced into rounds, leaving the tentacles in one piece, battered, and fried quickly in oil. Larger squid and cuttlefish are usually sliced and stewed as they need longer, slower cooking to become tender, but they, like octopus, can also be stuffed with a mixture of chopped tentacles, beaten eggs and herbs and braised with wine. For octopus, the beaklike mouth and anal portion are cut away. The ink sac can be used in the stew. The body is turned inside out and the internal organs, suckers and tips of the tentacles are removed. After cleaning, unless the octopus is young (under 2 lbs), the flesh should be softened by pounding and stewed for 2½ to 3 hours, until it is easily pierced with a knife.

Preparing snails and frogs' legs

Snails are widely available already prepared and frozen or, more usually, canned, but they can be prepared at home using either the common garden snail (*Helix aspersia*) or the more succulent variety used in France (*H. pomatia*). Before the creatures can be prepared, however, they must be starved for two days, then fed on lettuce for two weeks to purge them of any poisons they might have ingested. Their shells are then scrubbed and rinsed in several changes of water mixed with vinegar and salt. Snails whose heads do not come out should be discarded; the remainder dropped in boiling water and cooked for 5 minutes. Once drained and cooled, the snails are removed from their shells, their intestinal sacs discarded, and simmered in a *court bouillon* until tender. The shells are boiled briefly in water and bicarbonate of soda, drained, scrubbed, and rinsed.

Farms have been established in many countries to provide frogs' legs. Skinned and immersed in several changes of water to make the flesh swell and become whiter, the legs are prepared for specialty shops or for commercial canning and freezing.

Freshwater Fish

CARP

There are several varieties of this fish, native to eastern Asia but now found in ponds, lakes and rivers in most parts of the world. It is popular in America, France and England and, although available all year round, is at its best in winter. It tends to have a muddy taste and should be scaled, cleaned and soaked in mildly salted water for 3 to 4 hours before cooking. It can be baked, poached, fried, steamed or braised. In China, carp are often cooked with a sweet and sour sauce; in Europe they are stuffed and jellied.

Other members of the carp family include roach, dace, chub, tench, gudgeon, barbel and bream.

Carp

Pike

PIKE

Available in the northern hemisphere, pike can be bought fresh, whole (if small) or in fillets (if large). It can be baked, braised, poached, sautéed or broiled. It is particularly popular in central European cooking, where it is stuffed and baked with oysters, anchovies, butter and herbs.

EEL

This fish, which is spawned in the ocean and travels to fresh water to mature, is particularly popular in Europe, Japan and New Zealand. There are several varieties. It can be boiled, fried or broiled and made into soups and stews or jellied. Available all year round, it can be bought fresh, frozen or smoked.

Eel

SALMON

Found in cooler waters throughout the northern hemisphere, salmon is one of the world's finest food fish. Delicate and tasty, its firm, oily flesh can vary in color from pink to dark red; Pacific varieties tend to be darker. Most salmon mature at sea but return to coastal streams to spawn, depending on the variety, during several weeks from December to August when the fish is generally available fresh.

Canned salmon, frozen salmon steaks and smoked salmon are available all year round. Pickled salmon is excellent as an hors d'oeuvre, while marinated salmon or *gravad lax* is a mainstay of Scandinavian cuisine. There are many fine recipes for fresh salmon; it can be broiled or poached in *court-bouillon*, and served, hot or cold, with an appropriate sauce, or prepared cold in aspic.

Salmon trout

SALMON TROUT

Also called sea trout, this north Atlantic, Baltic, and North Sea fish is often confused with salmon as it returns from the sea to spawn in European coastal rivers. At its best during the northern summer months, its pale pink and delicate-tasting flesh is particularly good poached and served cold or used to prepare dishes such as salmon trout in aspic. All methods of preparing trout or salmon are applicable to salmon trout. It is quite often served as a substitute for salmon.

Salmon

TROUT

Native to Europe and now found worldwide, there are many varieties of trout: brook, lake, rainbow or steelhead, brown, salmon (see opposite), and arctic char. The type shown is a rainbow trout. It is usually cooked whole and can be bought fresh, frozen or smoked. Available all year round, trout can be prepared *au bleu, à la meunière, en papillote,* in aspic, baked, poached, sautéed, broiled or grilled.

Trout

OTHER FRESHWATER FISH

CATFISH
Most varieties are freshwater and include blue, channel, yellow or gonion, spotted or fiddle and bullhead or horned pout. There are a few species of sea catfish, including wolf fish and the spotted catfish. Caught in Northern waters, catfish is usually sold as fillets. Popular in the South, its sweet white flesh is often coated with cornmeal and deep- or pan-fried.

GRAYLING
This is a beautiful silvery fish with a thyme-like scent, hence its Latin name *Thymallus*. It is also an excellent table fish, best prepared *au bleu,* or stuffed with herbs, and baked. It is caught in the northern hemisphere.

WHITEFISH
These are herringlike freshwater fish found in lakes throughout the northern hemisphere. Other species and sub-species include the houting, powan, vendace and northern white. They can be successfully substituted for trout.

Seawater Fish

WHITEBAIT

The name given to the fry (young) of herrings and sprats, these tiny silvery fish are found in the Mediterranean and the Atlantic. Available all year round, they are at their best in spring and summer. They are sold fresh or frozen and are so small they do not need gutting or trimming. Deliciously flavored and tiny they are usually served whole as fritters in a light egg batter.

SARDINE

The many species of this strong-tasting oily fish, prolific in the Atlantic and the Mediterranean, can vary a great deal in size. The name "sardine" is reserved for the younger fish; older ones are called "pilchards" (3 or 4 larger fish will make a good portion). Available all year round, sardines are sold fresh, or canned in oil or various sauces. When fresh, they can be baked, fried, broiled or grilled.

HERRING

A small 7–16-inch oily fish found in the Atlantic and Pacific, the herring was once so cheap that it was dismissed as fit only for the poor. Now, however, it has become a great delicacy. Sold fresh either whole or filleted, it can be stuffed, baked, fried, broiled, casseroled, or made into salads. It is also available smoked or canned. Its extreme oiliness makes it ideal for curing, as in rollmops, soured and marinated herrings, buckling, matjes, bloaters, red herrings and kippers (pages 186–7, 191). Herrings are at their best during summer. There are several herringlike fish in the Pacific. There is even a freshwater variety.

Whitebait

Sardine

Smelt

Sprat

Herring

Mackerel

SMELT

Often confused with the sprat, the smelt is, in fact, a member of the salmon family and as such is far more delicate and less oily by nature. It is found generally in the Baltic and around Britain; another type is caught in the Gulf of St Lawrence. Its bones are so soft that it is often eaten whole. Smelt is usually eaten deep-fried.

SPRAT

A rich, oily fish closely related to the herring and found on the coasts of Europe, the sprat or brisling is available fresh, canned or smoked (page 188) and can be barbecued, baked, fried or broiled. Smoked sprats packed in oil are a popular delicacy in northern and eastern Europe.

MACKEREL

Scomber is the true mackerel caught in the Atlantic and Mediterranean, although there are several related species. These include the chub or Spanish mackerel, the scad or horse mackerel and the Jack mackerel, amberjack and pompano of American and Southeast Asian waters. A fatty, dark-fleshed fish, it lends itself particularly well to barbecueing, baking, smoking (page 187) or broiling. It can be cooked in white wine or eaten raw with lemon juice or a similarly acid garnish to counteract its richness. It is available all year round.

HADDOCK

Usually smoked and known worldwide as Finnan haddie or Arbroath smokies (page 187), this North Atlantic fish is also available fresh or frozen all year round as both fillets and steaks. Its firm flesh is particularly good sautéed with almonds.

Haddock

MONKFISH

A deep-sea fish found off the Mediterranean and Atlantic coasts of Europe, Africa and America, the monkfish or anglerfish has such an ugly, heavy head that usually only the tail is sold. Its flesh is firm, white and succulent and is said to resemble lobster in taste. It can be poached, baked, steamed, fried or broiled and is excellent served hot with an herbed butter sauce such as Choron or Hollandaise; cold with mayonnaise, or cubed, battered and deep-fried with tartar sauce.

COLEY

A soft-fleshed white fish related to cod and pollack, coley (or coalfish or saithe) is fished extensively all year round in the North Sea and north Atlantic. Usually sold as fresh or frozen fillets, the flesh is pinkish-grey but becomes white when cooked. Though it is not suited to broiling, it can otherwise be cooked like cod, and is generally used in soups, fish pies and casseroles. It is usually salted in Scandinavia; in Germany, where it is known as *seelachs*, it is mostly smoked, and canned in oil.

Coley

Pollack

POLLACK

Pollack is caught all year round off north Atlantic coasts from Newfoundland to northern Europe and is available fresh in many local markets. It has fairly firm white flesh and can be prepared like fresh hake or cod, though its taste is considered slightly inferior. It is good used in mixed fish soups such as the French *bourride* or *chaudré*, in stews, or poached and served with a sauce like Creole sauce. In America the Alaska or walleye pollack is salted, dried or pickled.

Monkfish

Ling

LING

Ling or sea turbot, a member of the cod family, was once so popular it was called "beef of the sea". Today, however, its soft white flesh is usually only available smoked. When found fresh, ling should be cooked like hake. Tusk is closely related.

GRAY MULLET

No relation to the smaller, firmer-fleshed red mullet, the gray mullet has a very distinct taste and oily flesh. Available in autumn and early winter, it can be bought whole or in fillets. The smaller fish are suitable for broiling; larger ones can be stuffed and baked.

SEA BREAM

Found in the Atlantic, Pacific and Mediterranean, the bream family contains over 200 species of red, gray and bluish varieties including the porgy and scup. All have firm, white flesh though the red bream or daurade is reputed by connoisseurs to have the best taste. Available all year round, sea bream is usually bought fresh and whole. The larger fish can be braised, baked and stuffed, while the smaller ones can be very good if broiled or barbecued whole.

Gray mullet

Whiting

WHITING

Whiting, or silver hake, is a European seawater fish found off coasts from the Baltic to the Mediterranean. The Norway trout and blue whiting are fished in the North Atlantic and Mediterranean. Available whole or in fillets, it can be fried, poached, baked or broiled. It is available all year round.

Sea bream

HAKE

Varieties of hake are found almost all over the world. Hake is a large seawater fish of the cod family with slightly firmer white flesh and is available all year round. Small pieces of hake weighing 2–3 lbs can be poached whole; larger hake are cut into fillets, steaks or cutlets and sold fresh or frozen, canned or smoked. These can be sautéed, fried or broiled, but they are usually poached in seasoned fish stock or *court bouillon* and served with lemon or herb butter. They are also poached, chilled and served with mayonnaise. Hake is an excellent fish to use in stews, casseroles and soups, and it can be used in any recipe that calls for cod or haddock.

Hake

Cod

COD

One of the world's most important food fishes, cod is found in the cold northern waters of the Atlantic, mainly off the coasts of New England, Newfoundland, Iceland and Norway. It has soft white flesh and can grow to a weight of 80 lbs. Codlings weighing under 2½ lbs are sometimes called "scrod", and their flesh is firmer and sweeter. Available in the northern hemisphere all year round, cod is sold whole when fresh and small (when it is particularly suited to poaching and baking), and in fresh or frozen fillets and steaks (which can be fried or broiled). It is also available salted, smoked and dried (page 185), in which form it is an important ingredient in Mediterranean and Caribbean cooking. Cod's roe is also sold fresh, canned and smoked (page 189).

SEA BASS

One of a large group of seawater fish which includes groupers, the sea bass (also called striped bass or loup de mer) is found in the north Atlantic and Mediterranean. Freshwater bass such as the large mouth, smallmouth, rock, white (or silver) and yellow bass are also available. Sea bass is a firm, white fish which can weigh up to 10 lbs – although sea bass caught off the Pacific coast can weigh twice this – but the ones sold for cooking purposes are usually a good deal smaller. Usually bought fresh, sea bass is available whole or in steaks and fillets, all of which are suitable for the kitchen. Ways of cooking sea bass include poaching, stuffing with fresh or dried herbs and baking, or broiling.

Sea bass

RED MULLET

This 1–2-lb fish is native to the Atlantic, and now also found in the coastal waters of the Mediterranean. Available all year round, but at its best during the summer months, it has firm, tasty white flesh and is suitable for frying, baking or broiling. Many people prefer to leave the liver inside during cooking. It is also known as the sea woodcock, since, like the same bird, it is often cooked and eaten whole and ungutted.

Red mullet

RED SNAPPER

This Gulf of Mexico fish can weigh up to 31 lbs and has choice white creamy flesh. Those under 5 lbs are usually baked whole and stuffed. Larger fish are cut into fillets or steaks and can be prepared in a variety of ways: broiled with lemon-butter, deep-fried and served with *rémoulade* sauce, sautéed, poached, or used in soups. Available all year round, it is usually sold fresh, although it is also available frozen in America. Species such as gray snapper are also available, but they are smaller and inferior in taste.

Red snapper

OTHER SEAWATER FISH

ARGENTINE
There are several varieties, including the lesser argentine or silver smelt, the larger argentine or great silver smelt and the eastern, deep-sea argentine of Japan. All these small, silvery fish may be broiled or fried. They are found in the north Atlantic, Pacific and Mediterranean.

BLUE FISH
This is found on the Atlantic coast of America and in the Mediterranena. It can be broiled, fried, or baked with tomatoes, onions and herbs.

BONITO
Caught in Atlantic, Pacific and Mediterranean waters, bonito is of the tuna family, and is generally marketed cut into steaks. It is also salted.

CONGER EEL
Although it can be stuffed and baked, conger eel is best used for soups and stews. It is caught off the Atlantic coast of Europe, Africa and in the Mediterranean.

CROAKER
Caught off the eastern coast of North America, this fish is cooked in the same way as bass.

DOLPHIN FISH
This large golden fish, caught in warm waters, is also known as lampuga or dorado. It is usually bought as fillets or steaks, which can be broiled, baked or fried.

GARFISH
The slightly oily flesh of this fish (also called the garpike or sea eel) is sometimes compared to mackerel. It can be fried or broiled.

GROUPER
This is a common Mediterranean fish, especially

along the north African coast. The steaks can be broiled or baked.

GULF HAKE
There are two varieties of gulf hake: the lesser or tadpole fish and the greater or forkbeard. The lesser is black-skinned; the greater resembles a small pollack. Both are cooked in the same ways as hake.

GURNARD
Also called the sea robin, this is an armor-plated, spiny fish, including the red gurnard and the ray gurnard. There are also several Mediterranean species. Gurnard can be baked or braised.

MEAGRE
The meagre is found in the Atlantic and Mediterranean. It can be prepared as for bass.

NEEDLEFISH
The needlefish, skipper or saury closely resembles the garfish, but is plumper. It can be fried or broiled

OCEAN PERCH
This is caught in the Atlantic and the Mediterranean, though there is also a freshwater European variety. Other related species are the Norway haddock and the blue mouth. All are rather coarse, and best used in soups and chowders.

OPAH
Also known as kingfish, sunfish or moonfish, this is a large, beautifully colored fish, with a plump oval body. It can be fried, and in Japan is eaten raw. It is available worldwide.

ROCKLING
There are several types of rockling found among the coasts of Europe and off Newfoundland. They should be cooked as for whiting.

SHAD
Shad are a larger, plumper type of herring found in the Atlantic, Mediterrean and Pacific, but mostly caught in rivers, where they come to spawn. Shad can be treated like herring, and are also smoked or canned in brine or oil.

STURGEON
The fish is famous for its roe, made into caviar (page 189), but less known for its flesh, which is also of good quality. It is caught in the Caspian, Black Sea and Danube.

SWORDFISH
Caught in warmer seas, the swordfish is usually sold as steaks. It may be baked or broiled or barbecued.

TILEFISH
A large, deep-water fish which can weigh up to 31 lbs; this is best cooked like cod.

TUNA
Familiar to most people canned, tuna – which has several names including tunny and longfin – is also sold fresh, when it can be broiled, barbecued, baked, or braised with wine, tomatoes and herbs. Tuna also features in *salade Niçoise*.

WEAVER
Caught in European shallow coastal waters, the spines and venom sacs of both the greater and lesser weaver have to be removed before cooking. They are used in *bouillabaisse*, broiled or deep-fried.

Flat Seawater Fish

BRILL
Found in European waters and the Atlantic, it is available all year. It can be cut in halves, slices or fillets and lends itself to baking.

DAB
A small flatfish, the dab is caught in north Atlantic waters off the coast of Europe. The American sand dab is of finer quality. Sold whole or in fillets in Europe, it can be broiled or fried. The best season is April to November.

FLOUNDER
Similar to plaice, the flounder is caught in the Baltic and European Atlantic waters, and there are sub-species in the Mediterranean. (In America the word often applies to several types of flatfish: blackhead, fluke, gray and American lemon sole from Atlantic and South Pacific waters.) Available all year, it is sold fresh and frozen. It can be fried or steamed, whole or in fillets.

Brill

Flounder

Dab

PLAICE
From the North Sea and north Atlantic, plaice is sold fresh and frozen, whole or in fillets. It can be fried or broiled and is available all year round.

Plaice

Skate

OTHER FLAT FISH

JOHN DORY
Acclaimed as one of the best eating fish, John Dory, or related species, is available whole or in fillets, all year, and is suited to all cooking methods.

SKATE
Many varieties are available throughout the world. It is sold fresh and only the "wings" are eaten. Available all year, skate, with its soft sweet flesh, can be poached and served with capers and a black butter sauce (a classic French recipe), fried or broiled.

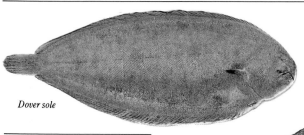

Dover sole

TURBOT

These large inhabitants of the Atlantic coast of Europe, North Sea, Black Sea and Mediterranean are available all year. Sold whole or as steaks or fillets, turbot may be poached or baked; steaks may also be fried, broiled or barbecued.

DOVER SOLE

Dover sole is caught in European waters from southern Norway to the coast of North Africa, and in the Mediterranean, and is exported all over the world. Available fresh or frozen, it can be fried whole or divided into fillets. One of the finest of the smaller flatfish, it is available all year.

Turbot

LEMON SOLE

A fish that is available all year, but at its best from December to March. Although less tasty than the Dover sole, it can be cooked in the same way. Lemon sole is available fresh or frozen, whole or in fillets.

HALIBUT

The largest of the flatfish, varieties include the Greenland halibut, and sub-species. Halibut is caught in the North Atlantic from Newfoundland to Norway, in the Barents Sea and the north Pacific. Steaks are sold fresh or frozen in the northern hemisphere, or frozen, canned or smoked elsewhere, it may be poached or baked.

Lemon sole

Halibut

Crustaceans

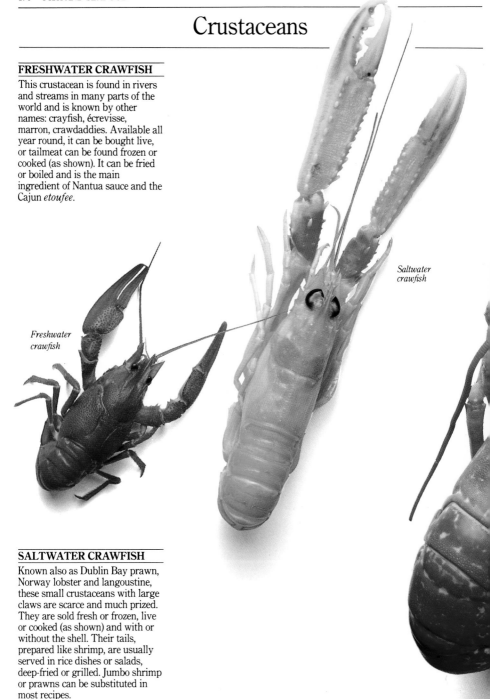

FRESHWATER CRAWFISH

This crustacean is found in rivers and streams in many parts of the world and is known by other names: crayfish, écrevisse, marron, crawdaddies. Available all year round, it can be bought live, or tailmeat can be found frozen or cooked (as shown). It can be fried or boiled and is the main ingredient of Nantua sauce and the Cajun *etoufee*.

Saltwater crawfish

Freshwater crawfish

SALTWATER CRAWFISH

Known also as Dublin Bay prawn, Norway lobster and langoustine, these small crustaceans with large claws are scarce and much prized. They are sold fresh or frozen, live or cooked (as shown) and with or without the shell. Their tails, prepared like shrimp, are usually served in rice dishes or salads, deep-fried or grilled. Jumbo shrimp or prawns can be substituted in most recipes.

Lobster

LOBSTER

Largest of the crustaceans, lobsters are prized for their flavor and generous meat yield. Lobsters are found in Atlantic coast waters from Nova Scotia to North Carolina, and Scandinavia to the Mediterranean. Their flesh is fine-textured and at its best when the animals weighs 1–2 lbs. In addition, the female or "hen" lobster can contain eggs in the form of red roe or coral. There are several varieties. Lobsters are available all year round and can be bought fresh or frozen, live or cooked in the shell. When alive they are dark blue; when cooked (as shown) they turn bright red. Lobster can be baked, steamed, boiled or broiled.

JUMBO SHRIMP

The terms for these small clawless crustaceans vary from country to country, and there are several varieties. Indigenous to the Mediterranean but now also found in the Atlantic and the Pacific, jumpo shrimp can be steamed, stewed or boiled; fried or broiled, and are often used in salads and cold buffet displays. Available fresh or frozen, they are sometimes available cooked, shelled or unshelled.

Cooked whole jumbo shrimps

Uncooked jumbo shrimp

Baby shrimp

Rock lobster

BABY SHRIMP

This tiny crustacean, also known as cocktail shrimp, reaches a maximum of 3 inches in length. They are often boiled on board fishing ship or on reaching port as a precaution against spoilage. Pale pink when raw, baby shrimp are available fresh, frozen or canned.

ROCK LOBSTER

Found worldwide in most temperate coastal waters, the rock lobster (also known as spiny lobster, or langouste), has no claws and weighs 3–8 lbs. Most of the flesh is contained in the tails. Available fresh or frozen, they can be steamed, boiled or grilled.

Crabs

Many species of this crustacean are found in coastal waters throughout the world. Atlantic coast favorites are the blue, Jonah, rock and stone crabs, while the Dungeness and king crabs are renowned on the Pacific coast, especially towards Alaska. Popular European varieties are the blue, common crab, the shore or green crab, and the spider crab. Crabs shed their shells many times before reaching maturity and in some places, from mid-spring to mid-autumn, they are in demand fresh as young "soft-shells" or "peelers", when they have just emerged from their latest shell. At this point they are smaller, with more flavor, and so tender that almost every part of the crab can be eaten. Crab is also sold canned and frozen.

Spider crab

Blue crab

BLUE CRAB

Native to the east coast of America, where it is very popular, the blue crab is also found in the North and South Atlantic and eastern Mediterranean. Available all year round, it can be bought as a soft-shelled crab in the summer. Otherwise it is sold live, uncooked in the shell (as shown), cooked (with or without the shell), fresh, frozen and canned. Blue crab can be baked, steamed or boiled; when cooked it turns red.

Common crab

SPIDER CRAB

Found in the south Atlantic and the Mediterranean, the spider crab is available all year round. It can be bought live uncooked in the shell (as shown), or cooked. It can be baked, steamed or boiled, and turns bright red when cooked.

COMMON CRAB

Found in the Atlantic and Mediterranean, this large crustacean has powerful claws – larger in the male than the female – which, as in other crabs, contain white meat (the shell contains dark meat). It can be bought live, uncooked in the shell (as shown), or cooked (with or without the shell). Available all year round, but at its best in the summer, the common crab can be baked, steamed or boiled. As with most crustaceans, when cooked it turns bright red.

Frogs' Legs and Molluscs

FROGS' LEGS

Prized for their delicate texture, the flesh tastes something like chicken. Only the hind legs of certain frogs (usually *Rana esculenta*) are used. Available frozen or fresh, they are mostly sold ready-prepared. The tender white meat goes well with a variety of flavors, and can be deep-fried or sautéed, stewed or broiled, and is often served with garlic butter. About 4 pairs should be allowed per person.

OCTOPUS

An eight-legged cephalopod mollusc found in all temperate waters, and prepared like squid, the flesh of the octopus should be beaten with a blunt object until no longer springy, and the suckers and end of the legs removed before cooking. When longer than 8 inches, the head is usually discarded, but it can be cleaned, stuffed with the chopped legs, and stewed. Smaller ones can be coated in batter and fried whole.

Frogs' legs

CUTTLEFISH

Found in the Mediterranean, Adriatic and temperate coastal waters, this is prepared like squid and does not require pounding. Those under 8 inches can be sautéed whole in oil, or stuffed and poached. In the case of longer cuttlefish, the body can be cut away and discarded, the 10 legs blanched (with the outer skin peeled away) and stewed.

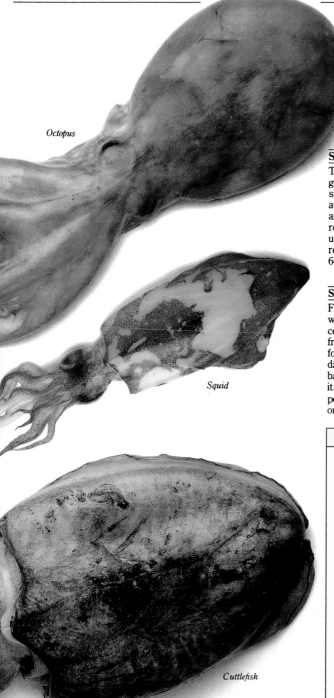

Snail

Octopus

Squid

Cuttlefish

SNAIL

The edible snail or escargot is a gastropod mollusc; gourmet fare since ancient Greece. Widely available canned or frozen, they are sometimes sold fresh. Slightly resilient in texture, they are usually served with garlic butter in reusable shells or dishes. Allow 6–8 per person.

SQUID

Found worldwide in temperate waters, the squid or calamari is a cephalopod mollusc. It is available fresh or frozen. Its ink sacs (only found in fresh animals) contain a dark brown liquid, often used as a basis for a sauce in which to cook it. Smaller squid can be sautéed, poached, boiled or broiled; larger ones are often stewed.

OTHER SEAFOOD

SEA URCHIN
Not a mollusc but an echino-derm, sea urchins are found off the coasts of America and Europe attached to coral. Salty-tasting, they have a texture like raw egg and a hard, spiny shell that must be cut open. They can be eaten raw or used to flavor omelets, sauces, or soufflés.

Molluscs

CLAMS

Found the world over in the wet sand of freshwater streams and sea coasts, clams are cultivated mostly in France and Portugal. They are, however, very popular in America where there are soft-shelled clams, which include round and long "razor" clams, and hard-shelled round clams – some types of hard-shells are shown. Larger, stronger-tasting hard-shells are usually reserved for chowders, while some of the smaller cherrystone varieties are eaten raw; the larger littleneck clams may be steamed open and served with melted butter. Imported clams are available canned.

MUSSELS

Closely related to the clam, mussels are found the world over. Varieties are usually specific to a certain area, but the blue mussel (*Mytilus edulis*) is found along the Atlantic coasts of both America and Europe where it is also farmed commercially. Mussels are generally sold fresh in their shells and may be eaten raw, steamed or used in salads, soups and pâtés. The large green-lipped mussel is found only in New Zealand.

Chowder clam

Cherrystone clam

Littleneck clam

SCALLOP

Scallops are commonly found along the American and European Atlantic coasts. There are many species but two basic types: the delicately flavored smallbay scallops and the larger deep sea scallops. They can be broiled, breaded and deep-fried, or poached and served in the shell with cream sauce, as *Coquilles Saint-Jacques*. They are also available pickled. In America only the white muscle is eaten; in Europe, as in Britain, the roe, or coral, is eaten too.

Mussel

Scallop

COCKLES

About 1 inch long, cockles are round marine molluscs mostly consumed in Europe. They are found in the Mediterranean, Baltic, and north-west Atlantic. Unless by the sea, where they are fresh and may be eaten raw, cockles are sold ready-cooked, shelled, and packed in ice, or canned, pickled in vinegar. They are good in salads, soups, and can be used in pasta dishes.

OYSTERS

There are many varieties of this mollusc, which is found in Mediterranean, Atlantic and Pacific waters, all of them varying in size. The recommended way of eating oysters is raw, straight from the half-shell complete with juices. If served hot, they should be only lightly cooked. The giant American Pacific oyster can be more than double the size of European varieties. They are usually not sold in the summer months when spawning makes them thin and less succulent.

Cockle

Periwinkles

Whelk

PERIWINKLES

A darkish brown shell is most common. Although available on both sides of the Atlantic, it is much more popular in Britain. Periwinkles are usually cooked in boiling salted water and may be served with a sauce.

WHELKS

Generally with a brownish or grayish shell, the whelk, sometimes known as a periwinkle, is indigenous to both sides of the Atlantic Ocean. They are usually cooked in a covered pot in a little water but some are sold canned and precooked or pickled.

OTHER MOLLUSCS

ABALONE
Abalone has very firm flesh that needs softening before cooking. It is usually tenderized and canned for use in soups and Oriental dishes, but fresh abalone is available all year. When fresh, it is tenderized, cut into thin steaks, and eaten raw or sautéed for a mere 45–55 seconds as it is easily overcooked.

CONCH
A pink-shelled, warm-water mollusc eaten mostly in Florida and the Carribbean Islands. It has a similar flavor and texture to scallops. Usually marinated and tenderized before cooking it is used in salads, fritters and chowders.

LIMPETS
Marine molluscs with a single tent-like shell, limpets cling to rocks around the world at low tide. Usually 1–2 inches across, they can be eaten raw, or cooked and used in soups and mixed seafood dishes.

Portuguese oyster

European oyster

PRESERVED FISH

THE PROCESS OF CURING foods, and thus preserving them, by methods of drying, smoking and salting, was a discovery of major importance and was, no doubt, the result of observing natural phenomena – for example, fish trapped in coastal salt deposits by the tidal flow would have been found to be preserved.

Methods of preserving
Unsalted fish are cleaned, headed and gutted, tied in pairs, and dried for about six weeks in a current of air. Heavy salt-cured fish are headed and gutted and their backbones removed. The split fish are piled in layers with a mixture of coarse and fine salt between each layer, about 30 lbs of salt to every 100 lbs of fish. They are then hung in a current of air, or machine-dried. Light-cured fish are headed, gutted, washed and split, and about one-third of the fish is salted with dry salt, using 8–10 lbs of salt to every 100 lbs of fish. The fish are laid in tubs until the juices dissolve the salt and form brine, in which the fish remain from two to three days. They are then taken out of the brine solution and sun- or machine-dried.

Pickled-cured fish are cleaned, eviscerated, packed with plenty of salt into wooden barrels and left for ten days to allow shrinkage to take place. The juices and salt form a brownish liquid called "blood pickle", which is drawn off, and then poured back to top up the barrel. The lid is then sealed and the barrel of fish ready for storage.

Anchovies are cleaned, dry-salted, pressed to remove fat, and sprayed with their own brine for several months at room temperature. Sardines are headed and gutted, then immersed in brine for about 15 minutes before being tunnel-dried.

There are two main types of smoke cure: cold-smoking, below 85°F, and hot-smoking, at 250°F, which also cooks the fish. Smoke is generated in kilns by sawdust, which is regularly recharged to give uniformity to the product. In both cases, fish are normally given a preliminary brine bath before smoking.

Fish roes
The ova or eggs of the female fish are called "roe", and that of the male fish "milt". Both are normally eaten smoked. The best roes come from the sturgeon and salmon but others commonly available include those of the carp, cod, pike-perch, gray mullet and herring. The roe of the sturgeon, caviar, is the most highly prized and, consequently, the most expensive.

Preserved fish in the kitchen
Dried fish, such as salt cod, require a preliminary soaking in water for a day, to soften the fish and remove some of the salt. Salt cod, or *bacalao*, common in the Mediterranean where it is sold on market stalls straight from the barrel, is transformed into such dishes as the French *brandade de morue*. In Spain and Portugal it is generally served braised, stewed or fried. It can also be eaten raw in salads.

Smoked fish may be pounded to make a savory paste or butter or used in pâtés. It also makes a pleasing addition to soufflés. Smoked fish have limited keeping properties that vary according to type. As a general guide, they will keep for up to five days at normal temperatures and up to fourteen days at temperatures below normal.

Pickled and canned fish, once opened, should be refrigerated if they are not to be consumed at once. Anchovies are used in salads and sauces, in pizza, and the Provençal *pissaladière*, in anchovy butter and paste. In Scandinavia, pickled fish are commonly used in everyday cooking and form an integral part of the traditional *smorgasbord*.

Dried Fish

BOMBAY DUCK

Despite its name, this is really an unsalted, sun-dried fish. In its fresh state it is from a long, silvery species called "bummalao", which is native to India, where it is often eaten fresh. Once dried, Bombay duck or bombil loses its fishy taste and adopts instead a curious flavor, rather like burnt oil or fat. It is used to flavor curries, or may be fried or pickled.

BACALAO/SALT COD

This is salted and dried cod. The fresh fish is caught in the north Atlantic, and then exported to various countries (often already dried). It can be bought either whole, as shown, or cut up in pieces, and is much used in Iberian cookery for stews and casseroles, one of the most famous of which is *bacalao a la vizcaina*. It needs overnight soaking before use.

Bombay duck

Bacalao/Salt cod

SHARK'S FIN

The dried cartilage of a shark's fin, this is much used in oriental cooking, where it is considered a delicacy. It requires overnight soaking before use and is best known as the basic ingredient for shark's fin soup.

Shark's fin

OTHER DRIED FISH

KATSUOBOSHI
A Japanese dried fish which can also be smoked.

LUTEFISK
The reconstituted unsalted cod from Norway known as stockfish or stockfisk. It is usually prepared in the early spring. In Sweden there is a smaller version made with dried ling.

MIGAKI-NISHIN
From Japan, this is a mixture of dried fish fillets and abalone.

Smoked Fish

KIPPER

The most common smoked fish in Britain, herring kippers should be plump, juicy and properly smoked, not dyed to disguise inadequate treatment, as if often the case. Kippers are sold whole – usually in pairs – or as fillets, which are often available frozen. They can be used to make pâté, and otherwise can be broiled.

Kipper

Smoked trout

Buckling

SMOKED TROUT

Both the rainbow and the brown trout can be smoked, but the rainbow trout is normally used. The fish are gutted with the head left on, brined, speared on rods, cold-smoked and then hot-smoked. Smoked trout requires no cooking and is usually served as an appetizer with thinly sliced brown bread and butter and lemon wedges.

SMOKED SALMON

The unrivalled king of all smoked fish, this is usually served as an appetizer, in paper-thin slices accompanied by wedges of lemon. The fish are headed, gutted and filleted, and string is passed through the lug bones to facilitate hanging. The skin is scored with a sharp knife, and the fillets dry-salted with fine salt. Some curers use traditional mixtures such as brown sugar, saltpetre and rum. The salmon is washed in cold water before being hung to dry for a day, then cold-smoked.

BUCKLING

Of the many versions of smoked herring, this is undoubtedly the best. Originally from Schleswig-Holstein in Germany, it is also prepared in Britain, the Netherlands and Norway. It is brined and hot-smoked, requires no cooking, and is eaten cold in the same way as smoked trout.

Smoked mackerel

Smoked salmon

SMOKED HADDOCK

Originally from the village of Finnan in Aberdeenshire, Scotland, from which it takes one of its names – finnan haddie – this haddock is traditionally cured over peat smoke. The fish is headed, gutted, split down the backbone and immersed in brine. Dyes are not added. After this, it is threaded onto spears, the protein gloss is allowed to develop, and then it is smoked. It can be eaten as it is, served with a rich egg sauce, or flaked and used as an omelet filler. It is also an important ingredient of kedgeree, the classic English breakfast dish of smoked fish, eggs and rice.

Smoked haddock

Arbroath smokie

SMOKED EEL

A good smoked eel is a succulent delicacy, so smooth and buttery in texture that it becomes virtually spreadable. The eel is gutted, headed and brined, and dry-salted. It is then washed, dipped in boiling water, and hung up to smoke. It is usually eaten cold in the same way as smoked trout.

ARBROATH SMOKIE

Another version of smoked haddock from the east coast of Scotland, this is usually headed and gutted but otherwise left whole. Whiting may also be used. The fish are headed and gutted, but not split, and tied in pairs. Arbroath smokies are usually served as an appetizer.

Smoked eel

SMOKED MACKEREL

Smoking intensifies the already rich, strong taste of the mackerel. It is ready for eating and is usually used for hors d'oeuvres, served with lemon wedges.

OTHER SMOKED FISH

BLOATER
First developed at Yarmouth England, in 1835, bloaters, which are whole herring, are said to own their special flavor to the activity of gut enzymes. The fish are dry-salted for about 12 hours, washed to remove surplus salt, threaded on metal "speats", and stacked in the kiln to smoke.

GLASGOW PALE
These are called "pales" because they are lightly smoked and undyed. They are first split and gutted, then brined and smoked.

RED HERRING
This is named for the color its skin turns after smoking. The whole fish is dry-salted or heavily brined, and smoked intermittently.

Smoked Fish and Roes

Smoked sturgeon

SMOKED STURGEON

This is a delicacy regarded as a sort of *objet d'art* of the gourmet world – very expensive and yet worth every effort to track down! It should be thinly sliced and served as an appetizer.

SMOKED HALIBUT

Usually it is the Greenland halibut which is smoked; it is quite a fatty fish and smoking seems to suit it. Serving suggestions include slices of the fish on open sandwiches, accompanied by lemon wedges.

SMOKED SPRAT

A German variety of sprat is smoked whole and eaten in the traditional German way with a dark rye bread and butter. The most famous are the Kieler Sprotten from the port of Kiel in Germany. The fish are washed and brined.

Smoked sprat

Smoked halibut

SOFT HERRING ROE

Sperm of the male fish, herring roe has a creamy smooth texture. It is often fried in butter and served with lemon slices. A hard variety is also available, though it is quite scarce.

Soft herring roe

SEVRUGA CAVIAR

Caviar is called after the species of sturgeon providing it. This one is the smallest-grained from the small Caspian sturgeon, and is sold fresh and pressed. Pressed caviar is made from damaged eggs, salted and crushed together.

BELUGA CAVIAR

The largest-grained caviar, and the most expensive, comes from the large Caspian sturgeon, which have been known to live for over 70 years, and reach a length of 12 feet. It is available fresh, pasteurized and pressed.

COD'S ROE

Also available uncooked and boiled, it is here shown smoked and in this form can be used to make a variety of *taramasalata*, the Greek dip. Boiled roe can be fried or broiled.

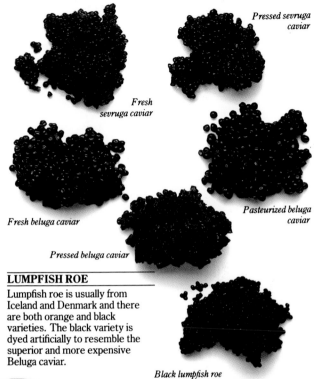

Pressed sevruga caviar

Fresh sevruga caviar

Pasteurized beluga caviar

Fresh beluga caviar

Pressed beluga caviar

LUMPFISH ROE

Lumpfish roe is usually from Iceland and Denmark and there are both orange and black varieties. The black variety is dyed artificially to resemble the superior and more expensive Beluga caviar.

Black lumpfish roe

Cod's roe

Orange lumpfish roe

SALMON ROE

Eaten in the same way as caviar, this is sometimes referred to as caviar, though the word should really apply only to sturgeon roe.

Salmon roe

OTHER ROES

BOTARGO CAVIAR
This Sardinian delicacy is made from compressed and salted mullet roe.

OSETR CAVIAR
A caviar taken from the Danube sturgeon, a fish also found in the Caspian Sea.

ROES
Japanese preserved roes include: hontarako, a salted and dried cod's roe; karasumi, made from the roe of the gray mullet or tuna, salted, pressed and dried; and tarako or momojiko, the salted roe of the Alaskan pollack.

Seaweeds and Canned and Pickled Fish

JELLYFISH SEAWEED

Although sold as a seaweed and usually thought of as such, this is, in fact, strips of jellyfish which have been dried and salted. It is used in Chinese, Japanese and Southeast Asian dishes.

Jellyfish seaweed

DULSE

A coarse northern seaweed which, when fresh, is red, dulse is harvested along the coasts of the British Isles, Iceland and parts of Canada. Usually sold dried, it can be cooked, like spinach, used to flavor soups, or chewed like chewing gum.

Dulse

CANNED ANCHOVY

A tiny, very fatty fish with a powerful flavor, it is cured by having most of its fat content removed by pressure and fermentation. Anchovies are usually filleted, brined and then preserved in oil, though they are also available salted in jars. Very strong-tasting, they are used in canapés, pastes, pizza toppings, *salade Niçoise*, anchovy paste (page 69) and anchovy butter.

KOMBU

A type of dried kelp which is particularly popular in Japan, where it is used to make the soup stock *dashi* and infused to make a tisane. It should be washed before use.

Kombu

MEKABU

A Japanese lobe-leaf seaweed similar to wakame (the traditional Japanese seaweed), this is available in the form of curled, dried strands. Used mainly in soups and salads and as a garnish, it should be soaked before use.

LAVER (*Nori*)

This seaweed has been gathered along the coasts of Britain and Eire for centuries. One type, sea lettuce, is used in salads, sauces and soups. A fine, silky plant, it is mashed and boiled and then sold as laverbread. The Japanese laver *Porphyra tenera* is pressed and dried to a thin, flexible, dark-brown sheet called nori, shown here. It is used in sauces, soups, sandwiches and *sushi*, a dish of rice and fish, and also as a garnish for other dishes.

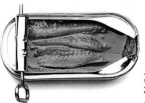

Canned anchovy

CARRAGEEN MOSS

This seaweed, also known as Irish moss, is hand-raked on the coasts of northern Europe and New England. A gum similar to agar-agar is extracted from it, and it is also cooked and eaten as a vegetable which is like spinach.

Carrageen moss

Mekabu

Laver (nori)

Canned tuna

CANNED TUNA

Tuna is usually preserved in oil, brine or water. Its firm flesh makes it useful in sandwiches, cold dishes and casseroles.

Canned sardine

CANNED SARDINE

These small fish of the herring family (page 164) are usually canned whole, in oil (as shown) or tomato sauce. The fish is thoroughly gutted before processing. The preserving process softens the bones, which means that they can be eaten as they are. Their main use is in appetizers and sandwiches.

ROLLMOP HERRING

The raw herring is headed, gutted, boned and left in the form of double fillets. It is then spread out flat, rolled up around pieces of pickled cucumber or onion and marinated in a spiced vinegar. After several days in the marinade it is ready for eating with dark bread and butter.

Whole matjes herring

Rollmop herring

Matjes herring fillet

MATJES HERRING

This is a young Netherlands herring caught in the spring, before it becomes too fatty. It is lightly salted and barrel-stored for a few days only, just sufficient to ferment the gut enzymes. It is usually bought whole and salted from the barrel, though salted fillets are also available. Both should be soaked in water before use.

OTHER PRESERVED FISH AND FISH PRODUCTS

BISMARCK HERRING
A German herring from the Baltic which is simply filleted and marinated in vinegar with onion rings for 2–3 days.

NUOC-MAM
A clear brown liquid with a cheesy smell and salty taste, this is prepared in Vietnam from small fish such as the clupeids (herring and sprats). The whole fish are pressed into tubs, salted and tightly sealed, and left for about 12 weeks before the liquid is drained off. Salting is heavy, and caramel, molasses, rice or boiled corn may be added as extra flavorings. Petis and nuoc-mam roc are variations.

OYSTERS
Oysters are steamed, brined, dipped in oil, then hot-smoked before being packed in oil in sterilized jars.

PRAHOC
A fish paste from Cambodia, prahoc is made with eviscerated fish which are scaled, washed and pressed under banana leaves. The fish are then mixed with coarse salt and sun-dried in order to lose some of their moisture, before being pounded to a paste. The product is then left to ferment.

SALMON
Canned salmon ranges from bright red to the less expensive pink varieties. It is used in patties, salads and sandwiches.

TRASSI
Also called trasi udang, this is a cured shrimp paste made in Sumatra from shrimp mixed with 10–15 per cent salt. The mixture is spread out in the sun for a few days, and it is then kneaded and dyes are added until a sticky red mass is obtained. Other ingredients may be included – potato peel, for example, and rice bran. Mature trassi keeps indefinitely and when cooked and mixed with chile peppers becomes *sambal goreng*, a popular condiment.

POULTRY AND GAME

THE WORD "POULTRY" IS used to describe all domestic birds which are bred especially for the table, and covers chickens, turkeys, ducks, geese, guinea fowl and domestic pigeons or squabs. Over the years, poultry farming has developed enormously. Selective breeding for meat and eggs has led to automated production techniques, and today poultry meat is more popular than the meat from any other animal or bird.

The standard and quality of poultry in America, is supervised by the US Department of Agriculture, and grades are given. "Grade A", for example, indicates that the bird is of a very high quality, as regards appearance and meatiness; the circular mark means it has been approved.

Poultry can be bought either whole or in a variety of individual portions – legs, wings, thighs, drumsticks, halves and quarters. It can also be bought fresh or frozen, with or without giblets (which are often used to make gravies and stuffings).

Cooking poultry

Chicken is a particularly delicate meat, and needs considerate cooking since it has a rapid rate of shrinkage in high heat, but much depends on the age of the bird: tender young poultry can be barbecued, fried, broiled or roasted; old birds need long, slow braising or stewing. Traditional dishes such as Scottish cock-a-leekie and French *coq au vin* are unlikely to have been prepared with cockerels, but with capons or boiling hens. The age and type of poultry therefore determines the method and the recipe. When frying chicken, cut-up pieces should be cooked in deep fat at 300–325°F in a thick-bottomed pan for about 20 to 25 minutes. Broiled chicken pieces need to be cooked at a distance of about 7–9 inches from the source of heat until they are well-browned and tender.

To roast a chicken, brush with oil or fat and, if it is to be stuffed, pack the stuffing loosely just before roasting; tightly packed stuffing will go soggy. Never stuff in advance; a chicken that, for convenience, has been stuffed the previous day may encourage bacterial activity.

Birds that are roasted in aluminum foil or in a ceramic "chicken brick" are in fact cooked by steam and not by radiant heat, and will need a final 20 to 30 minutes browning, uncovered. As a general guide, a 2–2½-lb bird will take 1 to 1¼ hours at 400°F. To test whether the bird is cooked, pierce the thigh or drumstick to the bone with a sharp pointed knife or fork. If the juices run clear and free of blood, or if the joints sever easily when pulled, the chicken is ready for serving.

Turkeys are usually roasted, and a meat thermometer will be a useful aid to this: a 12–17-lb bird will take about 3 to 3¾ hours uncovered, or until a meat thermometer inserted in the leg shows 185°F. A turkey of comparable weight, covered with foil and roasted at 450°F, cooks in 2½ to 3 hours. To roast a duck or goose, pierce the skin in several places during cooking to allow the excess fat to run off into the pan. A 3–5-lb duck takes 2½ to 3 hours, uncovered, at 325°F, a goose of 4–8 lb needs 2¾ to 3½ hours at 325°F.

When roasting guinea fowl, choose young birds of 1½ lb. Older (and probably tougher) birds of 2½–3 lb are more suited to casserole cooking and braising. A 1½-lb bird will need about 1½ hours at 350°F. Squab should be roasted for about 45 minutes – at the higher temperature of 425°F for the first 20 minutes and then turned down to 350°F for the remaining 25 minutes. Guinea fowl and squab should be roasted covered with strips of bacon or pork rind to stop the breasts drying out.

Storing poultry

Fresh, uncooked poultry should be used within two or three days of purchasing provided it has been kept in a refrigerator. Once cooked it should be kept in the refrigerator, loosely wrapped, and eaten within a few days. The meat can also be frozen, if separated from the stuffing and the gravy.

When thawing frozen poultry, it is best to do so gradually in a refrigerator, allowing about 15 hours for a 3–lb bird; alternatively it can be thawed by placing the bird in a sink and covering it with cold water (the water should be changed regularly until the bird thaws).

GAME

For culinary purposes, "game" is used to describe all birds and animals which are hunted for food, and although several are now reared domestically, they are still classified as game.

Basically, game is divided into two types: feathered and furred. Hares are decidedly game animals, but many people don't think of rabbits and pigeons as game, even though they are hunted for food. Game is further distinguished by the characteristic texture and taste of its meat, which differs from that of poultry and farmyard animals: it is generally darker, stronger-tasting and often tougher.

Wild animals, because of their diet and general lifestyle, have certain enzymes in their tissues which break down or metabolize meat proteins. These enzymes, which become active about 24 hours after the animal has been killed, soften the meat, making it gelatinous and palatable, and giving it that "gamey" flavor. While the enzymes are at work, the game carcass hosts anerobes, micro-organisms which also help to break down the protein, forming non-toxic ptomaines. Provided that there are no dangerous staphylococci present, the bacteria that affect game meat are harmless; it is curious that game and certain types of fish can be safely eaten and enjoyed at a stage of advanced putrefaction, when many white meats, notably pork, are positively dangerous.

Although the practice of hanging game is traditional, it is a mistake to think that game must be mature, and there is historical evidence to suggest that it may not always have been eaten when well matured.

Choosing game

The most important factor when buying game is to know its age, since this will determine the method of cooking (see below). Indications of age are by no means infallible, but there are some general guidelines when buying young birds. Look for clean and soft-textured feet, pliable breastbones and rounded spurs. When buying game animals, bear in mind that the ears of young hares and rabbits split easily.

Hanging game

Game bought from a dealer will probably have been correctly prepared and hung, but you can, of course, order in advance and specify your requirements. Here are some approximate hanging times for freshly killed game: pheasant, 6 to 14 days; partridge, 7 to 8 days; wood-pigeon, 2 to 3 days; snipe and woodcock, 7 to 10 days; hare and rabbit, 2 to 3 days; venison and boar, up to 3 weeks. Quail does not need to be hung at all.

Game should be hung in a cool, dry, airy place and protected from flies. Although there is no real need to hang game if you object to the taste, as a general rule, you should hang a carcass until you detect the first whiff of tainting – in birds this is around the crop or vent. Game is left intact during hanging, except venison, hares and rabbits, which may be "paunched" or gutted straight away.

Birds are usually hung by their heads, and rabbits and (particularly) hares with the head down. The blood of hares is usually collected in a receptacle as it drains off, and is used to thicken the sauce in jugged hare.

Cooking game

Game meat responds best to roasting. Young game birds, in particular, should be roasted, and it is traditional to leave them unstuffed. In practice, however, large birds such as pheasant may be stuffed with seasoned ground beef, which helps to keep the flesh moist. Older, tougher game should be casseroled, braised or made into pies, pâtés and terrines. Marinating in a mixture of oil, vinegar, wine or beer, herbs and spices helps to make meat tender and enhances the taste.

The oven should be set at 400°F, for the first 10 minutes, then at 350°F for the following times: grouse, 30 minutes; partridge, 30 minutes; pheasant, 45 minutes; pigeon, 60 minutes; quail, 25 minutes; snipe, 45 minutes; duck, 45 minutes; woodcock, 30 minutes. Roast a hare or a young rabbit at about 450°F, for about 45 minutes; venison should be roasted at 425°F, for 20 to 25 minutes, then at 350°F, according to the weight – a haunch takes about 1½ to 2 hours.

Poultry

STEWING CHICKEN

A mature bird weighing 2½–6 lbs, this is quite tasty but requires long, gentle cooking to soften its relatively tough flesh. The age of a bird is often determined by the state of its breastbone: in an older chicken the bone is hard and rigid. Stewing chickens are used in fricassees, in main dish pies, for ballottines and galantines and, most importantly, for soup.

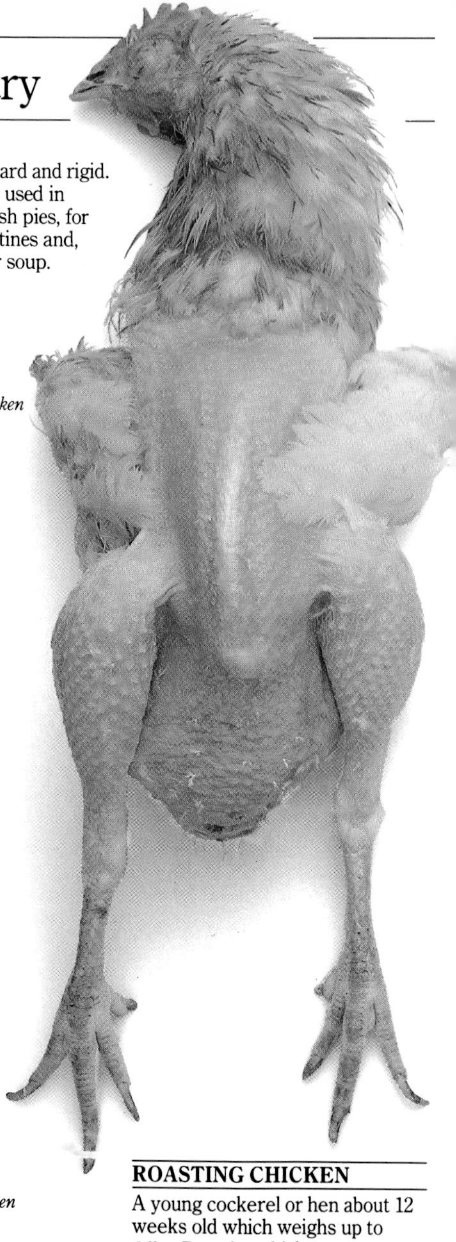

Stewing chicken

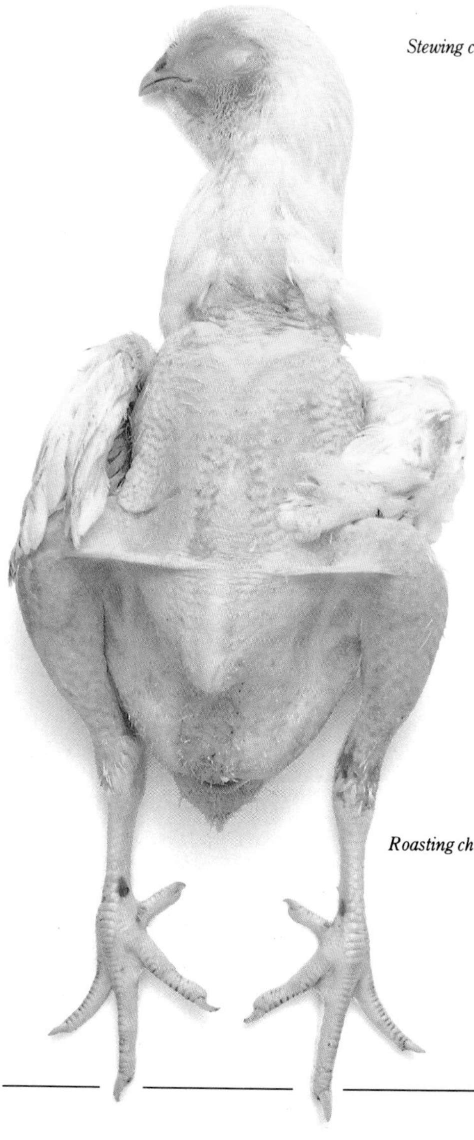

Roasting chicken

ROASTING CHICKEN

A young cockerel or hen about 12 weeks old which weighs up to 6 lbs. Roasting chickens are equally good cooked in an oven or on a rotisserie. Broiler fryers are 7- to 8-weeks old chickens weighing 1½ to 4 lbs. They are usually sold whole, halved, quartered or cut into pieces for frying and barbecuing.

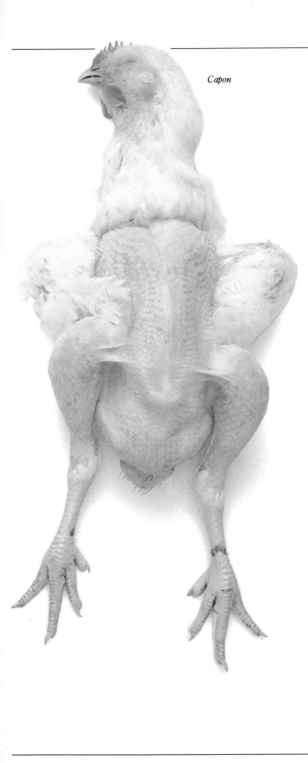

Capon

CAPON

A young cockerel which has been castrated and specially fattened, the capon is bred for its meat. From 6–10 lbs in weight, they are larger than most chickens. Capons are noted for their tenderness and have a large proportion of white meat to dark. They are usually roasted but can be prepared in the same ways as other chickens.

POUSSIN

This is a baby or young chicken weighing from 1–2 lbs. The bird should be old enough to have a firm flesh and good taste. The term "poussin" also describes a very small chicken of the Hamburg type. Poussins are similar in appearance to Rock Cornish Game Hens, which are a cross between Cornish and White Rock chickens. Poussins have delicate flesh and can be roasted, baked, sautéed or broiled. One serving usually consists of an entire bird.

Poussin

DUCK

Most of the duck eaten is the domestic variety, shown here. Ducks have a big frame and a high fat content, but not a great deal of meat. On the other hand, there is little wastage because the carcasses make an excellent soup stock and the livers are often used in pâtés. The French and Chinese are noted for their duck recipes. In the French dish *caneton à l'orange*, the acidity of the orange provides a perfect complement to the bird's richness. Ducks are available fresh or frozen and, on average, weigh around 4–6 lbs. Ducklings weigh 3½–4 lbs and are at their best roasted.

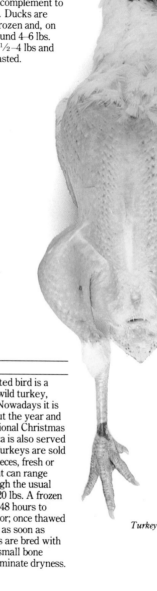

TURKEY

Today's domesticated bird is a descendant of the wild turkey, native to Mexico. Nowadays it is available throughout the year and considered a traditional Christmas bird, and in America is also served at Thanksgiving. Turkeys are sold whole or cut into pieces, fresh or frozen. Their weight can range from 6–30 lbs, though the usual weight is from 10–20 lbs. A frozen turkey takes about 48 hours to thaw in a refrigerator; once thawed it should be cooked as soon as possible. Most birds are bred with heavy breasts and small bone structure to help eliminate dryness.

Turkey

Duck

GUINEA FOWL

Originally, it is believed, these birds came from Africa. Related to the pheasant, they were once considered game birds, but they have been reared domestically for centuries in many parts of the world. Like game, they are best hung for two or three days before plucking, dressing and cooking. Their flesh is tender (the hens more so than the cocks) with a gaminess that is reminiscent of pheasant, and is suitable for roasting, casseroles, braising, and, in general, any recipe suitable for pheasant.

GOOSE

There are many varieties of table geese. The French Toulouse goose is bred for its contribution to *pâté de foie gras*, the Strasbourg for *confit d'oie* (cut-up pieces of goose preserved in goose fat). The larger domestic bird is sometimes too tough and usually too fatty to eat, but the younger bird (shown here) is delicate and tender. While table geese are expensive and their meat yield low by comparison to turkey, goose, with its slightly gamey flavor, is considered by many to be the best poultry. Available fresh or frozen, a goose usually weighs between 6–12 lbs, and is best roasted. The goose and gander are similar in appearance and size. When prepared for the oven, the word goose is applied to both.

Goose

OTHER POULTRY

SQUAB

A squab is a young pigeon specially bred for the table. It is normally about 4 weeks old, and weighs between 12–24 ounces. Squab is drawn and prepared in the same way as other domestic birds. It is tender, and can be roasted, sautéed, grilled, broiled or stewed.

Guinea fowl

Feathered Game

Woodcock

Grouse

GROUSE

Grouse is considered to be the most delicious of the game birds. The grouse family includes many varieties: the red grouse of Scotland (shown here), the blackcock or black grouse, the capercaillie or wood grouse, and the ptarmigan of northern Europe. The sage grouse, rugged grouse and prairie chicken of North America are close relatives. Like other game birds, its availability is limited by hunting seasons. Young birds are suitable for roasting or broiling, while older birds can be braised successfully. One bird is served per person.

WOODCOCK

Native to Europe and America, woodcock is now found worldwide, but its availability is often limited by hunting seasons. Woodcock should be well hung but the skin should remain intact on plucking. One woodcock should be served for each person. It is suitable for roasting, braising or broiling; like its relative, the snipe, if roasted, it is not drawn or decapitated, although the gizzard is removed.

Snipe

Partridge

Quail

SNIPE

This bird, native to Europe, is subject to the same availability restrictions as most other game birds. It is best roasted, although it is so small it can also be cooked under the broiler. It is often cooked with its entrails, which are regarded as a delicacy. One bird should be allowed per person.

PARTRIDGE

The type shown is native to Europe, but there are many other varieties, all related to the pheasant. Its availability is limited by hunting seasons. Partridge can be roasted, stewed, braised or casseroled. Young birds especially should be roasted and served with their own gravy as a sauce – when roasting, one bird should be allowed per person. In France, it is cooked with cabbage and other vegetables and made into a decorative mold flavored with *chartreuse* liqueur.

QUAIL

Native to the Middle East, the quail is a migratory game bird and, like the partridge, is related to the pheasant. Popular varieties include the Californian quail and the European quail, which is reared on quail farms and sold as a gourmet item to restaurants. Available all year round, it can be roasted, sautéed or broiled, and features in many *haute cuisine* dishes, especially when it is served in aspic. Since birds are small, allow at least one per person when serving.

Feathered and Furred Game

WILD DUCK

Originally from the northern hemisphere, the most famous and largest of the wild ducks is the mallard (the male is shown), from which all domestic varieties are descended. There are several other types, including teal (one of the smallest wild ducks), widgeon, shoveller, pochard and scaup. It can be bought fresh (though its availability is restricted by hunting seasons), or frozen. It is excellent for roasting and one bird will serve two or three people.

Hen pheasant

Wild duck

Cock pheasant

PHEASANT

Native to China, but now found in many countries, the cock and hen pheasant are often sold together as a brace. Though the hen pheasant is considered to be more tender, it will only serve about three people, whereas the cock will serve four. Perhaps the most popular game bird, it responds well to hanging. Bought fresh or frozen oven-ready, it is excellent for roasting, stewing, braising and serving *en papillote*.

HARE

Originally from Europe, the hare is now found worldwide, but its availability is restricted by hunting seasons. Though they belong to the same family as rabbits, hares are "gamier". They are also larger, and their flesh is darker and stronger-tasting. Young hares do not need hanging and can be fresh roasted; older animals of

Rabbit

Hare

OTHER FEATHERED AND FURRED GAME

BEAR
The European bear (*Ursus arctus*) and the American bear (*Ursus americanus*) are occasionally enjoyed for their steaks, but bear paws are considered to be the prime part. Bear is most popular in German and Russian cooking.

BOAR
The European wild boar (*Sus scrofa*), although plentiful on the Continent and in some parts of America, is still best known for its medieval associations. Only the meat of the young boar is really tender, older animals need to be hung for two or three days, and the flesh marinated before cooking. It is usually roasted, and is popular in German and Russian cooking.

DEER
The meat of any animal from the deer or Cervidae family is called "venison". It is one of the most popular game meats, but needs to be hung and marinated, unless the animal is very young. The best meat is taken from the buck in its second year, and the most popular cut is the haunch, although the loin and fillets also make good eating. Deer in general, and elk (*Alces alces*) in particular, are eaten for their meat and liver, while smoked elk tongue is a delicacy. Young, tender venison may be grilled or larded with pork fat and roasted (some cooks pour sour cream over the meat before roasting).

PIGEON
Pigeon is sometimes tough, and therefore best suited for stewing or braising. In North Africa, pigeons feature in *bstilla*, a delicate pie made with fine pastry, sugar and nuts.

RABBIT
Originally from Africa, but now found worldwide, rabbits have meat that is generally tender, but the animals need to be drawn (gutted) and hung for four to five days. Curiously, it has never become an *haute cuisine* ingredient, but has always been a countryman's dish, and countless recipes for rabbit pie and stew testify to this trend. Usually bought whole (domestic rabbits can also be bought cut up and frozen), they are used in casseroles, stews and roasts.

two years upwards should be hung and the meat made into casseroles, stews, pâtés and terrines. It is used in the German casserole with red wine *hasenpfeffer*, and in the French dish *lièvre à la royale*. Many classic French dishes call for the back or saddle (*râble*) or the saddle and hind legs (*train*) only.

SAUSAGES AND PRESERVED MEATS

An early culinary discovery was that meat would keep for an extended period if the moisture content could be reduced by drying, salting or smoking. In this way, regular year-around supplies of meat became available and a new era began that was eventually to see hams, bacon and sausages take their place as a staple part of our diet.

Inhabitants of hot climates pounded meat to release the juices and dried the strips in the sun or over a fire. The South African biltong is an example of this technique. In North America, the Red Indians invented pemmican – dried, lean buffalo meat, pounded and mixed with fat, vegetables and fruit (usually cranberries), then packed in hide skins and sealed with tallow. Meat is still sealed with fat in the preparation of pâtés and terrines.

In Mexico and Central America, buffalo meat was cut into strips and sun-dried. This *charqui* was later made by the pioneers, who knew it as "jerky" or "jerked beef". The peasants of Europe, and in particular those of Britain, lived for centuries on a diet of bread and beer, supplemented with bacon. Most of the beef that came to the table was powdered with dry salt. Ships' victuallers bought it by the ton for the British fleet.

Cooking techniques were devised to offset the saltiness; these included adding cereals such as barley to absorb the salt, or a variety of vegetables: the *pot-au-feu* of France and the boiled beef dinners of New England were dishes born of expediency. Spices, especially ginger and pepper, played an important role in enhancing the taste of salt meat and, during one period in the seventeenth century, piles of oranges were kept in the kitchens of wealthy households, so that the juice could be added to cooked meat dishes.

Although salt beef and sun-dried buffalo meat certainly played an important role regionally, much of the tradition of preserved meats actually rests firmly on the pig. French butchers in particular have a long history of charcuterie – the hams of Gaul were so famous that they were even exported to Rome.

An ancestor of the sausage (the word comes from the Latin *salsus* meaning "salted") was made by primitive peoples, using the paunch of an animal to contain other parts of the viscera, which would then have been cooked over a fire; Scotland's haggis is a probable descendant. The Greeks and Romans encouraged sausage-making and it is believed that the Germans, who claim to have invented the sausage, learned their skills from the Romans, but it was left to the French to develop the idea so imaginatively – the range and variety they have devised over the years is staggering. Following France, the most varied contributions to sausage-making come from Germany and Italy, with several other European countries also providing a significant number.

The European ways with hams and sausages spread to America – the French inspired the Creole-Acadian *boudins* and *andouilles*, the Italians the *bologna* and *salamis*, the Germans the *frankfurters* and *knackwursts*, and Spain and Portugal originated the *chorizos* of Latin America. The American diet of the nineteenth century consisted largely of salt pork (the *petit salé* of France and the pickled pork of Britain. Utility and poverty saw that every scrap of the animal was used, preferably salted and smoked, so that the products could last the months following pig-killing time. The tradition of using every part of the animal is still maintained: sausages, liver sausages and blood puddings use the inexpensive cuts, while the choicer portions – the belly, loin and legs – are reserved for the smoking and curing processes, to produce bacon and ham.

Processing

The word "cure" simply means that meat is cured of its propensity to putrefaction. In the past, dry-salting was often unsatisfactory because salt was coarse and unrefined, and could produce uneven results. Sugar, which helps soften the meat and adds flavor, was used only by the few who could afford it. Meat was thus dry, hard and very salty, but in the late eighteenth century some attempt was made to refine curing techniques.

Types of sausages and hams vary because local tastes, ingredients and techniques vary.

Hungarians add paprika to their sausages; Germans utilize the wild juniper that flavors Westphalian hams. Brine recipes vary too, and so do smoking techniques. The following are the most commonly used.

Brine cure: This is also known as "pickle" and, if sugar is added, it becomes a "sweet pickle". Most pickles are sweet – an exception is that used for Bayonne ham. Some brines are spiced and may contain juniper, coriander, ginger, and other flavorings. Saltpetre is added because it keeps the meat attractively pink – bacteria in the meat convert the salt to a nitrite (or nitrite is added to the brine). Nitrites stabilize the red pigment myoglobin in the blood, retaining the characteristic color of the meat.

Dry cure: Dry salt is rubbed into the meat, special attention being paid to the area around the bone, if any. The salt is moisture-absorbing and draws out the juices to form a brine which then penetrates the meat.

Smoking: Wood smoke contains several antiseptic tar products, and meat is usually smoked over hardwood logs and sawdust. Duration of smoking varies considerably, according to the product and the recipe.

Corning: In the sixteenth century the word "corn" was synonymous with "grain", and meat rubbed with grains of salt was thus corned. In New England saltpetre was omitted from the cure and the resulting gray color of the meat is still preferred. In Britain, corned beef refers to a product of cured, boiled, pressed and then canned beef.

Hams, bacons and other cured meats

Ham is the cured and smoked hind leg of pork, while bacon is usually the cured belly of pork, which accounts for its high fat content. Canadian bacon, however, is cut from the loin of the animal and so is much more meaty.

There are perhaps a hundred or more different hams, each country contributing to the selection, but most are cured in more or less the same manner – dry-salted or brined, smoked and matured. Bacon is available smoked and unsmoked in two forms, either sliced or as unsliced slab bacon. Other meats such as mutton and beef are sometimes cured.

Sausages

Sausages are made from the minced meat of pork, veal, beef, chicken, mutton, rabbit, even horseflesh and armadillo. Some countries add a certain amount of cereal to the mixture, notably Britain, while other countries, like Germany, forbid it. A rich variety of ingredients is used in sausage-making: eggs, cream, beer, wine, pigs' blood, tripe, bread-crumbs, oatmeal, potato flour, onion, garlic, herbs, spices, salt and pepper. Some sausages are precooked, others fresh, others cured, air-dried or smoked.

Sausage skins, or casings, are made of the intestines of sheep and pigs and there are also artificial casings. Those sausages to be smoked are first air-dried, then smoked over hardwood chips or sawdust, either cold-smoked or hot-smoked depending on the product.

There are literally thousands of sausages – Germany categorizes sausages into *bratwurst* (lightly smoked and scalded fresh sausages, to be cooked by the purchaser), *rohwurst* (salami-type sausages, raw, air-dried and smoked), and *kochwurst* (ready-cooked, used for spreading, or slicing and eating cold). French types are divided into large *saucissons*, which may be smoked (*saucissons fumées*), fresh *saucisses* and *saucisses fumées*, and the boiling sausages (*cervelat*). The most diverse and varied of all sausage types must certainly be the Italian *salami*. The diverse and varied of all sausage types must certainly be the Italian salami. The characteristic of this type of sausage is that it is brine-pickled, smoked, or both, and is made of raw ingredients.

With so many varieties made all over the world, the names of individual sausages can vary not only from country to country but even from region to region.

Fresh Sausages

LINK SAUSAGES

A general term covering fresh sausages, which may contain pork, pork and beef, or venison and seasonings. There are many varieties from different countries available under many names. All contain chopped or emulsified meat and seasonings. Occasionally herbs are added. The casings are usually made out of synthetic or natural materials.

Pork   *Beef*   *Venison*

Pork and beef

SKINLESS SAUSAGE

Sausage meat is also sold without a casing. The meat may also be shaped in patties.

CHIPOLATA

Made in small-sized casings, chipolatas or breakfast sausages are often used as a garnish. The one on the left contains pork; the one on the right is a pork and beef mixture.

BRATWURST

Made in longish links, this rather pale German bratwurst sausage contains pork and/or veal, bacon, milk and chopped onions. It is quite highly seasoned with salt, pepper and mace, and can be broiled or fried.

CUMBERLAND SAUSAGE

This is a coarse-textured English sausage consisting of roughly chopped pork and black pepper stuffed in to a long casing.

LUGANEGHE

A pure pork Italian sausage, which, like the English Cumberland, is not twisted into links. It is particularly associated with northern Italy. Luganeghe can be boiled or broiled.

Skinless sausage

Bratwurst

Chipolatas

Luganeghe

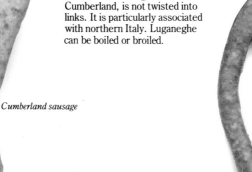

Cumberland sausage

MERGUEZ

A spiced sausage from north Africa made from goat or mutton and flavored with *harisa*, a mixture of hot chile peppers and cumin. It is usually grilled.

Merguez

LAP CHEONG

A Chinese sausage of chopped pork, cereal, soy sauce and paprika. (*Lap* means "wax" and *cheong* means "intestine".)

SALSICCIE CASALINGA

The name simply means "home-made sausage". They are usually made of pure pork and flavored with garlic and peppercorns, and may be poached, broiled or fried.

SALAMELLE

This is the Italian name for a variety of spiced sausage.

TOULOUSE SAUSAGE

A sausage from Toulouse in France made of pork and pork fat, coarsely chopped and flavored with pepper and a little sugar. These sausages feature in several French recipes, especially the regional dish *cassoulet*.

Toulouse

Lap cheong

Salsiccie casalinga

Spiced English sausage

Salamelle

Spiced French sausage

Paprika sausage

SPICED FRENCH SAUSAGE

A fairly coarse-textured sausage, highly spiced and well seasoned with garlic.

SPICED ENGLISH SAUSAGE

This is a pale pink sausage that incorporates pork and spices. Its texture is quite smooth. The Oxford sausage (shown here) is made from veal, pork, beef suet, herbs and spices, while the Cambridge sausage contains pork, herbs and spices.

PAPRIKA SAUSAGE

A dark, fairly coarse-textured sausage, made of lamb and beef and containing paprika, coriander, fennel and a variety of seasonings.

OTHER FRESH SAUSAGES

BOCKWURST
A delicately flavored, highly perishable German white sausage consisting of fresh pork and veal, chopped chives, parsley, eggs and milk.

HAGGIS
A Scottish sausage, served hot on festive occasions and at other times of the year. Haggis is made from the liver, lungs and heart of a sheep, chopped with onions, oatmeal, parsley and seasonings. The mixture is then stuffed into the stomach lining. It needs long cooking, but commercial ones are precooked and only require about 30 minutes.

THURINGER
A pork sausage that may also contain some beef or veal. It can be either fresh or cooked.

Fresh and Lightly Cooked Sausages

BLACK PUDDING

Traditionally, this black sausage is associated with the north of England, although it appears under different names in many areas. Main ingredients are pig's blood, groats, fat, oatmeal, onions, spices and seasonings. The German variety is called blutwurst, the Irish, drisheen, and the Italian, biroldo.

MORCILLA

The Spanish version of black pudding, morcilla is used as an ingredient of a national dish, *fabada*, which includes chorizo and bacon.

BOUDIN

Boudin noir (shown here) is a French version of black pudding, and contains pig's blood. Boudin blanc is a fresh sausage made with white meat and may also include pork, chicken or veal with eggs, cream, seasonings and spices. It is eaten hot, and may be poached or grilled.

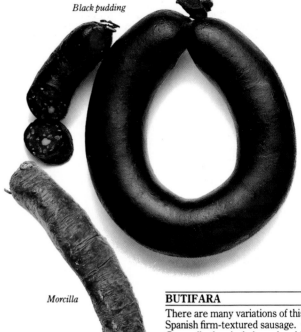

Black pudding

Morcilla

BUTIFARA

There are many variations of this Spanish firm-textured sausage. Generally they include pork, white wine, garlic, seasonings and spices. Butifara is preboiled and air-dried and may be eaten cold. It features in the Catalonian cooked dish *cazuela à la Catalana*.

ANDOUILLETTE

A French sausage which, like the larger andouille, is made of pork and/or tripe, chitterlings, calf mesentery, pepper and perhaps wine, onions, and spices. Sometimes smoked, it can be broiled or fried.

Boudin

Greek sausage

GREEK SAUSAGE

A dark, stubby sausage from Greece, this is usually quite heavily spiced.

Andouillette

Butifara

CREPINETTE

The term "crépinette" covers many varieties of small minced meat sausages, consisting of either lamb or pork. Wrapped in caul, crépinettes are coated with melted butter and breadcrumbs.

Crepinette

COTECHINO

An Italian lean and fat pork sausage with white wine and spices. In Italy they are made fresh, but a part-cured, part-cooked type is commercially distributed and exported. The fresh sausage needs several hours cooking, the commercial one only about 30 minutes. It is often served hot with beans.

Cotechino

TEEWURST

This quality German rohwurst sausage is made of the best meat. A mixture of finely minced pork and beef, it is sometimes highly spiced and lightly smoked. It is a spreading sausage.

Teewurst

FRANKFURTER

The original frankfurter is lean pork and salted bacon fat blended into a paste and smoked, but there are now many variations in ingredients as well as in size and shape, as shown here. Often the incredients include beef and chicken. Vienna sausage is a small "cocktail" frankfurter. Knackwurst is a small, plump lean-meat frankfurter containing pork and beef.

Frankfurter

Cervelat

Saveloy

ZAMPONE

An Italian pork sausage from Modena where the meat is stuffed into a boned pig's trottter, or foot instead of a casing.

Zampone

CERVELAT

The name originated from the Latin word for brains but nowadays it generally contains a finely minced mixture of beef and pork, seasoned with garlic and smoked until golden. There are many different varieties in many parts of Europe: a Swiss version is the landjaeger – a black, wrinkly and heavily smoked sausage – while the goettinger is a German cervelát made with spiced beef and pork. A variety of German cervelat is shown on page 211.

SAVELOY

An English version of cervelát, saveloy contains pork and seasonings. The addition of saltpetre gives it a red tinge.

Cooked and Lightly Smoked Sausages

SCHINKEN KALBFLEISCHWURST

This mixture of minced pork, beef and veal with ham pieces usually has a touch of garlic included, and is sometimes flavored with peppercorns and caraway seeds. It is sliced and eaten cold.

ZUNGENWURST

Often quite spicy, this large German smoked sausage is made of pork fat, large pieces of pork tongue, and sometimes liver and blood.

METTWURST

A German spreading sausage of pork and beef, this often contains paprika. There is a coarse version, shown here, and a smoother, pinker one. Both are available ready-to-eat, either as a spread or in slices.

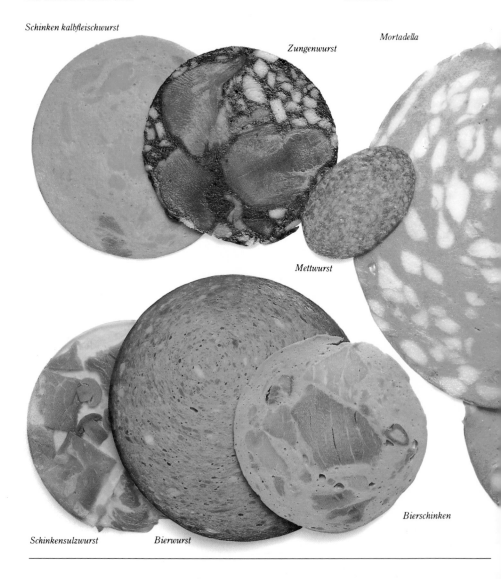

Schinken kalbfleischwurst

Zungenwurst

Mortadella

Mettwurst

Schinkensulzwurst

Bierwurst

Bierschinken

MORTADELLA

One of the largest types of sausage, the ingredients vary but usually consist of pork, garlic and seasonings. This bland sausage from Bologna is available plain or sometimes with pistachio nuts or coriander seeds. It should be thinly sliced.

SCHINKENSULZWURST

Pieces of ham and mushroom slices are set in jelly.

BIERWURST

A German pork or pork-and-beef sausage flecked with fat and smoked. It is usually spicy.

BIERSCHINKEN

Pistachio nuts and peppercorns are often included with the lean and fat pork and ham pieces in this German sausage.

EXTRAWURST

A pale-pink mixture of beef and pork or bacon fat, this German sausage is smooth in texture and slices easily. It is lightly smoked and may be poached or grilled.

KNOBLAUCHWURST

The strong, distinctive taste of garlic characterizes this German sausage, which contains fat and lean pork and is also flavored with salt, pepper and spice. It can be grilled or poached.

JAGDWURST

There are various types of this "hunter's" sausage, some large and round, others narrow and flat. They contain pork and spices and are smoked. Schinkenjagdwurst, shown here, contains finely minced pork with diced pork fat and pieces of ham.

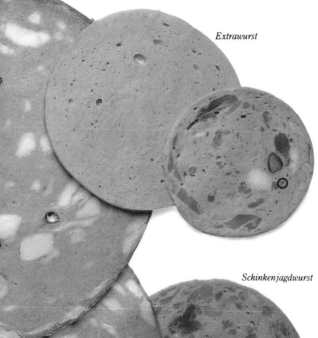

Extrawurst

Knoblauchwurst

Schinkenjagdwurst

Plain mortadella

OTHER COOKED AND SMOKED SAUSAGES

BERLINER
A pork and beef sausage mildly flavored with salt and sugar.

LINGUIC
This Portuguese pork sausage is cured in brine, seasoned with garlic, and spiced with cinnamon and cumin.

STRASSBURGER
A liver and veal sausage containing pistachio nuts.

WEISSWURST
This is a mildly spiced German sausage made of pork, veal, and/or chicken.

Smoked Sausages

PEPPERONI

A dry Italian sausage that consists of a mixture of coarsely chopped beef and pork and is highly seasoned with ground red pepper and other spices. It is commonly served on pizzas.

Kabanos

Pepperoni

Katenrauchwurst

KABANOS

A Polish sausage made of minced pork and beef, with herbs.

CHORIZO

A Spanish (and Latin-American) spicy sausage made with pork and cayenne, pimento or other hot chile pepper, usually in narrow casings. Some chorizos are fresh, but most are dried and smoked. Longaniza is a Portuguese version.

Chorizo

KATENRAUCHWURST

This dark-skinned sausage is firm in texture and contains coarsely cut smoked pork. Originally it was produced in *katen* or peasant huts, hence its name. It was hung in the chimney to be smoked. It is similar to Mettwurst.

BIRNENFORMIGE SALAMI

The name means "pear-shaped"; a perfect description of this German salami before slicing.

Birnenformige salami

NETZ SALAMI

A German salami that takes its name from the string in which it is hung.

Netz salami

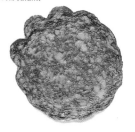

LAND SALAMI

A country-style salami usually with spices or herbs mixed into the pork.

Land salami

EDEL SALAMI

The name "edel" means "noble". It is a rich salami of mixed pork and beef.

Edel salami

KIELBASA

A Polish sausage of ground pork and beef that is garlicky and well seasoned, and available fresh or smoked. The word means "sausage", as does the Russian "kolbasa", which is similar.

Kielbasa

SAUCISSON FUME

Saucissons are large and can be air-dried or smoked. The saucisson fumé is typically made from pork, with flecks of back fat or bacon, peppercorns and garlic and herbs. Saucisson fumé aux herbes, shown here, has a generous coating of dried herbs.

Saucisson fumé

OTHER SMOKED SAUSAGES

KALBWURST

Generally a German veal smoked sausage, it may also contain pork, pork fat and pistachio nuts.

SMOKIES

Smoked, cooked links of pork and beef spiced with pepper.

CERVELAT

German minced beef and pork sausage that is smoked to a golden brown. Its meat is more finely ground than Italian salami and usually less highly seasoned.

Cervelat

PLOCKWURST

A German beef or beef and pork rohwurst. There are several varieties, including the pfeffer-plockwurst shown here. It is one of the few square sausages, and is coated with coarsely ground black pepper.

Plockwurst (pfeffer plockwurst)

Salami

There is a vast range of salami sausages available, including versions from Germany, Italy, America, Denmark, Hungary and France. All are made with uncooked meat which may be pork, beef or a mixture of the two, and variously flavored. Some are decorated with pistachio nuts, peppercorns or coriander seeds. Kosher salami is an all-beef type flavored with garlic, mustard, coriander and juniper. Salami may be air-dried, smoked or both. It is usually thinly sliced and eaten cold, although chopped slices find their way into many Italian cooked dishes, including pizza. Salamini are smaller versions of the usually large sausage.

Milano salami

MILANO SALAMI

An Italian salami made with lean pork, beef and pork fat. It is seasoned with garlic, pepper and white wine (see Milano-style).

MILANO-STYLE SALAMI

Another variety of Milano salami. Both are often used for antipasto.

TOSCANA

Fiorentino is the best known of the Tuscan salamis. Larger than average, they often consist of pure pork mingled with pieces of lean meat and fat.

Milano-style salami

Toscana

DANISH SALAMI

An even-shaped salami which is useful in sandwich-making. A mixture of pork, veal, spices and sometimes garlic.

Danish salami

FRENCH PEPPER SALAMI

Pork and beef are mixed with coarse fat and seasoned with whole black peppercorns. It is often used in hors d'oeuvres.

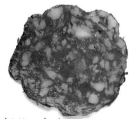

French pepper salami

FRENCH HERB SALAMI

A small beef and pork salami coated with herbs. Useful for picnics, it is also served in hors d'oeuvres.

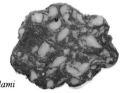

French herb salami

FELINETTI

From Parma, this is a delicate salami containing white wine, peppercorns and a little garlic.

Felinetti

GENOA SALAMI

Popular as an antipasto, this is seasoned with garlic, peppercorns and red wine and contains a mixture of pork and veal.

Genoa salami

Country-style salami

GERMAN SALAMI

The German varieties generally are a finely ground beef and pork mixture and tend to be more heavily smoked than any of the Italian salamis.

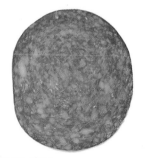

German salami

FARMER-STYLE SALAMI

A salami that is usually a coarse-cut beef and pork mixture with whole peppercorns and garlic.

COUNTRY-STYLE SALAMI

The basic sausage mixture is bound with twine and left to dry and mature instead of being eaten immediately. It contains pork, pork fat, garlic, herbs and peppercorns.

HUNGARIAN SALAMI

Very fatty pork is mixed with a blend of several spices in this salami. The casings are lightly smoked and the taste of this salami improves with age.

NAPOLI SALAMI

A long thin salami made with pork and beef. It is seasoned well with both black and red pepper to make it quite hot. Similar to Pepperoni.

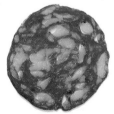

Napoli salami

Farmer-style salami

Hungarian salami

Preserved Meats and Bacons

CORNED BEEF

Also called salt beef, this is a cut of beef – usually brisket – cured in brine and spiced.

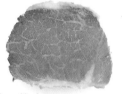

Corned beef

TONGUE

Usually beef tongue, it is salted, poached and served in cold slices with salads. It can also be smoked or corned.

Tongue

SMOKED TURKEY

The meat is soaked in pickling brine and then smoked. It is usually sliced for sandwiches.

Smoked turkey

BRESAOLA

This dried salt beef is a speciality from Lombardy, Italy. Cut thinly, it is served as an hors d'oeuvre.

Bresaola

GALANTINE

This is made from boned meat or poultry prepared in a gelatin stock and set.

Galantine

RILLETTES

From France, this is potted pork belly, sometimes with goose or rabbit added.

Rillettes

BOLOGNA

There are a number of versions of this famous sausage which is basically a mixture of cooked smoked pork and beef. Devon, fritz and polony are other names.

Bologna

PASTRAMI

Romanian cured meat taken from either goat, mutton, beef, pork or goose. The meat is dry-cured with a mixture of salt, saltpetre, black pepper, nutmeg, paprika, garlic and allspice, before smoking. The American version, (shown here), is cured, smoked plate (underside) of beef. It is usually thinly sliced and used for sandwiches.

Pastrami

DUCK TERRINE

Duck, lean ham and bacon fat are mixed with seasonings, spices and sometimes brandy.

Duck terrine

LIVERWURST

Originally from Germany, liver sausage is now made in many different countries. Most varieties are made of ground pork, pork or veal liver, onions and seasoning, and may also contain truffles, peppercorns or flecks of fat back. They are usually finely minced and lightly smoked and are ready to eat, as slices or a spread.

Liverwurst

OTHER PRESERVED MEATS AND BACONS

PATE DE FOIE GRAS

Made from the liver of specially reared geese, mixed with spices and seasonings to a smooth texture, this pâté is a luxury item.

Pâté de foie gras

TERRINE DE PYRENEES

A semi-smooth-textured terrine which includes mushrooms.

Terrine de Pyrénées

PATE DE FORESTIER

Possessing a much coarser texture than terrine de Pyrenées, pâté de forestier is surrounded by a pastry crust.

Pâté de forestier

BAUERNSPECK

Austrian belly and flank of pork is cured in brine with juniper berries, then cold-smoked.

BRAUNSCHWEIGER

A cooked, smoked liver sausage containing eggs and milk.

BRAWN

A cooked meat speciality product containing small pieces of pig's head bound together by gelatin.

BUNDERFLEISH

This Swiss dried beef is brined, rubbed with spices, then air-dried.

DUTCH LOAF

This is a cold cut comprised of pork and beef.

FENELAR

In this Norwegian smoked mutton the leg is dry-salted with salt, saltpetre and sugar, rubbed with the mixture for several days, then brined in a

sweet pickle after which it is smoked and air-dried.

HONEY LOAF

A mixture of pork, beef, honey, spices and pickles.

SCRAPPLE

A speciality product of cooked pork and cornmeal; very popular in the American South.

SOUSE

Pieces of pork meat in a vinegar-spiked gelatin base to which dill pickles, sweet red peppers and bay leaves may be added.

SPINKGANZ

This is German smoked goose. Only the breast is used, which is dry-salted with salt, saltpetre, sugar and pepper, then smoked.

Smoked Canadian bacon

Unsmoked Canadian bacon

CANADIAN BACON

Available smoked and unsmoked, this is available in pieces or thinly sliced and can be served hot or cold.

Canadian back slab bacon

SLICED BACON

This is cut in individual slices, either unsmoked or smoked. Because of the evenness of the slices it is usually more popular than the slab bacon.

Unsmoked sliced bacon

Smoked sliced bacon

SLAB BACON

Below left, smoked bacon with rind, below right, unsmoked bacon without rind, and right, back bacon. The first two are cut from the belly and are quite fatty.

Smoked slab bacon with rind

Unsmoked slab bacon without rind

Hams

BAYONNE

Almost every region of France has its own salted and smoked ham. This one from the Basque country is one of the best known. Cured at Orthez in south-west France, this is a raw ham type – a *jambon cru*. The brine contains red wine, rosemary and olive oil. After brining, it is wrapped in straw and smoked.

PROSCIUTTO

A fine-quality raw ham (*prosciutto crudo*), cured at Langhirano near Parma in Italy. Hams are rubbed with a mixture of salt, sugar, nitrates, pepper, allspice, nutmeg, coriander and mustard. They are packed together for 10 days, then the process is repeated. After maturing, the hams are pressed, steamed and rubbed with pepper.

WESTPHALIAN

One of the most famous of the German hams, this is a raw ham, like Bayonne and Parma. After curing (with salt, sugar and saltpetre) and smoking, this rich, dark ham undergoes a lengthy ageing process.

Westphalian

Bayonne

Parma

VIRGINIA

Fully cooked boneless ham sometimes glazed with apple or pineapple juices and studded with cloves. Baked deli ham is often called Virginia ham.

SUGAR-GLAZED

A rolled boneless cooked ham with a sugar glaze; it is sold whole, in halves or sliced.

ARDENNES

A Belgian ham of great quality which is considered to rank in taste with Parma, York and Bayonne hams.

Ardennes

Virginia

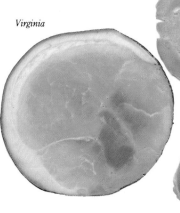

Sugar-glazed

Suffolk

YORK

This English ham enjoys a worldwide reputation. Firm and tender, it is noted for its delicate taste. It is often cured with dry salt instead of brine and then lightly smoked. The one shown has been coated with breadcrumbs.

SUFFOLK

This expensive English ham is soaked in molasses rather than salt – a process which turns its skin a distinctive black.

York

SMITHFIELD

This ham takes its name from a town in Virginia where its particular curing process was first developed. The hams are given two rubbings of salt and saltpetre, washed, and heavily smoked with hickory. They are then rubbed with pepper, and matured for up to 18 months.

Bradenham (slice)

Smithfield

Smithfield (sliced)

Bradenham

BRADENHAM

This ham is from Chippenham in England. The ham is dry-cured, treated with spices and molasses (which gives it its characteristic black skin), and then hung for many months to age.

OTHER HAMS

COUNTRY
A dry-cured bone-in ham, treated with the cure throughout the maturing process. Country hams come from rural areas of several states and are labeled with their state or region of origin – Georgia, Kentucky, Tennessee and Virginia are major producers of Country ham.

DEVILLED
A prepared spread made of finely ground ham and seasonings.

IRISH
Usually dry-cured and smoked over peat. Limerick and Belfast are two well-known types.

VARIETY MEATS

VARIETY MEATS OR OFFAL, meaning the "off-fall" or off-cuts from the carcass – have been both enjoyed and condemned for centuries, condemned because certain items such as the brain and heart were thought to provoke melancholy, while the head – and especially the boar's head – has been invested with symbolic significance of victory, similar to the fox's brush after the hunt.

Many people are still reluctant to eat brains, sweetbreads and tripe, and many more are unable to actually identify or pinpoint the location of caul, mesentery and chitterlings. Some forms of variety meats are unpopular for social, economic and religious reasons; others have always been in considerable demand, especially liver and kidneys – and particularly those of the calf. A tour around the anatomy of an animal will reveal some less familiar cuts.

Variety meats in the kitchen

All variety meats should be purchased as fresh as possible. If they are stale, they are usually dark in color with a dry appearance.

Brains, sweetbreads and tongues need a preliminary soaking. Brains should be soaked in cold water until all the blood is leached away and the arteries and fibers should then be removed. Sweetbreads require soaking for an hour or more, then blanching (parboiling) in acidulated water (about 7 minutes for lambs'; 10 for calves'). Tongues should be soaked in acidulated water for an hour if fresh, or in plain water overnight if salted. Small tongues should be blanched for 10 minutes, larger ones for 30

minutes, and they should then be plunged in cold water before removing the skin.

Beef and pork kidneys can be soaked in acidulated water for about 30 minutes. Other items, such as liver, tripe, trotters (pigs feet) and calves' feet, hearts and heads are usually prepared by the butcher.

Calves' and sheeps' heads may be boned or left whole. They may also be served whole – but more often than not divided into pieces – with appropriate sauces, the garnish being the sliced tongue and the brain. Pig's head is used mainly for charcuterie, in cold cuts and sausages. Pigs' and calves' ears can be grilled or stuffed. Calves' feet and pigs' trotters are highly gelatinous, and used to thicken stocks. They are also boned, stuffed, fried. Tails can be braised or boiled; sheeps' tails are made into a pie. Oxtail, which is rich in gelatin and has plenty of flavor, responds to long, moist cooking in casseroles and soups.

Many variety meats are from the inside of the animal. Examples are the spleen (the pig's is used as a sausage ingredient, while that of the ox and calf can be stuffed) and intestines (pigs' intestines are used as casings for sausages, and chitterlings or "chitlins" are famous in the South, served with collard greens). Calf's mesentery (part of the peritoneum) is also a sausage ingredient, but may be fried or prepared in the manner of tripe, while the lungs or "lights" are for stewing. Pig's caul (the lace-like membrane around the stomach) is the binding for *crépinettes* (small sausages – page 207).

BRAINS

Lamb brains and veal brains (the most popular) are pale pink and delicate in texture. They are often sautéed or chopped and fried or creamed. Veal, or calf, brains are sometimes served with black butter sauce or fried and cooked in batter.

Lamb brains   *Veal (calf) brains*

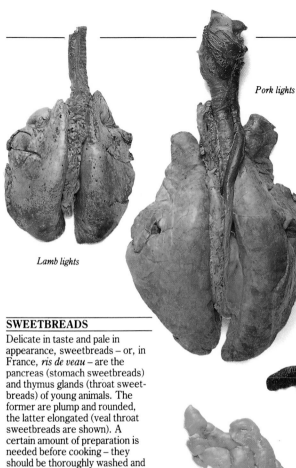

Pork lights

Lamb lights

LIGHTS

These are the lungs of an animal, which in America and Britain are generally reserved for pet foods, but they are cooked for the table in some countries. Not very substantial in themselves, they are either served with a nutritious sauce, added to stews or used by pork butchers as an ingredient in *pâté de foie*.

MELT

This is the spleen of animals (a pig's melt is shown). Although cooked for the table they are often sold in western society for pet food. Generally not highly regarded by gourmets, they are used either in sausage-making or, with the heart and lungs, are incorporated into stews. Ox and calves' melts can be stuffed.

SWEETBREADS

Delicate in taste and pale in appearance, sweetbreads – or, in France, *ris de veau* – are the pancreas (stomach sweetbreads) and thymus glands (throat sweet-breads) of young animals. The former are plump and rounded, the latter elongated (veal throat sweetbreads are shown). A certain amount of preparation is needed before cooking – they should be thoroughly washed and soaked. They can then be braised, fried or sautéed, and are often eaten with flavorful sauces. Recipes for veal and lamb sweetbreads are more or less interchangeable.

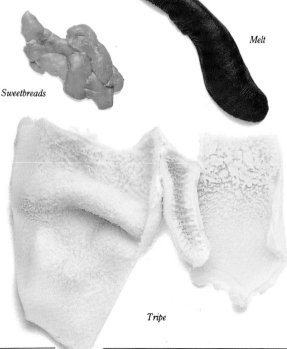

Melt

Sweetbreads

TRIPE

Tripe comes from the two stomachs of oxen and cows. Plain tripe comes from the first stomach or rumen, and honeycomb tripe (generally more tender) from the second stomach or reticulum. All tripe is sold cleaned, washed and blanched, and sometimes it is fully cooked. When bought raw, however, it needs long, slow cooking – the classic dish is a white stew with onions. Perhaps the most famous recipe is the French *tripe à la mode de Caen*.

Tripe

EYEBALLS

Eyeballs (particularly sheeps eyeballs, as shown) are considered a great delicacy in the Middle East. They are usually removed from the head after it has been roasted or boiled and are eaten straight away, with or without extra sauce or seasonings.

Sheeps eyeballs

HEART

Hearts are nutritious and contain very little waste. Lamb and veal hearts have the finest taste and are suitable for stuffing, pork hearts are larger and slightly coarser, and beef hearts are the least tender of all. All require long, slow cooking.

MARROWBONE

The shoulder or thigh bones of oxen or calves contain large quantities of marrow, a soft, fatty substance which is extracted from the bones after they have been cooked. Marrow is used in sauces, soups, stews and risottos; it is also eaten hot as a spread for an hors d'oeuvre.

TAIL

Tasty, nourishing and relatively inexpensive, tails are usually sold skinned and jointed for use in soups and stews. Oxtails should have creamy white fat and deep red meat, with an equal proportion of meat to bone. Rich in gelatin and with plenty of flavor, they respond to long, moist cooking in casseroles and soups. Sheeps tails, usually obtainable at Chinese butchers, may be made into a pie.

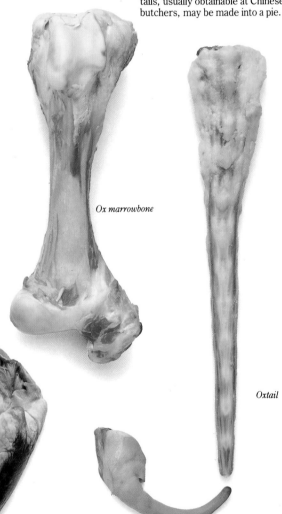

Ox marrowbone

Pork heart

Lamb heart

Chicken heart

Beef heart

Pig's tail

Oxtail

TONGUE

In some markets, tongue is sold ready to serve, but it is also available fresh, smoked or pickled for cooking and eating hot or cold, with or without sauce. Salted tongue is used cooked, pressed and sliced cold (page 214), while fresh tongue may be braised with wine, or boiled and served with various garnishes. Beef and veal tongues are the most common, lamb tongues the most tender.

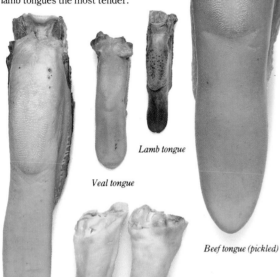

Lamb tongue

Veal tongue

Beef tongue (pickled)

Beef tongue

Pigs' trotters

TROTTERS and FEET

Pigs' trotters and calves' feet are bought whole or split in half and are used for making strong, gelatinous stock, consommés and aspic. They may also be broiled and eaten hot with sauce, added to stews for extra richness, jellied for eating cold, or boned, stuffed and fried.

Calves' feet

OTHER VARIETY MEATS

CHITTERLINGS
Pigs' intestines which are often used in sausage-making, they are particularly popular in America and France. They can be grilled or fried.

EARS
Pigs' and calves' ears can be grilled or stuffed. In China, pigs' ears are cooked with spices.

HEAD
Pig's head is used mainly in charcuterie, in brawn and sausages. It is also often boiled – with the tongue and brains removed – or marinated. Calves' and sheeps' heads may be boned or left whole, and are usually prepared by the butcher. They may also be served whole, but are usually divided into pieces and served with a sauce. Bath chaps, the smoked cheeks of the pig, are mainly boiled and eaten cold like ham.

MESENTERY
This is a membrane which forms part of the peritoneum. Caif's mesentery is a sausage ingredient, but may be fried or prepared in the same way as tripe.

TESTICLES
Also known as fries or animelles, lambs' and calves' testicles can be fried in batter, sautéed or cooked in a *court-bouillon* and served with vinaigrette.

LIVER

A rich source of iron, liver is probably the most popular variety meat eaten in western countries. Several varieties are shown, of which the finest in quality and flavor, and therefore the most expensive, is calf's liver. Although all types can be fried or broiled (with the exception of ox liver, which is usually used in stews and casseroles), sautéeing is the best cooking method to retain its moistness. Lamb's liver is more strongly flavored and often less tender than calf's liver. It is generally fried with bacon, but is often spit-roasted in the Middle East. Ox liver is inexpensive, with a strong flavor, but usually tough, while pig's liver is also strongly flavored and largely used in charcuterie, where it is one of the ingredients in pâtés. Chicken and goose livers are also most often used to make pâtés.

Calf's (veal) liver

Beef (ox) liver

Goose liver

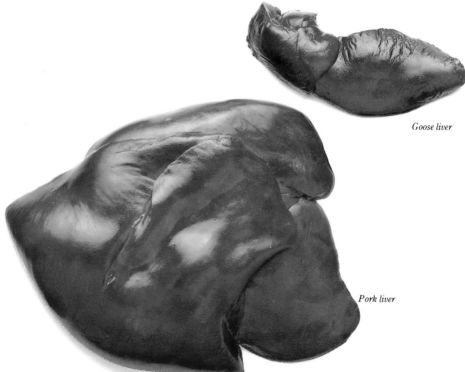

Pork liver

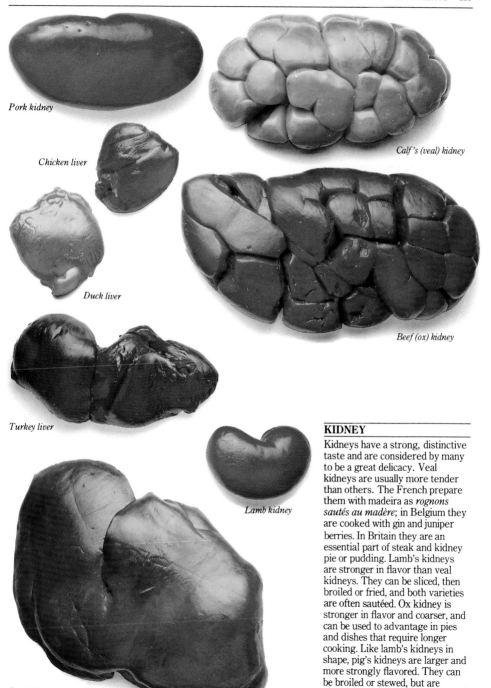

Pork kidney

Chicken liver

Calf's (veal) kidney

Duck liver

Beef (ox) kidney

Turkey liver

Lamb kidney

Lamb liver

KIDNEY

Kidneys have a strong, distinctive taste and are considered by many to be a great delicacy. Veal kidneys are usually more tender than others. The French prepare them with madeira as *rognons sautés au madère*; in Belgium they are cooked with gin and juniper berries. In Britain they are an essential part of steak and kidney pie or pudding. Lamb's kidneys are stronger in flavor than veal kidneys. They can be sliced, then broiled or fried, and both varieties are often sautéed. Ox kidney is stronger in flavor and coarser, and can be used to advantage in pies and dishes that require longer cooking. Like lamb's kidneys in shape, pig's kidneys are larger and more strongly flavored. They can be broiled or stewed, but are usually used in terrines.

MEAT

FROM THE EARLIEST TIMES, man has been a carnivorous animal. Though today there is a reappraisal of the importance of meat in the diet – whether its drawbacks, like cholesterol and high prices as well as ethical considerations, outweigh its value as a protein-provider – meat is still the most expensive item in the budget and a great deal of thought should be put into choosing and using it wisely.

The meat used in the bulk of recipes comes from the three main types of domestic farm animals – cattle, sheep and pigs, giving us beef and veal, mutton and lamb, and pork. While regional preferences, religion and climate may have certain influences, these meats feature in the majority of national cuisines, and may be supplemented by other domestic types, such as horsemeat, goat and reindeer.

Butcher's meat today is largely a product of selective breeding and feeding techniques, whereby animals are carefully reared to reach high standards and specific needs: the present-day demand is for lean and tender meat, and modern cattle, sheep and pigs are well-fleshed yet compact creatures compared to their forebearers of a century ago.

Cuts of meat

The consumer's requirements (affected by social and economic trends), religious custom and the animal's anatomy influence the way in which the butcher cuts his carcasses. Regional climates, family occupations and the use of local ingredients, such as herbs, fruits and vegetables, influence cooking methods and therefore demands for cuts. Butchering techniques vary considerably, not only from country to country, but even within cities and towns. (In America, however, such regional variations were standardized in the 1970's).

Meat from specific parts of an animal may be cut and cooked according to local custom and, more strictly, by religious observance – particularly in Jewish kosher and Muslim *halal* butchery, for example.

Choosing meat

Meat is a natural, and therefore not a uniform, product, varying in quality from carcass to carcass, while flavor, texture and appearance are determined by the type of animal and the way it has been fed. There is no reason to think that flavor is only obtained in meat which possesses a proportion of fat, although it does give a characteristic flavor to meat and helps to keep it moist during roasting. The color of meat is also no guide to quality. Consumers are inclined to choose light-colored meat – bright red beef, for example – because they think that it will be fresher than an alternative dark red piece. Freshly butchered beef is bright red because the pigment in the tissues, myoglobin, has been chemically affected by the oxygen in the air. After several hours, the color changes to dark red or brown as the pigment is further oxidized to become metamyaglobin. The color of fat can vary from almost pure white in lamb to bright yellow in beef. Color depends on the feed, on the breed and, to a certain extent, on the time of the year.

The most useful guide to tenderness and quality is a knowledge of the cuts of meat and their location on the carcass. The various cuts are described under their respective headings, but in principle the leanest and tenderest cuts, the "prime" cuts, come from the hindquarters. The "coarse" cuts, or meat from the neck, legs and forequarters, those parts of the animal that have had plenty of muscular exercise and where fibers have become hardened, provide meat for braising and stewing. Many consider these cuts to have more flavor, although they require slow cooking to make them tender.

The meat from young animals is generally more tender and, since tenderness is a prime factor, animals may be injected before slaughter with an enzyme, such as papain, which soften the fibers and muscles. But this merely speeds up a natural and more satisfactory process: meat contains its own proteolytic enzymes which gradually break down the protein cell walls as the carcass ages. That is why meat is usually hung from 10 to 20 days in controlled conditions of temperature and humidity before being offered for sale. Meat which is aged for longer becomes more expensive – the cost of refrigeration is high and the meat itself shrinks in size.

Meat in the kitchen

Meat is an extremely versatile product that can be cooked in a multitude of ways, and matched with practically any vegetable, fruit and herb. The cut (shin, steak, brisket), the method of heating (roasting, braising, broiling) and the time and temperature all affect the way the meat will taste. Raw meat is difficult to chew because the muscle fiber contains an elastic protein (collagen) which is only softened by grinding – as in steak tartare – or by cooking. When you cook meat, the protein gradually coagulates as the internal temperature increases. At 171°F coagulation is complete, the protein begins to harden, and further cooking makes the meat tougher.

Since tenderness combined with flavor is the aim in cooking meat, much depends on the ratio of time and temperature. In principle, slow cooking retains the juices and produces a more tender result than fast cooking at high temperatures. There are, of course, occasions when high temperatures are essential: you need to broil a steak under a hot flame for a very limited time in order to obtain a crisp, brown surface and a pink, juicy interior – using a low temperature would not give you the desired result. But in potentially tough cuts, such as brisket, or where there is a quantity of connective tissue, as with neck of lamb, a slow rate of cooking converts the tissues to gelatin and helps to make the meat more tender.

Meat on the bone will take longer to cook because bone is a poor conductor of heat. Tough or coarse cuts of meat should be cooked by braising, pot-roasting or stewing. Marinating in wine or wine vinegar helps to tenderize the meat, and imparts an additional flavor. Searing meat in hot fat, or in a hot oven before roasting or stewing, helps to produce a crisp exterior by coagulating the protein but does not, as is widely supposed, seal in the juices. However, if the external temperature is too high and cooking prolonged, rapid evaporation and contraction of the meat will cause considerable loss of juices and fat. Salt sprinkled on meat before cooking will also hasten loss of moisture since salt is hygroscopic and absorbs water.

Meat bones are useful for giving flavor to soup and stock, especially beef ones with plenty of marrow. Veal bones are gelatinous and help to enrich and thicken soups and sauces. Fat can be rendered down for frying, or else used as an ingredient when suet or lard is called for.

Cooking meat

Briefly, meat cooking can be broadly divided into the following categories: quick cooking at moderate to high temperatures, as when broiling, barbecuing and frying (suitable for such prime tender cuts as steaks, chops, veal escalopes, or cutlets, and kebobs); slow to moderate cooking, as when roasting or using a rotisserie (suitable for prime tender joints such as beef sirloin, leg of lamb, cuts of pork and veal); and slow cooking in a liquid, as when stewing, braising or pot-roasting (suitable for coarse cuts such as thick flank, leg, shank and neck cuts). One big advantage to braising and stewing is that any quantities left over can be easily re-heated. In fact, many dishes are improved by allowing them to "mature" and then re-heating. Roasts are less adaptable, and cold roast meat is rarely successfully re-heated, since it lacks the essential moisture. Re-heated meat must be heated through thoroughly, and then only once, to avoid the possible risk of food poisoning.

When you are preparing meat for cooking, never wash it, simply wipe the surface with a damp cloth. Use a meat thermometer when roasting; many are graded with temperature scales and also scaled according to the type of meat and the cut. They record the internal temperature of the meat. Meat that requires carving should rest for 15 minutes so that it loses its springiness and is easier to carve, and juices do not escape so readily. Always carve on a non-slip surface, and one where the juices can be collected. Use a sharp knife, otherwise the meat will simply tear along the grain, and a guarded carving fork.

Beef and Veal

Domestic cattle, from which we derive our beef, have been gradually developed over thousands of years. Their ancestors were the wild aurochs, *Bos primigenius*, first domesticated in Anatolia and Greece in about 6000 BC. The lineage of this ancient breed was so enduring that the last known specimen of aurochs was recorded in Poland in 1627. The Greeks and Romans prepared their beef dishes with an abundance of pepper and other spices, not because the meat was not fresh or lacked flavor, but because spices were an expensive item, and so was beef. Such fine ingredients were used on special occasions, and denoted the wealth of the household.

Beef in the kitchen

Beef has always been an expensive meat. During the Middle Ages, the infrequent fare of the common man was salt pork and mutton, and beef the privilege of the wealthy. In Britain, farmers maintained herds of cattle and sheep, only slaughtering a part of their stock as winter approached and grazing ended. Beef would then be eaten fresh, the remainder salted for the coming months. Yet by the eighteenth century the English had a reputation as a nation of beef-eaters. In London an event took place that was, in some respects, a culinary revolution – the introduction of the beefsteak.

In France, the *bifteck* had been noted by the epicure Brillat-Savarin. Here, as in London, butchering techniques were gradually improving, yet only city butchers could be relied upon to cut a steak for the grill: "It would seem", wrote one steak fancier, "that country butchers have not learned the secrets of proper cuts".

In America, beef has always been the most sought-after meat and steak was established as the favorite by the mid-nineteenth century. It was often served to travellers at coach stops or "porterhouses", as they were called. At this time, too, the reflector oven was introduced; this replaced the spit as the principal cooking apparatus for roast beef.

The early American desire for beef was met by the successful transplantation of Spanish cattle to Texas. Bred to withstand the heat and lack of water in Andalusia, the Texas Longhorns overcame the rigors of being herded to the railroad centres for shipment. And if the cattle supplied Americans with their favorite meat, the cowboys who herded them popularized a favorite way of cooking it – the barbecue. Although the Texas Longhorns, the staple of the American meat economy, have long been displaced by meatier breeds from Britain, today it is America, and not Britain, that has become a nation of beef-eaters – Americans eat and import more beef than any other country in the world, consuming some 65 lbs per head of the population every year, in the form of barbecued sirloin steaks, hamburgers broiled T-bone and porterhouse steaks, New England boiled dinner with corned beef, the Southwest's chili con carne and other beef dishes.

Choosing and using beef

The cuts of beef vary considerably, from the very tender fillet steak to the tough brisket or the shank, and there is a greater variety of cuts in beef than in other meat. In America meat is graded according to quality and yield, and such other factors as marbling, maturity, color, firmness, texture, and the ratio of usable meat to fat and bone.

There are seven primary cuts from a side of beef, each one composed of muscle, fat, bone and connective tissue. The least-developed muscles, usually from the inner area, yield cuts that can be roasted or broiled, while leaner and more sinewy meat is cut from more highly developed external muscles. An exception is rib and loin cuts, which come from external, but basically immobile muscles.

Knowing where the cuts come from helps determine the cooking method. The forequarter, which normally weighs from 155 to 190 pounds, produces four primary cuts: chuck, rib of beef, brisket and short plate. Chuck comes from the neck and shoulder – one of the most mobile sections. Cuts from this part are likely to be sinewy with large amounts of connective tissue. Moist cooking such as braising, stewing or pot-roasting produces the best results, but some small, tenderchucks steaks suitable for broiling and frying can be produced. Rib of beef is an immobile primary cut from the center of the back and yields the tenderest steaks and roasts. Brisket is cut from above the leg, and being fibrous it requires long, slow, moist cooking. Curing, as for corned beef, can also produce more tender meat. Short plate, which is part of the breast bone, produces cuts that need grinding or moist cooking with the exception of skirt steak however, which is produced from the same area and is of a more tender cut.

The hindquarter, which normally weighs 145–180 lbs, is made up of three main sections: full loin, whole flank, and round beef. Full loin is the tenderest part, produces porterhouse, sirloin, filet mignon, as well as tenderloin roast. Whole flank produces the London broil cut, as well as chopped meat trimmings. Round of beef, the hind leg, is a lean, mobile section comprising of the rump (requiring moist cooking) and six other roasts; these include the tender side of round and top round, as well as the less tender bottom round, the shank and heel which are more suitable to moist cooking or grinding.

VEAL

Veal is the meat from dairy calves usually slaughtered at three months of age. Today this meat is in short supply – due to more efficient dairy production from fewer animals – and expensive: young animals have a coddled upbringing and many are completely milk-fed. The association of milk and veal goes back at least to Norman times, when chefs prepared *blancmange* – veal cooked with milk and almonds – and taught English cooks to make *veel bukkenade* with veal, eggs, milk and spices, a medieval *blanquette de veau*.

One particular veal dish, the breaded escalope (cutlet), has had a curious, military history. It probably originated in Spain, and was introduced to Milan when the city was a part of the Spanish Empire in the sixteenth century. They called it the *scallopine Milanese*, perhaps after the scallop shell, the emblem of Spain's patron saint, St James, and it featured in Milan

homes as a delicacy. When Milan was later occupied by Austrian soldiers under Marshal Radetsky, the Marshal introduced the dish to the kitchens of Emperor Franz Josef, where it became the famed *Wiener schnitzel*.

Not as much veal is eaten in America as in Europe. French dishes include the provincial *blanquette de veau*, and the grand *selle de veau Orloff*. Italy, already replete with *scallopine*, is known for its cold veal with a sauce of tuna fish (*vitello tonnato*); the Tuscan stew *stufatino* and the famous *ossobuco*, veal knuckle stewed with tomatoes. Romanians mince veal and make a casserole, while the Bulgarians stew it with horseradish.

Choosing and using veal

Unlike beef, veal may be judged by the color of the meat. The whiter it is, the greater proportion of the calf's diet has been milk and the more likely the meat is to be tender with a delicate flavor. More mature veal is pink or rosy pink, with creamy white fat. A dry, brown, or mottled appearance indicates staleness. Veal is inclined to dryness as it has little internal fat and for this reason it is often larded with pork fat or bacon if roasted, pot-roasted or braised to make it moist.

The veal carcass is divided into two sections – the foresaddle and the hindsaddle. There are six primary cuts of veal. The three from the foresaddle are the shoulder (chuck); rack and breast; and foreshack. The not very tender shoulder may be cut into roasts, chops, steaks, and shoulder cutlets. Most cuts should be moist-cooked, but dry cooking is possible with extra fat. The rack is usually cut into chops and escalopes (cutlets) for sautéeing or braising, but it may also be roasted whole as a crown roast. The breast and foreshank are usually best braised. Most of the better cuts come from the three divisions of the hindsaddle: the legs and hindshanks, the loin, and the flank. The leg is usually divided into roasts with or without the bone, whereas the hindshanks should be braised. The loin provides expensive chops for broiling, sautéeing or braising; it can also be sold boneless as a roast. Flank meat usually comes cubed or ground.

Shank cross cut

SHANK CROSS CUT

Taken from the hindshank or foreshank perpendicular to the bone, it is used for braising.

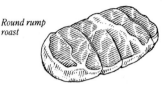

Round rump roast

ROUND RUMP ROAST

This boneless roast is usually tied and can be roasted or braised.

Top loin steak

TOP LOIN STEAK

A boneless cut from the short loin, used for broiling or grilling.

Bottom round rump roast

BOTTOM ROUND RUMP ROAST

An irregular thick cut from the hindquarters that is braised.

Round tip roast

RIB EYE ROAST

Also called a Delmonico Pot Roast, this is the large center muscle of the rib. All other muscles, bones and seam fat, are removed. This is for roasting.

Rib eye roast

Chuck T-bone steak

CHUCK T-BONE STEAK

Taken from the center or nearer the rib end of chuck, it is usually pot-roasted.

Porterhouse steak

PORTERHOUSE STEAK

The best short loin steak, it contains top loin and tenderloin; best broiled, pan fried or grilled.

SIRLOIN

This contains top sirloin and tenderloin muscles. It can be broiled, pan fried or grilled.

Sirloin

ROUND TIP TOAST

This comes from the hind quarters, but can also come from the sirloin. If high quality, it can be roasted; otherwise braised.

Rib roast

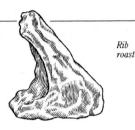

RIB ROAST

Removing the short-rib ends produces a tender seven-rib roast that may be divided into smaller roasts or steaks. All of them bone-in or boneless.

Chuck short ribs

CHUCK SHORT RIBS

These are pieces of layered meat for containing rib bones. They are usually braised or pre-cooked and barbecued.

RIB EYE STEAK

Also called Delmonico Steak, it is cut across the grain from rib eye roast. It can be broiled, panfried or grilled.

Rib eye steak

FLANK STEAK

This popular cut comes from the tail end of the loin, and can be broiled, pan fried, and barbecued.

Flank steak

OTHER BEEF CUTS

CHATEAUBRIAND

A thick steak cut from the center of the tenderloin, or fillet; suitable for broiling or sautéeing.

RIB ROAST

A tender cut sold either on the bone (Standing Rib Roast) or boned and rolled.

SKIRT STEAK

A marginally tender steak, suitable for broiling if from top quality or tendered beef. Otherwise, it is best braised or marinated and grilled.

TENDERLOIN (FILLET)

The tenderest cut of beef, taken from the middle of the loin. It can be roasted, cut into steaks for broiling or sautéeing, or cubed for Beef Stroganoff or Fondue Bourguignonne.

TOP LOIN CHOPS

The tenderloin is removed. These chops can be broiled, pan fried, or grilled.

Top loin chops

RIB CHOPS

This contains part of the chine bone; it can be broiled, pan fried, or grilled.

Rib chops

LOIN CHOP

A meaty chop containing backbone and tenderloin; it can be broiled, pan fried, or grilled.

Loin chop

BREAST RIBLETS

Quite long cuts with ribs. They are suitable for braising.

Breast riblets

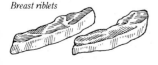

Leg rump roast

LEG RUMP ROAST

An irregularly shaped roast containing round muscle; it can be roasted or braised.

Leg rump roast boneless

LEG RUMP ROAST BONELESS

Usually rolled and tied to keep its shape. It can be roasted or braised.

Shoulder blade steak

SHOULDER BLADE STEAK

This contains blade bone ribs and back bone. It can be broiled or braised.

RIB ROAST

Contains up to 12 ribs and part of the chine bone. Used for roasting ask the butcher to loosen chine bone for easier carving.

Rib roast

STEW MEAT

This is boneless meat cut into chunks, usually from the fore-end, shoulder or shank. They are cooked in liquid, in stews, and casseroles.

Stew meat

BREAST

A fairly lean cut containing lower ribs. It can be roasted or braised; it is often boned, stuffed, and rolled.

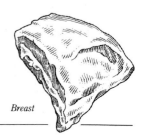

Breast

Lamb and Mutton

Sheep and goats have an ancestry that certainly predates that of cattle and pigs, going back to around 9000 BC. Like cattle, which yield both milk and meat, sheep have a two-fold purpose to provide wool and meat, and of the two, meat is today by far the most important.

Technically, lamb is the meat from a sheep under a year old. Baby, or milkfed lamb, is 6–8 weeks old. Spring lamb, which, despite its name, is available all year round, is marketed between 5 and 6 months of age; it is the type of lamb commonly found in the U.S. At one year, lamb becomes yearling mutton. At two, it is full-scale mutton, which is neither popular nor easy to find in this country. France's prized "pré salé" lamb, is lamb that has grazed in the salt marshes ("prés salés") of Brittany and Normandy. Much of the lamb consumed in the U.S. comes from New Zealand and Australia.

Lamb in the kitchen

Lamb is a popular meat in many parts of the world, and different countries have their own lamb dishes. In Middle Eastern and North African cooking, lamb features as the whole, spitted and roasted carcass called *mechoui*, or as *shish kebab*, which in fact means "skewered lamb". Minced lamb with cracked wheat is widely eaten, either raw or cooked. In Iran, mutton is stewed; in Tunisia it is cooked with spices and raisins. The French are particularly fond of roasting the leg. Lamb, or originally mutton, created the immortal Irish stew and the Lancashire hotpot.

Lamb is well suited to certain fruits and adjuncts: mint sauce with lamb and caper sauce with mutton are favourites in Britain. Algerians cook it with prunes and almonds, Moroccans with lemons and olives, the Belgians with endives, the Swedes with dill. Other herbs include rosemary and juniper berries. Lamb should be cooked so that it is still pink, and carved very thinly.

Choosing and using lamb

Good-quality lamb should have a fine, white fat, with pink flesh where freshly cut; in mutton the flesh is a deeper color. Lamb has a very thin, parchment-like covering on the carcass, known as the fell, which is usually left on roasts to help them maintain their shape during cooking. It should, however, be removed from chops. The flesh of a younger lamb is usually more tender. A good way to judge age is through weight – especially with legs of lamb: the highest quality weighs about 5 lbs and never more than 9 lbs. Smaller chops are also more tender and therefore more expensive.

A lamb carcass weighs between 45 and 60 pounds and is divided into halves – foresaddle and hindsaddle. The foresaddle contains the chuck, rack, foreshanks and breast. Even though chuck is cut from the mobile neck and shoulder, it is less developed and therefore more tender than other cuts of meat. The neck meat is usually ground although shoulder, loin chops, and kebob meat are obtainable. The rack produces some of the most desirable meat in the form of lean rib chops; it can also be roasted whole as a crown roast. The front legs or foreshanks, provide inexpensive meat that is usually braised. The breast can be boned and ground, or sold as riblets for braising. The hindsaddle is made up of the flank and two desirable cuts: the loin and leg. Most of the flank is ground as it is quite stringy. The loin is the most tender part and is usually cut up and sold for broiling. The leg is the meatiest part and can be roasted whole or divided into two parts: the shank and the rump, the shank being the meatier of the two. Two legs that are still attached are known as a "baron".

Leg shank half

Noisettes medallions

Leg

LEG SHANK HALF

Sirloin is half-removed; the lower half of the leg and the round leg bone are included. It is covered with fat and "fell", and is suitable for roasting.

NOISETTES/MEDALLIONS

These are small round slices, about two inches thick, cut from the loin. They are roasted or pan fried.

LEG

The whole leg contains the sirloin section with the hip bone, and the shank portion with the round bone. It has a covering of "fell" and is used for roasting.

Leg shank

SHOULDER CHOP

This contains cross sections of round arm bone and rib bones, it is usually braised.

Breast riblets

LEG STEAK

This is cut from the sirloin portion of the leg and contains backbone as well as some hip bone. It can be broiled or pan fried.

Shoulder chop

BREAST RIBLETS

Long cuts from the breast, they contain ribs, meat, and fat layers. They are used for braising, precooked and barbecued.

Rib roast

SHOULDER BLADE CHOP

This contains part of the blade and backbone and is used for braising.

Shoulder neck slices

RIB ROAST

This contains the ribs and the backbone. It is used for roasting.

Shank

Shoulder blade chop

SHOULDER NECK SLICES

These are cross cuts of neck with small bone. They are used for braising.

LAMB SHANK

A cut from the arm of shoulder containing the leg bone and section of shoulder bone. It is used for braising.

BREAST

A long cut that is part of the foresection with ribs. It is sometimes boned and stuffed, and can be roasted or braised.

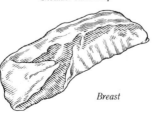

Breast

LOIN CHOP

This includes part of the backbone. It can be broiled, grilled, or pan fried.

Loin chop

Pork

The first people to taste roast pork were probably the Chinese, and Neolithic sites excavated in China show that pigs, used as food, were the only domestic animals. In the eighteenth century an Asian variety, *Sus scrofa vittatus*, was introduced. Most modern pig strains are descended from this Asian stock.

One of the most controversial aspects of pork is the fact that it is taboo in certain religions. It has been variously proposed that pork is basically unhygienic, and in hot climates presents a health hazard. Another view is that the pig was once a tribal emblem, and thus is sacrosanct. It is possible that as religion grew out of primeval rites, the pig became associated with primitive human sacrifice, and was then condemned as food.

Be that as it may, pork is greatly esteemed by many nations as a prime and tender meat. The pig's later associations with man have been very close. For centuries the diet of the European peasantry was supplemented by salt or pickled pork from their own pig; navies rationed it to their seamen who grew to despise it, and so did the aristocracy, who viewed pork as the food of the poor. Pigs were a feature of every homestead, however humble; pigs went with the settlers to the New World, and became so prolific that pork was a main item in American cooking long before beef took command, so that pork dishes feature among America's earliest recipes. The pigs were left to fatten in the woods and then, as today, they were utilized to the last ounce, including the head, entrails and trotters (see pages 202–217, and 218–223). Today, pork is America's second favorite meat after beef.

Pigs will eat almost anything – they are nature's vacuum cleaners, omnivorous and greedy – but pig farmers have to control their animals' diet to produce the right combination of fatness, weight, and meat quality. Pigs cannot eat grass alone, and are fed cereals, proteins, minerals and compound vitamins; diet influences the flavor of the meat, and it is likely that the free-ranging, ancestral pigs, though probably tougher and fattier than today's breeds, had a more natural flavor.

Pork in the kitchen

The pig's hardy, omnivorous, scavenging nature is the quality which has made it so enduring in a wide variety of climates and conditions. Perhaps because of its long association with salt, pork is often cooked or served with fruit: America, England and many European countries serve it with apple sauce; Danish cooks stuff pork with prunes, so do the Germans, who also stew pork in beer, serve it with sausages and potatoes, or with sauerkraut. In Russia, Italy, Greece and Poland suckling pigs are spitted whole and spit-roasted – suckling pig is an essential part of the Polish Easter festivities. But it is the Chinese who really excel with a wide variety of pork dishes – pork is shredded and stir-fried, spiced with star anise and ginger or braised with mushrooms.

Choosing and using pork

Pork should be pale pink with firm, white fat. Nearly all cuts of pork are prime, that is, they can be broiled or roasted because porkers are slaughtered at a young age and the meat is therefore tender throughout. The majority of cook books recommend that pork be well done to the point of dryness to minimize the danger of the parasite trichina; however, scientists have now recommended a new safe internal temperature for pork – 170°F – so that the meat remains moist and tender. Grill or fry chops and steaks, brushed with a little oil, for 15 to 20 minutes.

The four most commonly available cuts of fresh pork are the leg (fresh ham), the loin, the breast and the shoulder (the belly and jowl are sold to processors for bacon; the feet – or trotters – are used mainly to flavor stocks). Fresh ham is sold whole, boned, or as butt or shank roast (shank steaks are cut from the ladder). Loin cuts include blade, center, crown and sirloin roasts, as well as chopped cutlets and tenderloins. The breast is sectioned into ribs: the popular spare ribs, back ribs, and meaty country style ribs. Shoulder cuts include the Boston butt, sold as a whole or in cubes for stewing, as well as the relatively fatty picnic.

SIRLOIN CHOPS

Chops that have been cut from the end of the pork loin: these can be broiled or pan fried.

Sirloin chop

SHOULDER ARM ROAST

A cut that has the shank end removed; suitable for roasting.

Shoulder arm roast

LOIN CHOPS

High-quality chops containing part of the tenderloin; they can be broiled, grilled, or pan fried.

Loin chop

LOIN BLADE ROAST

A cut from the shoulder end of the loin; this is used for roasting. It can be a 5-rib or 7-rib roast.

Loin blade roast

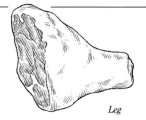

Leg

LEG

This lean tender cut contains the hind leg bone and is suitable for roasting. It can be boned and rolled.

Shoulder blade roast boneless

SHOULDER BLADE ROAST BONELESS

A tender fore end cut that is usually tied with string to keep its shape: it is roasted.

SPARE RIBS

A bony cut, suitable for baking, braising, or barbecuing.

Spare ribs

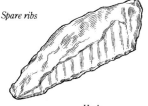

Hock

HOCK

A small bony cut from the hand, often cured as "ham hocks"; it is stewed, braised, or used in soups.

SHOULDER BLADE STEAK

Cut from the shoulder butt. It can be pan fried or braised.

Shoulder blade steak

RIB CHOPS

Chop from the rib end of the loin; these are suitable for broiling, pan frying, stuffing, or baking.

Rib chops

SIRLOIN CUTLETS

Tender boneless cuts from the sirloin; suitable for pan frying or braising.

Sirloin cutlets

SHOULDER ARM PICNIC

A cut from the shoulder: suitable for roasting or braising.

Shoulder arm picnic

INDEX

Page numbers set in italic refer to illustrations

· C ·

· D ·

· N · O ·

· P ·

· Q · R ·

ACKNOWLEDGMENTS

Designers: Christine Wood, Hilary Krag
Editor: Sydney Francis
Photographer: Philip Dowell, except pp 10/11, 12/13, 14/15, 16/17, 20/21, 36/37, 40/41, 42/43, 88, 114/115, photographer: Stephen Oliver
Home economist: Mandy Wagstaff
Illustrator: John Woodcock
Studio: Lorraine Abraham, Beverley Waldron
Typesetter: Bournetype, Bournemouth and MS Filmsetting Limited, Frome
Reproduction: Colourscan, Singapore

Dorling Kindersley
Managing editor: Jemima Dunne
Managing art editor: Derek Coombes
Americanization: Elizabeth Wolf-Cohen
Editorial assistance:
Candida Ross-Macdonald, Julia Harris-Voss
Design assistance: Mark Regardsoe
Production: Jeanette Graham

Reader's Digest Fund for the Blind is publisher of the Large-Type Edition of *Reader's Digest.* For subscription information about this magazine, please contact Reader's Digest Fund for the Blind, Inc., Dept. 250, Pleasantville, N.Y. 10570.